I0189725

A
Guide to
the Literature
of Tennis

A
Guide to
the Literature
of Tennis

Angela Lumpkin

Greenwood Press
Westport, Connecticut • London, England

Library of Congress Cataloging-in-Publication Data

Lumpkin, Angela
  A guide to the literature of tennis.
  Bibliography: p.
  Includes index.
  1. Tennis—Bibliography. I. Title.
Z7514.T3L85 1985 [GV995]   016.796342   85–9941
ISBN 0-313-24492-8 (lib. bdg. : alk. paper)

Copyright © 1985 by Angela Lumpkin

All rights reserved. No portion of this book may be
reproduced, by any process or technique, without the
express written consent of the publisher.

Library of Congress Catalog Card Number: 85-9941
ISBN: 0-313-24492-8

First published in 1985

Greenwood Press
A division of Congressional Information Service, Inc.
88 Post Road West
Westport, Connecticut 06881

Printed in the United States of America

∞

The paper used in this book complies with the
Permanent Paper Standards issued by the National
Information Standards Organization (Z39.48-1984).

10 9 8 7 6 5 4 3 2 1

Contents

Acronyms

ILTF	International Lawn Tennis Federation
LTA	Lawn Tennis Association (British)
USLTA	United States Lawn Tennis Association
USNLTA	United States National Lawn Tennis Association
USTA	United States Tennis Association

Acknowledgments

Several individuals have helped tremendously in making this book a reality. Kay Smiley, Michelle Neal, and the staff at the inter-library loan of Davis Library of the University of North Carolina at Chapel Hill furnished invaluable assistance in securing books for review. Delaine Marbry, Cindy Atkins, and Mattie Hawkins typed the manuscript while John Billing provided additional departmental support. Phillip and Patricia Lumpkin gave me a convenient home and encouragement while researching at the Library of Congress. Janice and Carol Lumpkin and Vernell Berry constantly encouraged me and helped me persevere. I am greatly indebted to the these individuals and to the editorial staff of Greenwood Press, because without their assistance this project would not have been completed.

Introduction

Tennis, as played on the green lawns of English estates and American country clubs beginning in the 1870s, boomed in popularity worldwide in the 1970s, tapering off only slightly in the 1980s. Some analysts credit the Billie Jean King–Bobby Riggs "Battle of the Sexes" extravaganza viewed by millions on television on September 20, 1973, as the spark for the increase in interest and participation in the sport. The tennis boom, though, actually started five years earlier when the amateur façade of the sport was removed. Open tennis, which permits players to accept prize money for their tournament victories, aborted the steady exit of the top players into professional tours away from tournament play. The return of the leading stars combined with the addition of younger players to enhance the quality of competition and led to a major increase in fan interest. Television exposure, commercial sponsorship, and an enthusiasm for fitness also contributed to tennis' becoming the sport of the 1970s and an enduring passion for many.

One index of the popularity of tennis is the publication of books about the sport. In 1874 *The Game of Sphairistrike* and later *The Major's Game of Lawn Tennis*, both written by the game's English promoter, Walter Wingfield, came with the purchase of tennis equipment. The All-England Cricket and Croquet Club formalized the first rules for tennis in 1877. L. S. F. Winslow included them in his *The Lawn-Tennis Annual* in 1882 along with records of matches held in 1881. The *Rules of Lawn Tennis as Adopted by the Cricket and Tennis Clubs of Philadelphia* in 1880 and the *Rules of Lawn Tennis as Authorized and Adopted by the United States National Lawn Tennis Association with a Description of the Game* in 1881 were the first rules for players in the United States. Julian Marshall authored the first tennis technique book, *Lawn-Tennis*, in 1879. Wilfred Baddeley's *Lawn Tennis* characterizes many of the early books as it briefly describes the history of the game, stroke technique, handicaps, practice hints, court demeanor, ladies play, umpiring, tournaments, and court construction. *Lawn Tennis as a Game of Skill* by Solomon Peile includes hints to beginners, general principles and rules, and a chapter for the ladies. Also available in London are Eustace Miles' *Lessons in Lawn Tennis*, Robert Osborn's *Lawn Tennis, Its Players, and How to Play, with the Laws of the Game,* Herbert Wilberforce's *Lawn Tennis,* and Sarah Whittelsey's *A Manual of Lawn Tennis.* Tri-authors Julian Marshall, James Spoons, and Arnan Tait's *Tennis, Rackets, and Fives* and *Tennis, Lawn Tennis, Rackets, and Fives* by John Heathcote, et al., were the first of numerous books written about similar ball sports. Henry Jones provided *Rules for Lawn Tennis* in 1890 while Fred Foster contributed *A Bibliography of Lawn Tennis 1874–1897.*

While Whittelsey was the first woman to author a tennis book, America's James Dwight and Henry Slocum were the first championship players to offer written instruction. Dwight taught in *Lawn-Tennis* in 1886 and in *Practical Lawn Tennis* in 1893. Slocum's *Lawn Tennis in Our Own Country* offers hints on stroke development, singles and doubles play, and ideas about courts and equipment. He also tells the early history of tennis, describes the United States National Lawn Tennis Association's Championships, and discusses intercollegiate tennis. Valentine Hall provides biographical sketches of players in *Lawn Tennis in America* while two other books focus on technique. Henry Chadwick in *Lawn Tennis Manual for 1885* explains how to play the game and its various strokes while Oliver Campbell in *Campbell's Lawn Tennis and the Way to*

Play It tells how to execute the strokes for singles, doubles, ladies', and children's play. D. W. Granbery and Company in 1884 published a *Lawn Tennis Catalogue and Directions for Playing* that combined instructions on technique with an equipment catalogue.

Two books dealing with the administrative side of tennis are Charles Bourne's *Lawn Tennis Score Book and Rules for Playing with Definitions of Terms* and Charles Dodgson's *Lawn Tennis Tournaments: The True Method of Assigning Prizes with a Proof of the Fallacy of the Present Method.* Bourne's 1884 book includes fifteen pages of score cards, four pages of rules plus an additional page on the game for three or four players, and two pages of terms. Dodgson in 1883 provided proofs that, except for first prize, the awarding of prizes lacks meaning and the present method of scoring in matches often leads to unjust results. He offers rules for conducting tournaments that include having a match last only half a day and awarding only three prizes. He provides an example of how to organize a draw of thirty-two. His equitable scoring system excludes sets with the winner being the player who first wins twenty-eight games or who achieves a sixteen-game margin. Tournament administrators might wish to give Dodgson's ideas some consideration today.

Instructions on how to play predominate the many categories of tennis books. Over 950 English language titles about tennis existed in 1984 and of this number, over 475 partially or completely deal with playing technique. Instructions written for children comprise over thirty-five of these. Former American champions or internationally ranked players are authors of over 120 biographical and instructional tennis books sharing their experiences and expertise. Children's books, especially in the last decade, have proliferated as this new audience learns about many aspects of tennis through 100 publications. Histories of the game of tennis, its tournaments, its champions, or special places or events number over 100 volumes. Autobiographies and biographies about champions from the United States and around the world personalize and enrich the interested reader's understanding of the sport. Over twenty-five titles emphasize relaxation, concentration, mental preparation, and related topics as the psychological perspective gains increasing favor with aficionados. Conditioning along with medical and rehabilitative advice comprise fifteen books. Twenty-two works focus on the rules of tennis. Tournament administration, from planning events to training umpires, is the subject of thirty publications. The construction of tennis courts comprises over twenty books which inform cities, clubs, and individuals how to build and to maintain tennis facilities. Equipment, travel, and humor are important aspects of the game with detailed information available about each of them. The numerous films and video cassettes available generally present overviews of the sport while emphasizing instruction and highlights of tennis matches.

Tennis books, both in number and diversity of topic, parallel the growing popularity of the sport. In the first twenty-five years of the sport's existence, twenty-five books were written wholly or mostly about the game, and these generally focus on rules and techniques of play. In the 1970s, however, over 350 books were published on topics ranging from biographies to psychology and from humor to travel. The appetite of the public for the sport has resulted in a massive construction of courts and in millions watching others play. Even though the tennis boom may have peaked, the residual popularity results in aspiring champions learning the game early (to emulate Tracy Austin, a player at age two), in star players becoming millionaires, and in sales of tennis clothing and equipment remaining profitable. Books will continue to reflect the level of interest in tennis in the United States. This guide should help individuals locate the books they need to enhance their understanding of tennis as well as their performance levels.

BIBLIOGRAPHY

Baddeley, Wilfred. *Lawn Tennis*. London: G. Routledge and Sons, 1895.

Bourne, Charles R. *Lawn Tennis Score Book and Rules for Playing with Definitions of Terms*. New York: Charles R. Bourne, 1884.

Campbell, Oliver Samuel. *Campbell's Lawn Tennis and the Way to Play It*. New York: Street and Smith Publishers, 1891.

Chadwick, Henry. *Lawn Tennis Manual for 1885*. New York: A. G. Spalding, 1885.

Dodgson, Charles Lutwidge. *Lawn Tennis Tournaments: The True Method of Assigning Prizes with a Proof of the Fallacy of the Present Method*. London: Macmillan and Company, 1883.

Dwight, James. *Lawn-Tennis*. Boston: Wright and Ditson, 1886.

———. *Practical Lawn-Tennis*. New York: Harper and Brothers, 1893.

Foster, Fred W. *A Bibliography of Lawn Tennis 1874–1897*. Surrey, England: Richmond-Surrey, 1897.

Hall, Valentine Gill. *Lawn Tennis in America*. New York: D. W. Granbery and Company, 1888.

Heathcote, John Moyer, et al. *Tennis, Lawn Tennis, Rackets, and Fives*. London: Longmans, Green, and Company, 1897.

Jones, Henry. *Rules for Lawn Tennis*. London: Thomas De LaRue and Company, 1890.

Lawn Tennis Catalogue and Directions for Playing. New York: D. W. Granbery and Company, 1884.

Marshall, Julian. *Lawn-Tennis*. New York: C. F. A. Hinrichs, 1879.

Marshall, Julian, Spoons, James, and Tait. J. A. Arnan. *Tennis, Rackets, and Fives*. New York: F. A. Stokes and Company, 1891.

Miles, Eustace Hamilton. *Lessons in Lawn Tennis*. London: Gill, 1899.

Osborn, Robert Durie. *Lawn Tennis, Its Players, and How to Play, with the Laws of the Game*. London: Strahan and Company, 1881.

Peile, Solomon Charles Frederick. *Lawn Tennis as a Game of Skill*. London: William Blackwood and Sons, 1885.

Rules of Lawn Tennis as Adopted by the Cricket and Tennis Clubs of Philadelphia. Philadelphia: Lippincott, 1880.

Rules of Lawn Tennis as Authorized and Adopted by the United States National Lawn Tennis Association with a Description of the Game. Philadelphia: J. B. Lippincott and Company, 1881.

Slocum, Henry Warner. *Lawn Tennis in Our Own Country*. New York: A. G. Spalding and Brothers, 1890.

United States Lawn Tennis Association. *The Association Tennis Book*. New York: D. W. Granbery and Company, 1889.

———. *Official Lawn Tennis Rules*. Boston: Wright and Ditson, 1884.

Whittelsey, Sarah Scovill. *A Manual of Lawn Tennis*. London: Butterick Publishing Company, 1894.

Wilberforce, Herbert William Wrangham. *Lawn Tennis*. London: George Bell and Sons, 1889.

Wingfield, Walter C. *The Game of Sphairistrike*. London: Harrison
    and Sons, 1874.
———. *The Major's Game of Lawn Tennis*. London: n.p., 1874.
Winslow, L. S. F. *The Lawn-Tennis Annual*. London, 1882.

A
Guide to
the Literature
of Tennis

1

A Historical Overview of Tennis

Tennis' heritage for over a century is a rich, colorful one, nationally and internationally. The evolution of this sport includes changes in playing styles, clothing, court surfaces, equipment, and most importantly its major expansion following open championships in 1968, which allowed professional players to compete in the major events. Over 100 of the tennis books focus on its development into one of today's most popular sports, on memorable matches, and on outstanding players and their contributions to the game. These works include specific histories of clubs, general histories of the sport from both national and international perspectives as well as twenty-one volumes that describe the famous All-England Championships at Wimbledon.

Lawn Tennis in America by Valentine Hall includes records of tournaments between 1884–1888 along with portraits of leading players and descriptions of tennis as played abroad. *Lawn Tennis, Its Past, Present and Future*, written by Jahial Paret in 1904, provides information about the origin and development of the game. National and international matches comprise one aspect of the ninety-eight pages on history in this comprehensive volume about tennis. Arthur Myers also combines a historical account of the game with playing instructions in *The Complete Lawn Tennis Player*. Davis Cup matches of

1900–1907 are a part of Myers' historical account. The *Growth of Lawn Tennis in California* describes the success of native players from that state in 1913 while George Hillyard looks at *Forty Years of First-Class Lawn Tennis* from the British perspective in 1924.

Arthur Myers examined *Twenty Years of Lawn Tennis* in this 1921 book. Although international in its coverage of Davis Cup matches, American players, Riviera recollections, and places and players in Europe, Myers emphasizes memories of the Wimbledon champions from 1877–1921. The United States Lawn Tennis Association in celebration of its anniversary in 1931 published *Fifty Years of Lawn Tennis in the United States*. This comprehensive volume provides tournament results, describes outstanding matches, and highlights the nation's leading players. It also includes thirty-eight signed articles by writers and players such as Helen Wills Moody, Bill Tilden, Hazel Wightman, Dwight Davis, Richard Sears, and Mary Browne. Teddy Tinling describes his love of tennis in *Tinling: Sixty Years in Tennis*.

Several general histories recount the origins and developments of tennis. *The Story of Tennis* by Morys Aberdare describes the early origins of the game including its evolution from real tennis through the professional tennis tours of Bill Tilden, Mary Browne, and Vincent Richards. George Alexander in *Lawn Tennis: Its Founders and Its Early Days* credits Walter Wingfield with initially marketing, but not founding, the game and James Dwight and others with popularizing the sport in the United States. Malcolm Whitman thoroughly examines the background of the game in *Tennis: Origins and Mysteries*. He proves that Mary Outerbridge first brought the implements of tennis to the United States and set up the game at the Staten Island Cricket and Baseball Club in 1874. Early tennis history is the focus of Terry Todd's *The Tennis Players: From Pagan Rites to Strawberries and Cream*. He looks at the ancient origins of the sport, the initial rules, the first championships and champions, tennis attire, professionalization of tennis, and the social side of tennis, especially at the All-England Championships. John Smyth from an Englishman's perspective in *Lawn Tennis* traces the evolution of the game by eras of time: before World

War I, years between the wars, and post–World War II. He includes information about the Davis Cup and Wightman Cup competitions, the professional game, and the greatest players. Angela Lumpkin, in *Women's Tennis: A Historical Documentary of the Players and Their Game*, focuses on the outstanding women players and their contributions. Her coverage is international with an emphasis on players from the United States. She compares playing styles, looks at clothing changes, examines tennis beyond the major championships, and recounts the struggle for identity by the women's professional circuit. Gerald Gurney looks at the histories of three racket sports in *Tennis, Squash and Badminton Bygones*.

Three of the most comprehensive histories are *American Tennis: The Story of a Game and Its People* by Parke Cummings, *Tennis, Its History, People and Events* by Will Grimsley, and the *United States Tennis Association Official Encyclopedia of Tennis* by Bill Shannon. Cummings describes the major developments of the game in a chronological and topical manner including the social aspects of tennis, clothing and equipment transitions, and champion players. Grimsley's history reveals the evolution in equipment and in scoring. He describes the major events such as the All-England Championships, the United States Nationals, and the Davis Cup and the Wightman Cup events. Julius Heldman analyzes the styles of twenty of the outstanding players for this book. Grimsley includes descriptions of his ten most historic tennis games. Bill Shannon served as editor for the third edition of the *United States Tennis Association Official Encyclopedia of Tennis*. Its history section focuses on the leading players as the chronicle unfolds. Results and records of national and international competitions are also available therein, as are the rules and stroke-production principles.

Several specific histories add color and drama to the evolution of tennis. Edward Potter recounts many rich traditions in *The West Side Tennis Club Story: 60th Anniversary, 1892–1952*. This famous Forest Hills, New York, club hosted the Davis Cup matches initially in 1914, the men's nationals (1915–1977), the women's nationals (1921–1977), and numerous Wightman Cup matches. The *Seabright Lawn Tennis and*

Cricket Club Jubilee Year Book briefly describes the forty-year
history of this club along with results and champions. Ronald
Lerry, a writer for *The Birmingham* (England) *Post* describes
the *Cradle of Lawn Tennis: The Story of Warwickshire and Its
Clubs*. Over 100 clubs have existed in the county of Warwickshire since 1872 with the Leamington Lawn Tennis Club led
by T. H. Gem and J. B. Perera predominating. The first woman
winner at Wimbledon, Maud Watson, came from Warwickshire. Lloyd Garrison tells about *Tennis in Santa Barbara: A
History, 1878–1982*. His approach is to recount the achievements of high school, college, and club players in this California
locale. Other accounts of club events include *From Bustles to
Shorts: Four Generations at the Cincinnati Tennis Club, 1880–
1963* by Stanley Lewis and *The Fitzwilliam Story: 1877–1977*
by Ulick O'Connor. The short-lived existence of tennis as a
team sport is the story told in Greg Hoffman's *The Art of World
Team Tennis*. He discusses each of the three seasons, explains
the innovative format, scoring, and officiating, and provides
yearly results and statistics.

Four books record the classic matches, each nation's leading
players, and the results of the Davis Cup, the international
men's team competition. *The Story of the Davis Cup* by Arthur
Myers, *The Quest of the Davis Cup* by Stephen Merrihew, *A
History of the Davis Cup: Being the Story of the International
Lawn Tennis Championship, 1900–1948* by Dennis Coombe,
and *The Davis Cup* by Edward Potter describe this annual
competition from 1900 through 1913, 1928, 1948, and 1969
respectively. Merrihew details the beginnings, tells about major successes by United States' players, and includes British,
Australian, and French victories. Coombe, captain of the 1947
New Zealand team, briefly describes the competitions in three
time frames: 1900 to 1914, 1919 to 1939, and 1946 to 1948.
While providing detailed match results, Potter topically examines the leading nations which challenge for the Cup and
their outstanding players.

Three books chronicle the national tournaments held at the
West Side Tennis Club in Forest Hills, New York. Julian May's
Forest Hills and the American Tennis Championship is a mostly

pictorial work written for children. It focuses on outstanding champions such as Bill Tilden, Don Budge, Alice Marble, Althea Gibson, Arthur Ashe, Billie Jean King, Jimmy Connors, and Chris Evert. *Carnival at Forest Hills: Anatomy of a Tennis Tournament* by Marty Bell uses the backdrop of the 1974 championships to explain the various components of this event. Bell explains the tournament milieu, the rise of youthful stars, rivalries, and the outcomes of the tournament matches. Billie Jean King and Jimmy Connors triumph in the singles competition, as do King and Rosemary Casals in women's doubles and Bob Lutz and Stan Smith in men's doubles. Robert Minton provides more in-depth pictures and descriptions in his *Forest Hills: An Illustrated History*. He explains how the West Side Tennis Club began, describes its hosting of the great Davis Cup match of 1914, recounts the financial battles of 1919–1941, and discusses how the club confronted commercialization. Between 1942 and 1975 Minton focuses on the big game, leading players, the rape of the lawn, and the spirit of West Side.

Grace Lichtenstein in *A Long Way, Baby: Behind the Scenes in Women's Pro Tennis* describes the day-to-day happenings on the women's circuit and discusses the players who compete in its events. Peter Bodo's *Inside Tennis: A Season on the Pro Tour* takes a similar look at the men's circuit and provides insights into the struggles, challenges, and successes of male professional players. Marty Riessen tells how he handles the mental pressures of top-level tennis competition in *Match Point: A Candid View of Life on the International Tennis Circuit*. Riessen and Richard Evans describe Riessen's conflicts with amateurism, his becoming a contract pro, playing when hurt, jet-age tennis, along with some instructional hints. Michael Mewshaw visited the leading international tournaments for men in 1982 and in *Short Circuit* provides insights into the character of each site and into the aura surrounding events in Genoa, Strasbourg, Milan, Nice, and Monte Carlo as well as at the Italian, French, English, and United States Championships. The tennis world Mewshaw describes is filled with arrogant players, money-hungry promoters, drug abuse, and fraudulent financial practices, such as "tanking," or deliberately losing a match, and appearance guarantees. Menshaw's muckraking may be cynical yet still on target with some problems that do exist in the world of tennis.

Arthur Myers recalls in *Fifty Years of Wimbledon: The Story of the Lawn Tennis Championships* the early history of the All-England Championships that occurred first in 1877 for men and in 1884 for women. Myers analyzes the championships year by year while describing the leading players and playing innovations. Francis Burrow, an eyewitness of most of the early championships, chronicles, in *The Centre Court and Others*, the outstanding occurrences, especially between 1918–1936. His reminiscences provided colorful insights into the aura of Wimbledon and its famed center court. This followed Burrow's earlier work *The "Last Eights" of Wimbledon, 1877–1926*. Players are the focus of the 1934 *Wimbledon Who's Who and Tennis Celebrities*. Norah Cleather told the *Wimbledon Story* in 1947 in a topical and chronological manner. From the early days through the Suzanne Lenglen and Bill Tilden years and from non-English champions to a salute to the spectators, Cleather provides an illustrated and lovingly described view of Wimbledon. From his perspective as lawn tennis correspondent for the London *Daily Telegraph*, John Olliff describes the old Wimbledon, the new Wimbledon, and Wimbledon today (1949) in *The Romance of Wimbledon*. Between 1868–1921 the first Wimbledon emerged as the venue for the triumphs of the Doherty brothers, Norman Brookes, Anthony Wilding, Suzanne Lenglen, and Bill Tilden. The new Wimbledon of 1922–1939 featured French champions, an English renaissance, and dramatic changes in the attire of the ladies. Wimbledon today also portrays the romance of the fortnight. In 1957 Maurice Brady told the *Centre Court Story*. Archibald Macaulay and John Smyth take their readers *Behind the Scenes at Wimbledon* for a look at how Wimbledon works, the players, and the fans. Part I of this book describes the championships prior to 1945 highlighting Suzanne Lenglen, victories by French and United States players, and the triumph of England's Fred Perry. Among the outstanding post-war champions were Maureen Connolly, Lew Hoad, Maria Bueno, Angela Mortimer, and Rod Laver.

John McPhee in *Wimbledon: A Celebration* based his pictorial and descriptive history on the 1970 Wimbledon championships. He provides glimpses about the nature of Wimbledon, its beauty, its traditions, and a sense of why Wimbledon is Wimbledon. He details the players and their games while taking time to applaud the efforts of groundskeeper Robert Twynam. *Wonderful Wimbledon* by Alistair Revie traces the history of these championships while highlighting players and developments such as Suzanne Lenglen, Fred Perry, Ellsworth Vines, the liberation of the ladies, and open tennis. Magic is a part of the setting according to Gwen Robyns in *Wimbledon: The Hidden Drama*. Female players are the focus of this history as Suzanne Lenglen, Elizabeth Ryan, Helen Wills Moody, Helen Jacobs, Maureen Connolly, Maria Bueno, Althea Gibson, Angela Mortimer, Ann Jones, and Christine Truman along with other male and female stars and their performances add to the legacy of the championships. Written for juvenile readers, Julian May's *Wimbledon World Tennis Focus* uses pictures of the stars to portray the championships at Wimbledon. May includes stories about Helen Wills Moody, Helen Jacobs, Don Budge, Rod Laver, Margaret Court, Billie Jean King, Jimmy Connors, Chris Evert, and others.

Lance Tingay's *100 Years of Wimbledon*, Maxwell Robertson's *Wimbledon 1877–1977*, and James Medlycott's *100 years of the Wimbledon Tennis Championships* describe the centennial existence of the championships. Tingay recounts the victories of the Renshaws, the Dohertys, and Dorothea Lambert-Chambers along with the move of the All-England Club from Worple Road to Church Road. Leading players are the focus of the later years of Tingay's history and in the biographical sketches he includes. Maxwell Robertson divides his history into brief eras of time and then selects representative players from each to discuss. The Four Musketeers dominated in 1922–1931 as did players from the United States between 1946–1950. Billie Jean King in 1966–1968 and Jimmy Connors in 1973–1976 dominated their respective fields. Robertson in 1981 continued his chronicle in *Wimbledon: Centre Court of the Game*. This third one-hundred-year history also tells the story but focuses more on championship personalities, great games, and fashion. Medlycott provides match highlights of Suzanne Lenglen's 1919 victory over Dorothea Lambert-Chambers and Arthur Ashe's defeat of Jimmy Connors in 1975.

Charles Landon offers yet another history in *Classic Moments of Wimbledon* that emphasizes the Renshaws, the Dohertys, foreign invasions, Suzanne Lenglen, Fred Perry, Helen Wills Moody, and champions from Australia and the United States. Ronald Atkin and Eamonn McCabe's brief *The Book of Wimbledon* describes the fortnight of the championships as an honored British tradition. Using photographs extensively, they tell about the early years, the open era, the lay-out and organization of the All-England Lawn Tennis and Croquet Club (with its exclusive membership of 375), and about these extraordinary championships. Geoff Peters examined *Wimbledon on Camera* in 1981 while John Parsons takes an in-depth look at *The Championships Wimbledon Nineteen Eighty-Three*. In honor of one hundred years of the ladies championships, former champion Virginia Wade and Jean Rafferty tell about the *Ladies of the Court: A Century of Women at Wimbledon*. Each chapter highlights an outstanding champion and some unique characteristic about her. Some of these players include prototype pro Dorothea Lambert-Chambers, woman warrior Maureen Connolly, reluctant ambassador Althea Gibson, Margaret Court's grand slam greatness, go for the big one by Billie Jean King, first teenage prodigy Chris Evert, and Martina Navratilova's staking a claim to greatness.

Yearbooks, even before the end of the nineteenth century, provide results of championships and often a historical perspective of the game. *A Manual of Lawn Tennis* beginning in the 1880s furnished readers with the history, rules, equipment, stroke technique, and tournament results. *Spalding's Lawn Tennis Annual* under the various editorships of Frederick Alexander, Samuel Hardy, and Jahial Paret provides rules, results, and stories as early as 1890. Spalding also publishes *The Lawn Tennis Manual* as a yearbook. In England the *Lawn Tennis Almanack (Annual)*, *Dawson's International Lawn Tennis Almanac* by Clarence Jones, *Gamage's Lawn Tennis Annual* since 1912, *Ayres' Lawn Tennis Almanack and Tournament Guide* since 1910, and *Annual of Lawn Tennis*, provided similar information on an annual basis. *The Lawn Tennis Association*

Official Handbook, the annual publication of the British Lawn Tennis Association since 1912, lists the affiliated associations, tournament results, rules, and tournament regulations. *Lowe's Lawn Tennis Annual and Compendium* by Gordon Lowe (since 1932) gives results of championships and team matches (Davis Cup and Wightman Cup), reviews the past year's results, and offers hints on how to play the game. The United States Lawn Tennis Association's (United States Tennis Association since 1975) *The Official Yearbook and Tennis Guide with the Official Rules* began in 1941 to furnish tournament results, committee listings, rankings, records, and rules.

BIBLIOGRAPHY

Aberdare, Morys George Lyndhurst Bruce. *The Story of Tennis*. London: Stanley Paul, 1959.

Alexander, George E. *Lawn Tennis: Its Founders and Its Early Days*. Lynn, Massachusetts: H. O. Zimman, 1974.

Annual of Lawn Tennis. Hampshire, England: n.d.

Atkin, Ronald, and McCabe, Eamonn. *The Book of Wimbledon*. London: David and Charles, 1982.

Ayres' Lawn Tennis Almanack and Tournament Guide. London, 1910.

Bell, Marty. *Carnival at Forest Hills: Anatomy of a Tennis Tournament*. New York: Random House, 1975.

Bodo, Peter. *Inside Tennis: A Season on the Pro Tour*. New York: Delta Books, 1979.

Brady, Maurice. *Centre Court Story*. Slough, England: Foulsham, 1957.

Burrow, F. R. *The Centre Court and Others*. London: Eyre and Spottiswoode, 1937.

———. *The "Last Eights" at Wimbledon, 1877–1926*. Lawn Tennis and Badminton, 1927.

Cleather, Norah Gordon. *Wimbledon Story*. London: Sporting Handbooks, 1947.

Coombe, Dennis. *A History of the Davis Cup: Being the Story of the International Lawn Tennis Championship, 1900–1948*. London: H. Locke, 1949.

Cummings, Parke. *American Tennis: The Story of a Game and Its People*. Boston: Little, Brown, 1957.

Gamage's Lawn Tennis Annual. London, n.d.

Garrison, Lloyd W. *Tennis in Santa Barbara: A History, 1878–1982*. Santa Barbara, California, 1983.

Grimsley, Will. *Tennis, Its History, People and Events.* Englewood
    Cliffs, New Jersey: Prentice-Hall, 1971.
Growth of Lawn Tennis in California. San Francisco: Wright and
    Ditson, 1913.
Gurney, Gerald. *Tennis, Squash and Badminton Bygones.* Cincinnati:
    Seven Hills Books, 1984.
Hall, Valentine Gill. *Lawn Tennis in America.* New York: D.W. Gran-
    bery and Company, 1888.
Hillyard, George Whiteside. *Forty Years of First-Class Lawn Tennis.*
    London: Williams and Norgate, 1924.
Hoffman, Greg. *The Art of World Team Tennis.* San Francisco: San
    Francisco Book Company, 1977.
Jones, Clarence Medlycott. *Dawson's International Lawn Tennis Al-
    manac.* London: Dawson's of Pall Mall, n.d.
Landon, Charles. *Classic Moments of Wimbledon.* Ashbourne, Der-
    byshire, England: Moorland Publishers, 1982.
The Lawn Tennis Almanack. London: Dunlop Sports Company, n.d.
The Lawn Tennis Association Official Handbook. London: British Lawn
    Tennis Association, 1912.
The Lawn Tennis Manual. New York: A. G. Spalding and Brothers,
    n.d.
Lerry, Ronald. *Cradle of Lawn Tennis: The Story of Warwickshire and
    Its Clubs.* Birmingham, England: Stanford and Mann, 1947.
Lewis, Stanley W. *From Bustles to Shorts: Four Generations at the
    Cincinnati Tennis Club, 1880–1963.* Cincinnati; 1963.
Lichtenstein, Grace. *A Long Way, Baby: Behind the Scenes in Women's
    Pro Tennis.* New York: Morrow, 1974.
Lowe, Francis Gordon, ed. *Lawn Tennis Annual and Compen-
    dium.*London: Eyre and Spottiswoode, 1932.
Lumpkin, Angela. *Women's Tennis: A Historical Documentary of the
    Players and Their Game.* Troy, New York, Whitston Publishing
    Company, 1981.
Macaulay, Archibald Duncan Campbell, and Smyth, John. *Behind the
    Scenes at Wimbledon.* New York: St. Martin's Press, 1965.
McPhee, John A. *Wimbledon: A Celebration.* New York: Viking Press,
    1972.
A Manual of Lawn Tennis. New York: Butterick Publishing Company,
    n.d.
May, Julian. *Forest Hills and the American Tennis Champion-
    ship.*Mankato, Minnesota: Creative Education, 1976.
————. *Wimbledon World Tennis Focus.* Mankato, Minnesota: Crea-
    tive Education, 1975.

Medlycott, James. *100 Years of the Wimbledon Tennis Championships.* London: The Hamlyn Publishing Group, 1977.

Merrihew, Stephen Wallis. *The Quest of the Davis Cup.* New York: American Lawn Tennis, 1928.

Mewshaw, Michael. *Short Circuit.* New York: Atheneum, 1983.

Minton, Robert. *Forest Hills: An Illustrated History.* Philadelphia: Lippincott, 1975.

Myers, Arthur Wallis. *The Complete Lawn Tennis Player.* Philadelphia: George W. Jacobs and Company, 1908.

——. *Fifty Years of Wimbledon: The Story of the Lawn Tennis Championships.* London: "The Field," 1926.

——. *The Story of the Davis Cup.* London: Methuen, 1913.

——. *Twenty Years of Lawn Tennis.* New York: George H. Doran Company, 1921.

O'Connor, Ulick. *The Fitzwilliam Story: 1877–1977.* Dublin: Richview Browne and Nolan, n.d.

Olliff, John Sheldon. *The Romance of Wimbledon.* London: Hutchinson, 1949.

Paret, Jahial Parmly. *Lawn Tennis, Its Past, Present and Future.* New York: Macmillan Company, 1904.

Parsons, John. *The Championships Wimbledon Nineteen Eighty-Three.* Topsfield, Massachusetts: Merrimack Publishers Circle, 1984.

Peters, Geoff, ed. *Wimbledon on Camera.* New York: State Mutual Book and Periodical Service, 1981.

Potter, Edward Clarkson. *The Davis Cup.* New York: A. S. Barnes and Company, 1969.

——. *The West Side Tennis Club Story: 60th Anniversary, 1892–1952.* New York, 1952.

Revie, Alastair. *Wonderful Wimbledon.* London: Pelham, 1972.

Riessen, Marty, and Evans, Richard. *Match Point: A Candid View of Life on the International Tennis Circuit.* Englewood Cliffs, New Jersey: Prentice-Hall, 1973.

Robertson, Maxwell. *Wimbledon: Centre Court of the Game.* London: BBC Publications, 1981.

——. *Wimbledon 1877–1977.* London: Barker, 1977.

Robyns, Gwen. *Wimbledon: The Hidden Drama.* New York: Drake Publishers, 1974.

Seabright Lawn Tennis and Cricket Club. *Seabright Lawn Tennis and Cricket Club Jubilee Year Book.* New York, 1926.

Shannon, Bill, ed. *United States Tennis Association Official Encyclopedia of Tennis.* New York: Harper and Row, 1981.

Smyth, John George. *Lawn Tennis.* London: Batsford, 1953.

Spalding's Lawn Tennis Annual. New York: American Sports Publishing Company, 1890.

Tingay, Lance. *100 Years of Wimbledon.* Enfield, England: Guinness Superlatives, 1977.

Tinling, Ted. *Tinling: Sixty Years in Tennis.* Topsfield, Massachusetts: Merrimack Publishers Circle, 1984.

Todd, Terry. *The Tennis Players: From Pagan Rites to Strawberries and Cream.* Guernsey, British Isles: Vallency Press, 1979.

United States Lawn Tennis Association. *Fifty Years of Lawn Tennis in the United States.* New York: United States Lawn Tennis Association, 1931.

————. *The Official Yearbook and Tennis Guide with the Official Rules.* Lynn, Massachusetts: H. O. Zimman, 1941.

Wade, Virginia, and Rafferty, Jean. *Ladies of the Court: A Century of Women at Wimbledon.* New York: Atheneum, 1984.

Whitman, Malcolm Douglas. *Tennis: Origins and Mysteries.* New York: Derrydale Press, 1932.

Wimbledon Who's Who and Tennis Celebrities. London: Burrow, 1934.

2

A History of Championship Players and Performances

As a single chronicle of passing events and times, history seems lifeless. The addition of the individuals who frame the happenings and make them occur as they do brings color, uniqueness, and style. What follows are books which use one of five approaches to describe the players and their achievements: a) using a player focus to trace the development of the game; b) looking at players' personalities and records in encyclopedic fashion; c) examining the issues confronting the game through the activities of the players; d) viewing players' perspectives through their writings; e) relying primarily on photographs to highlight their tennis triumphs.

Arthur Myers, writer for *The Daily Telegraph* for thirty years, compiled many of his narratives in *Great Lawn Tennis: Pen Pictures of Famous Matches*. He describes championship performances of Anthony Wilding, Norman Brookes, Suzanne Lenglen, Helen Wills Moody, Bill Tilden, Rene Lacoste, Henri Cochet, Jean Borotra, Jack Crawford, Fred Perry, and many others. *Inside Tennis* by Norman Cutler focuses on several of the lesser-known players such as Bob Falkenburg, Ted Schroeder, Budge Patty, Hamilton Richardson, Beverly Baker, Louise Brough, Doris Hart, Frank Sedgman, and Vic Seixas. Susan Noel in *Tennis in Our Time* examines tennis from an English perspective as does Cutler. Biographies of players are a focal point for Noel's work, yet she also discusses English tennis, international championships, tournament administration, and open tennis. The performances of over 100 men and women comprise Edward Potter's *The World's Leading Tennis Players.* *Kings of the Court: The Story of Lawn Tennis* also by Potter is a history of the game with players central to its approach. Willie and Lawford Renshaw and Reggie and Laurie Doherty are among the players who dominated tennis during their respective eras. Potter places Bill Tilden and Suzanne Lenglen atop his top-twenty all-time players' lists. Against the backdrop of Maurice McLoughlin's career from 1914 through his induction into the Tennis Hall of Fame, Al Laney describes *Covering the Court: A 50-Year Love Affair with the Game of Tennis.*

Allison Danzig and Peter Schwed borrow articles from the *New York Times* (1919–1971), *World Tennis* magazine (1954–1969), the *Boston Globe, Sports Illustrated,* the *Los Angeles Times,* and several books to compile *The Fireside Book of Tennis.* Although it includes a brief history of the game, of Wimbledon, and of the Davis Cup and Wightman Cup matches, players are the subjects of most of the essays. These include Suzanne Lenglen, Helen Wills Moody, Maurice McLoughlin, Bill Tilden, Bill Johnston, Jacques Brugnon, Jean Borotra, Henri Cochet, Rene Lacoste, Ellsworth Vines, Helen Jacobs, Don Budge, Fred Perry, Jack Kramer, Pancho Gonzales, Alice Marble, Maureen Connolly, Ken Rosewall, and Rod Laver. The second part of the work describes great tennis moments and matches. Richard Evans gathered newspaper articles, magazine pieces, and book chapters into his *Tales from the Tennis Court: An Anthology of Tennis Writing.* Portraits of Jimmy Connors, Helen Wills Moody, Pancho Gonzales, Arthur Ashe, and Bjorn Borg are among the essays that seem to disproportionately describe recent tennis players. *The Complete Book of Tennis: A New York Times Scrapbook History* and Gene Brown's *Tennis* both use articles from *The New York Times* to tell the history of tennis. Herbert Wind reprinted articles from *The New Yorker* in his *Game, Set, and Match: The Tennis Boom of the 1960s and 70s.* He discusses Rod Laver's and Margaret Court's Grand Slam victories, describes tennis' and Wimbledon's 100-year histories, recounts the Billie Jean King–Bobby

Riggs match, and reflects about the United States championships at Forest Hills. He also acclaims the outstanding play of
John Newcombe, Pancho Gonzales, Ken Rosewall, Jack Kramer, Arthur Ashe, Roy Emerson, Chris Evert, and others. Michael Bartlett and Bob Gillen gather essays from multiple
authors for *The Tennis Book*. This anthology includes articles
about the professional tours, champions and challengers, strokes
and strategies, great matches, outstanding players, and the
leading championships.

Individuals and their styles of play are the focus of Paul
Metzler's *Tennis Styles and Stylists* and *Love and Faults: Personalities Who Have Changed the History of Tennis in My Lifetime* by Teddy Tinling and Rod Humphries. Tinling, a tennis
official and dress designer, and Humphries focus on the leading
ladies in the game, such as Suzanne Lenglen, Helen Wills
Moody, Elizabeth Ryan, Helen Jacobs, Alice Marble, Gussy
Moran, Maureen Connolly, Billie Jean King, and Chris Evert.
They also recall the achievements and personalities of outstanding male stars like Bill Tilden, Henri Cochet, Fred Perry,
Don Budge, Jimmy Connors, and Bjorn Borg. Memorable
matches, biographies, and records comprise five histories of
tennis for children. These are Joseph Cook's *Famous Firsts in
Tennis*, Bryan Cutress' *Tennis*, Andrew Lawrence's *Tennis:
Great Stars, Great Moments*, Lawrence Lorimer's *The Tennis
Book*, and Maureen Reardon's *Match Point*. Reardon and Cutress describe the structure of the game, its champions, and its
major events after which Reardon summarizes tennis by calling
it the "hottest game around." Lorimer provides an encyclopedia
of terms, players, and championships including the greatest
stars and famous matches.

Maxwell Robertson in *The Encyclopedia of Tennis* combines
a history of the game with entries describing players, countries,
tennis associations, clubs, championships, and terms. The history of tennis is told through signed essays by journalists and
a few players. Lance Tingay chronicles the game in three eras
of time. Allison Danzig tells the story of tennis in the United
States, while Fred Perry, Bud Collins, and Gladys Heldman
discuss the professional game. Some essays describe playing
technique while others explain and report the championships.

Allison Danzig, Harry Hopman, and Lance Tingay rank the
top male and female players. Bill Talbert and Pete Axthelm
in *Tennis Observed* report the highlights of the United States
Championships between 1881–1966. Richard Schickel in *The
World of Tennis* explains tennis as played at the international
level using the leading singles players as representatives of
each time period. The climax of his book is a look at the United
States Championships in 1974. *World Tennis* is actually an
annual publication in both New York and London with great
similarity in content, but some changes in focus depending on
the audience. Both volumes record the facts and figures for all
the major events and circuits for the past year along with championship rolls of past seasons. *The Concise Dictionary of Tennis*
by Martin Hedges contains a listing of players from early champions to current stars, tournament venues, and tennis terms.
The biographical sketches contain the major championships
won by each player. Bud Collins and Zander Hollander provide
a history of the game yet focus on players in *Bud Collins'
Modern Encyclopedia of Tennis*. Allison Danzig profiles the
twenty-five greatest players between 1914–1945 while Bud
Collins highlights the twenty-five greatest players between
1946–1979. Barry Lorge describes the 1946–1979 era focusing
on the myth of amateurism through the open era. George Sullivan's *Tennis Rules Illustrated* covers rules, scoring, United
States champions, Wimbledon champions, rankings, money
winners, and great matches. Maurice Brady offers two other
volumes covering historical and biographical aspects of the
game in *The Encyclopedia of Lawn Tennis* (1958) and *Lawn
Tennis Encyclopedia* (1969). Gene Brown provided *The Complete Book of Tennis* in 1981. Bill Shannon in 1982 compiled a
comprehensive *U.S. Open Record Book* that provides facts and
figures about open championships in the United States. Three
recent books provide a wealth of facts, features, and feats. David
Emery includes 125 players in his *Who's Who in International
Tennis*. This volume tells about players on the professional
circuits from established stars to teenage would-be champions.
Each citation gives biographical information, career highlights, and a brief personality sketch. Fred Nebling in 1984
provided *Tennis Trivia* for the real fan. *The Guinness Book of*

Tennis Facts and Feats by Lance Tingay appeases any tennis buff's quest for the trivial or the significant. Tingay lists the first, the longest, the shortest, the greatest, and most every other possible piece of information sought. Results abound about the Wimbledon championships, the United States championships, international team competitions, events on the professional circuits, and even for tennis events no longer held.

Another approach taken to describe tennis is to look at the issues and major occurrences in the sport. Rex Bellamy, tennis journalist for *The Times* of London, attempts to capture the character of the men's and the women's international tennis circuits and to recall the drama and humor of the open competitions between 1968–1971 in *The Tennis Set.* He writes about the five major international tournaments (French, German, Italian, English, and United States) plus focuses on the United States as the hub of the professional scene. Bellamy also discusses the leading players who are split into opposing camps by the disputes between the ruling organizations in tennis. Murray Janoff analyzes the recent history of tennis from an issue orientation in both *Game! Set! Match!* (1973) and *Tennis Revolution* (1974). The first book focuses on Davis Cup matches but also includes player profiles and women's contributions to the sport. Janoff specifically looks at the changes in the Davis Cup, the role of Harry Hopman as captain of the Australian teams, and the 1972 quest for the Davis Cup. In *Tennis Revolution* Janoff examines the Van Alen Streamlined Scoring System, the press, the various groups vying for control of tennis, such as World Championship Tennis, tennis as a game played for money, team tennis, the rebels, strengthening umpiring, and who is number one. The politics of tennis provide the framework for Rich Koster's *The Tennis Bubble: Big Money Tennis, How It Grew and Where It's Going.* He discusses the rebels Bill Roirdan and Jimmy Connors, the World Championship of Tennis, the Association of Tennis Professionals, world team tennis, the women's circuit, and television and the fans. Catherine Bell and Roy Peter, in *Passing Shots*, portray tennis in the early 1980s featuring the stars, their styles of play, and the atmosphere at the major tournaments. They show both the triumphs and the defeats. *Short Circuit* by Michael Mewshaw reveals problems with finances and drugs on the men's professional circuits in 1982. He alleges that promoters and players are guilty of fraudulent financial practices.

Often players provide their viewpoints about the development of tennis and about its personalities. Bill Tilden in *The Common Sense of Tennis* goes beyond the fine points of playing and watching tennis to include descriptions about international tournaments, women's play, and tennis personalities in this 1923 work. Tilden later describes *Shooting Stars: Pen-Pictures of the World's Greatest Lawn Tennis Players of 1930*. The United States Lawn Tennis Association's *Fifty Years of Lawn Tennis in the United States* chronicles the emerging popularity of the game using thirty-eight essays by writers and players. *Match Point, Game, Set, and Match*, and *Points for Victory* (*The Nestle Books of Tennis #1, #2, #3* respectively), contain short articles written by players, teaching professionals, and journalists. While some articles in the first book describe topics such as concentration (Angela Mortimer) and fashion (Angela Buxton), primarily the essays are historical. Rod Laver tells about his dream come true, Ken Rosewall describes his world champion's viewpoint, and Lance Tingay recalls famous Wimbledon battles. Books #2 and #3, edited by David Young, continue this same format. In *Game, Set and Match*, Roy Emerson explains why fitness is essential, Lesley Turner describes the highs and lows of tennis, Rod Laver suggests ways to play percentage tennis, Peter Wilson portrays the stars of the Wimbledon stage, Margaret Smith tells her story from Albury to Wimbledon, and Maria Bueno describes her tennis comeback. Ann Jones recalls her most memorable match in *Points for Victory*, while Peter Wilson analyzes Wimbledon's greatest final, Fred Stolle proves that a backhand changed a match, and Jaroslav Drobny recounts Wimbledon's longest match. These are but a few of the numerous articles in these three books.

Frequently the color and drama of the history of tennis is shown through pictorial essays or at least by works which use the visual medium primarily. Lamont Buchanan tells *The Story of Tennis in Text and Pictures* through many early pictures about the game and action shots of the stars. Lance Tingay traces the origins, growth, and popularity of tennis through five eras of time in *History of Lawn Tennis in Pictures*. Tingay uses a similar approach in *Tennis, A Pictorial History* four years later as does Alain Deflassieux in *Tennis*. Eugene Scott uses photographs extensively to depict *Tennis: Game of Motion*. He shows the history, twenty outstanding aces, examples of the championship strokes, doubles action, tournament sites, and the greatest matches. Using 1,200 black and white illustrations and forty color photographs, Gianni Clerici offers *The Ultimate Tennis Book*. He shows the ancients, the pioneers, the stars of the golden age, and contemporary jet-age champions. Examples of the players he focuses on are the Renshaws, the Dohertys, Suzanne Lenglen, Bill Tilden, Rene Lacoste, Jack Kramer, Fred Perry, Helen Wills Moody, Alice Marble, Don Budge, Maureen Connolly, Pancho Gonzales, Frank Sedgman, Ken Rosewall, Althea Gibson, Maria Bueno, Rod Laver, Margaret Court, Billie Jean King, and Jimmy Connors. *An Illustrated History of Australian Tennis* by Richard Whitington focuses on the outstanding male players from that country. These stars are Norman Brookes, Gerald Patterson, Jack Crawford, John Bromwich, Adrian Quist, Frank Sedgman, Ken McGregor, Lew Hoad, Ken Rosewall, Neale Fraser, Roy Emerson, Rod Laver, and John Newcombe. Geoff Peters provides a glimpse of *Wimbledon on Camera*. Joseph Cook provides juvenile readers with *Famous Firsts in Tennis*. Cook briefly describes and pictures the first world championship, the first men's and women's champions in the United States, and the first Davis Cup and Wightman Cup matches. He continues with personality profiles of players who are the first, such as the following: stylist, Suzanne Lenglen; offensive star, Fred Perry; big game player, Jack Kramer; master of all court surfaces, Tony Trabert; black to win a major tennis championship, Althea Gibson; and tennis player to affect society, Billie Jean King. Julian May relies extensively on photographs of the champions to tell about *Forest Hills and the American Tennis Championship*. Robert Minton's *Forest Hills: An Illustrated History* uses photographs to portray these championships, too.

Five of the histories of Wimbledon include numerous photographs. *Wimbledon: A Celebration* by John McPhee uses the photographs by Alfred Eisenstaedt to capture the beauty and mood of Wimbledon as well as the drama of the players in action. James Medlycott devotes about 75 percent of the *100 Years of the Wimbledon Tennis Championships* to photographs. Lance Tingay tells about the history of the *100 Years of Wimbledon* through text and pictures. Ronald Atkin and Eamonn McCabe average a picture per page in their brief work, *The Book of Wimbledon*. Photographs of champions in action predominate in *Ladies of the Court: A Century of Women at Wimbledon* by Virginia Wade and Jean Rafferty. They focus on outstanding representative players and their achievements.

BIBLIOGRAPHY

Atkin, Ronald, and McCabe, Eamonn. *The Book of Wimbledon*. London: David and Charles, 1982.

Bartlett, Michael, and Gillen, Bob, eds. *The Tennis Book*. New York: Arbor House, 1981.

Bell, Catherine, and Peter, Roy. *Passing Shots*. New York: Beaufort Books, 1983.

Bellamy, Rex. *The Tennis Set*. London: Cassell, 1972.

Brady, Maurice. *The Encyclopedia of Lawn Tennis*. London: R. Hall, 1958.

———. *Lawn Tennis Encyclopedia*. South Brunswick, New Jersey: A. S. Barnes, 1969.

Brown, Gene. *The Complete Book of Tennis*. New York: Arno Press, 1981.

———. *Tennis*. New York: Arno Press, 1979.

Buchanan, Lamont. *The Story of Tennis in Text and Pictures*. New York: Vanguard Press, 1951.

Clerici, Gianni. *The Ultimate Tennis Book*. Chicago: Follett, 1975.

Collins, Bud, and Hollander, Zander, eds. *Bud Collins' Modern Encyclopedia of Tennis*. Garden City, New York: Dolphin Books, 1980.

The Complete Book of Tennis: A New York Times Scrapbook History. New York: Bobbs-Merrill Company, 1980.

Cook, Joseph J. *Famous Firsts in Tennis*. New York: Putnam, 1978.

Cutler, Norman. *Inside Tennis*. London: Evans Brothers, 1954.

Cutress, Bryan. *Tennis*. Morristown, New Jersey: Silver Burdett, 1980.

Danzig, Allison, and Schwed, Peter, eds. *The Fireside Book of Tennis*. New York: Simon and Schuster, 1972.

Deflassieux, Alain. *Tennis*. London: Barrie and Jenkins, 1977.

Emery, David. *Who's Who in International Tennis*. New York: Facts on File Publications, 1983.

Evans, Richard. *Tales from the Tennis Court: An Anthology of Tennis Writing*. London: Sidgwick and Jackson, 1984.

Hedges, Martin. *The Concise Dictionary of Tennis*. New York: Mayflower Books, 1978.

Janoff, Murray. *Game! Set! Match!* New York: Stadia Sports Publishing, 1973.

————. *Tennis Revolution*. New York: Stadia Sports Publishing, 1974.

Koster, Rich. *The Tennis Bubble: Big Money Tennis, How It Grew and Where It's Going*. New York: Quadrangle/New York Times Book Company, 1976.

Laney, Al. *Covering the Court: A 50-Year Love Affair with the Game of Tennis*. New York: Simon and Schuster, 1968.

Lawrence, Andrew. *Tennis: Great Stars, Great Moments*. New York: Putnam, 1976.

Lorimer, Lawrence T. *The Tennis Book*. New York: Random House, 1980.

McPhee, John A. *Wimbledon: A Celebration*. New York: Viking Press, 1972.

Match Point. The Nestle Book of Tennis No. 1. London: Stanley Paul, 1963.

May, Julian. *Forest Hills and the American Tennis Championship*. Mankato, Minnesota: Creative Education, 1976.

Medlycott, James. *100 Years of the Wimbledon Tennis Championships*. London: Hamlyn Publishing Group, 1977.

Metzler, Paul. *Tennis Styles and Stylists*. New York: Macmillan, 1969.

Mewshaw, Michael. *Short Circuit*. New York: Atheneum, 1983.

Minton, Robert. *Forest Hills: An Illustrated History*. Philadelphia: Lippincott, 1975.

Myers, Arthur Wallis. *Great Lawn Tennis: Pen Pictures of Famous Matches*. London: Cassell and Company, 1937.

Nebling, Fred. *Tennis Trivia*. Great Neck, New York: Todd and Honeywell, 1984.

Noel, Susan. *Tennis in Our Time*. London: W. H. Allen, 1954.

Peters, Geoff, ed. *Wimbledon on Camera*. New York: State Mutual Book and Periodical Service, 1981.

Potter, Edward Clarkson. *Kings of the Court: The Story of Lawn Tennis*. New York: Charles Scribner's Sons, 1963.

————. *The World's Leading Tennis Players*. New York, 1954.

Reardon, Maureen. *Match Point*. Milwaukee: Advanced Learning Concepts, 1975.

Robertson, Maxwell, ed. *The Encyclopedia of Tennis*. New York: Viking Press, 1974.

Schickel, Richard. *The World of Tennis*. New York: Random House, 1975.

Scott, Eugene. *Tennis: Game of Motion*. New York: Crown Publishers, 1973.

Shannon, Bill. *U.S. Open Record Book*. New York: Harper and Row, 1982.

Sullivan, George, ed. *Tennis Rules Illustrated*. New York: Cornerstone Library, 1981.

Talbert, William F., and Axthelm, Pete. *Tennis Observed*. Barre, Massachusetts: Barre Publishers, 1967.

Tilden, William Tatem. *The Common Sense of Lawn Tennis*. London: Methuen, 1924.

———. *Shooting Stars: Pen-Pictures of the World's Greatest Lawn Tennis Players of 1930*. Savory Publishing House, 1930.

Tingay, Lance. *The Guinness Book of Tennis Facts and Feats*. Enfield, Middlesex, England: Guinness Superlatives, 1983.

———. *History of Lawn Tennis in Pictures*. London: T. Stacey, 1973.

———. *100 Years of Wimbledon*. Enfield, England: Guinness Superlatives, 1977.

———. *Tennis, A Pictorial History*. Glasgow: Collins, 1977.

Tinling, Teddy, and Humphries, Rod. *Love and Faults: Personalities Who Have Changed the History of Tennis in My Lifetime*. New York: Crown Publishers, 1979.

United States Lawn Tennis Association. *Fifty Years of Lawn Tennis in the United States*. New York: United States Lawn Tennis Association, 1931.

Wade, Virginia, and Rafferty, Jean. *Ladies of the Court: A Century of Women at Wimbledon*. New York: Atheneum, 1984.

Whitington, Richard S. *An Illustrated History of Australian Tennis*. New York: St. Martin's Press, 1976.

Wind, Herbert Warren. *Game, Set, and Match: The Tennis Boom of the 1960s and 70s*. New York: Dutton, 1979.

World Tennis. London: Queen Ann Press.

World Tennis. New York: Simon and Schuster.

Young, David. *Game, Set, and Match: The Nestle Book of Tennis No. 2*. London: Stanley Paul, 1964.

———. *Points for Victory: The Nestle Book of Tennis No. 3*. London: Stanley Paul, 1965.

3

Rules and Administration

Tennis strokes and styles of play faintly resemble the leisurely upper-class pastime of the 1870s, yet the early rules remain the standards for play with only minor revisions and interpretations. With highly structured leagues and plentiful competitions replacing afternoon diversions, tournament directors and officials can benefit from the few books available on tennis administration.

RULES

Walter Wingfield published the first rules for tennis in 1874 as *The Game of Sphairistrike* and *The Major's Game of Lawn Tennis*. This English entrepreneur borrowed the scoring system and racket from the old game of rackets, the rubber ball and lawn surface from field tennis, and the hour-glass shaped net and net height from badminton and marketed his invention as sphairistrike. Upper-class men and women in England eagerly adopted his game, but by 1877 the All-England Cricket and Croquet Club changed the game, codified its rules, and began the Wimbledon Championships. Julian Marshall published these rules in *Lawn Tennis with the Laws Adopted by the M.C.C. and A.E.C. and L.T.C. and Badminton*.
Rules of Lawn Tennis as Adopted by the Cricket and Tennis

Clubs of Philadelphia predates the first national championships for men in 1881 and for women in 1887. The United States
National Lawn Tennis Association first published its rules in
1881 in *Rules of Lawn Tennis as Authorized and Adopted by
the United States National Lawn Tennis Association with a
Description of the Game.* This same governing association continues to provide the rules in *Official Lawn Tennis Rules* (1884),
*The Playing Rules of Lawn Tennis as Adopted by the United
States Lawn Tennis Association, Umpires Manual and Rules
of Lawn Tennis with Cases and Decisions, Rules of Tennis and
Cases and Decisions,* and its *Official Yearbook and Tennis Guide
with Official Rules* (annually since 1941). Four other books
focus solely on the rules. These include *The Playing Rules of
Lawn Tennis* (1886), *Lawn Tennis: Its Laws, Rules ... etc.* (1887),
Henry Jones' *Rules for Lawn Tennis* (1890), and *The Law of
Tennis* by Reginald Woods and Pembroke Vaile. Often, books
about tennis technique include the rules, such as the *Lawn
Tennis Catalogue and Directions for Playing,* Jahial Paret's
Lawn Tennis, Its Past, Present and Future (1904), George
Wright's *Rules of Lawn Tennis: With a Description of Important
Strokes* (1932), Pauline Betz Addie's *Tennis for Everyone, with
Official USLTA Rules* (1973), and James Wagenvoord's *Tennis
Notes* (1981). Joseph Whittelsey for years edited *The Wright
and Ditson Officially Adopted Lawn Tennis Guide,* which since
1897 has provided the rules, tournament results, club, inter-
collegiate, and interscholastic champions, and information about
regional events. *Spalding's Lawn Tennis Annual* listed the
rules and records, too.

To broaden tennis players' understanding of the rules, several interpretive books are available. Jack Stahr in 1979 and
Nick Powell in 1983 each discuss rules and officiating in their
books, both entitled, *A Friend at Court.* Nick Powell's *The Code*
summarizes the procedures and unwritten rules which tradition and custom dictate for tennis. The premise of this work is
that on close calls, a player will give the benefit of the doubt
to their opponent. Since rules are sometimes tedious to read,
George Sullivan uses diagrams in *Tennis Rules Illustrated.* Bob
Adams takes a humorous approach in his presentation of *The
Official Hacker's Rules of Tennis.* Burt Cutler in *So You Think*

You Know Tennis! and Peter Schwed in *Test Your Tennis I.Q.* assess the reader's knowledge of the rules. The *Rules and Standing Orders of the International Tennis Federation* and *Rules of Tennis and Cases and Decisions* explain the rules and rule interpretations of the International Tennis Federation and the United States Tennis Association respectively.

ADMINISTRATION

Tennis officials must know the rules. Except for Valentine Hall's *Lawn Tennis in America*, an 1888 publication which briefly lists rules and umpiring hints, not until 1951 did the United States Lawn Tennis Association publish its *Umpires Manual and Rules of Lawn Tennis with Cases and Decisions*. In 1923 Alfred Crawley's *Lawn Tennis Umpire and Referee: What He Must Know, and What He Should Do* became available in London. Crawley includes the rules, scoring, and handicapping. He explains umpiring the lines, foot faults, systems of the draw, and some of the knotty points about officiating. Francis Pearce published *Lawn Tennis Hints on Umpiring* also in England in 1936. Jack Stahr and the United States Tennis Association offer training materials for officials in *Tennis Umpire's Clinic Kit* while the United States Tennis Association currently provides the *USTA Umpires Handbook*. Nick Powell's *The Code* is a required reference for all USTA-sanctioned tournaments since this booklet summarizes the procedures and unwritten rules of the game as dictated by tradition and custom. Dave Parker adds a self-study workbook for umpires in *What's the Score?* Barbara Hultgren in consultation with the United States Tennis Association describes proper preparation of another group of vital tournament officials in *Ball Persons: A Trainer's Manual*.

The availability of tournaments is important to players of all skill levels. In London the annual *Ayres' Lawn Tennis Almanack and Tournament Guide* first provided this information. In the United States the *Official United States Tennis Tournament Directory* lists tournaments by state and by circuit, addresses of major tennis organizations, and tennis publications. Robert Snibbe's *Pro-Am Tennis Guide* also offers extensive information about events. Four resource guides list events and programs for special groups: *Junior Year Book, United States College Tennis Guide, Directory of Tennis Programs for Seniors,* and *Directory of Tennis Programs for the Disabled.* David Benjamin's *Competitive Tennis: A Guide for Parents and Young Players* describes tournament possibilities for youthful enthusiasts. The United States Tennis Association provides information about tournament procedures, rules, and etiquette in *A Handbook for Junior Tennis Tournament Players.*

Tournament administration necessitates considerable planning and skill although relatively limited information is available about this subject. Eleanor Owens describes how to rapidly replace players as they complete matches in *Tennis: Easy On— Easy Off.* Eve Kraft and Eunice Whiting explain the many facets of tournament planning in *A Handbook for Chairmen of Junior Tennis Tournaments: A Guide to the Planning and Direction of Junior Tournaments.* They discuss the committee responsibilities, budget, entries, publicity, supplies, hospitality, housing, transportation, the tournament draw, and handling problems and complaints. Lois Blackburn in a *Handbook for Planning and Conducting Tennis Tournaments* explains how to establish a tournament, to obtain a sanction, and to secure sponsors. She then describes the actual organization from officiating to scheduling to promoting to conducting the event. *The Tennis League Handbook* by Julie Kelly and Nancy Kirwan gives instructions for planning and operating a tennis league along with draw schedules for singles, doubles, and progressive partner doubles. Bill Shertenlieb and Phronie Sanders describe the administration of ladders, mixers, and leagues in *Focus on Competition: A Tennis Manual.*

Charles Bourne filled a void for tournament scoring in 1884 with his *Lawn Tennis Score Book and Rules for Playing with Definitions of Terms* which provides fifteen pages of score cards. In 1893 Joseph Whittelsey's *Official Lawn Tennis Score Book* also provided blanks for scoring. The *USTA Score Book for Coaches* by the United States Tennis Association and Reed Heller's *The Tennis Score Book* in recent years provide statistical forms for record keeping by teams and clubs. Coaches and

players can learn ways to improve their play by using Peg
Greeley's *Tennis Charting: The Graphic Way*.

The classic book about the administrative aspects of tennis
is Charles Dodgson's *Lawn Tennis Tournaments: The True
Method of Assigning Prizes with a Proof of the Fallacy of the
Present Method*. According to the explanations and tables in
this 1883 publication, tournament directors can assign the top
three prizes equitably by changing the length of matches and
the manner of the draw and by using total games won rather
than sets.

BIBLIOGRAPHY: RULES

Adams, Bob. *The Official Hacker's Rules of Tennis*. Massachusetts:
    Adams, 1982.
Addie, Pauline Betz. *Tennis for Everyone, with Official USLTA Rules*.
    Washington, D.C.: Acropolis Books, 1973.
Cutler, Burt. *So You Think You Know Tennis!* Los Angeles: Price/
    Stern/Sloan Publishers, 1977.
International Tennis Federation. *Rules and Standing Orders of the
    International Tennis Federation*. London: International Tennis
    Federation.
Jones, Henry. *Rules for Lawn Tennis*. London: Thomas De La Rue
    and Company, 1890.
Lawn Tennis: Its Laws, Rules ... etc. Manchester, England: J. Hey-
    wood, 1887.
Lawn Tennis Catalogue and Directions for Playing. New York: D. W.
    Granbery and Company, 1884.
Marshall, Julian. *Lawn Tennis with the Laws Adopted by the M.C.C.
    and A.E.C. and L.T.C. and Badminton*. New York: CFA Hin-
    richs, 1879.
Paret, Jahial Parmly. *Lawn Tennis, Its Past, Present and Future*. New
    York: Macmillan Company, 1904.
The Playing Rules of Lawn Tennis. New York: Peck and Snyder, 1886.
Powell, Nick. *The Code*. Lynn, Massachusetts: H.O. Zimman, 1981.
———. *A Friend at Court*. New York: United States Tennis Associ-
    ation, 1983.
*Rules of Lawn Tennis as Adopted by the Cricket and Tennis Clubs of
    Philadelphia*. Philadelphia: Lippincott, 1880.

Schwed, Peter. *Test Your Tennis I.Q.* Norwalk, Connecticut: Tennis
  Magazine, 1981.
Spalding's Lawn Tennis Annual. New York: American Sports Pub-
  lishing Company, 1890.
Stahr, Jack. *A Friend at Court.* Lynn, Massachusetts: H.O. Zimman,
  1979.
Sullivan, George, ed. *Tennis Rules Illustrated.* New York: Cornerstone
  Library, 1981.
United States Lawn Tennis Association. *Official Lawn Tennis Rules.*
  Boston: Wright and Ditson, 1884.
———. *Official Yearbook and Tennis Guide with the Official Rules.*
  New York: A.S. Barnes, 1941.
———. *The Playing Rules of Lawn Tennis as Adopted by the United
  States Lawn Tennis Association.* New York: Peck and Snyder,
  1888.
———. *Umpires Manual and Rules of Lawn Tennis with Cases and
  Decisions.* New York: United States Lawn Tennis Association,
  1951.
United States National Lawn Tennis Association, *Rules of Lawn Ten-
  nis as Authorized and Adopted by the United States National
  Lawn Tennis Association with a Description of the Game.* Phil-
  adelphia: J.B. Lippincott and Company, 1881.
United States Tennis Association. *Rules of Tennis and Cases and
  Decisions.* New York: United States Tennis Association, 1983.
Wagenvoord, James. *Tennis Notes.* New York: St. Martin's Press,
  1981.
Whittelsey, Joseph T., ed. *The Wright and Ditson Officially Adopted
  Lawn Tennis Guide.* Boston: Wright and Ditson, 1897.
Wingfield, Walter C. *The Game of Sphairistrike.* London: Harrison
  and Sons, 1874.
———. *The Major's Game of Lawn Tennis.* London, 1874.
Woods, Reginald F., and Vaile, Pembroke Arnold. *The Law of Tennis.*
  Chicago: T.E. Wilson and Company, 1919.
Wright, George. *Rules of Lawn Tennis: With a Description of Impor-
  tant Strokes.* Boston: Wright and Ditson, 1932.

BIBLIOGRAPHY: ADMINISTRATION

Ayers' Lawn Tennis Almanack and Tournament Guide. London: F.H.
  Ayres, 1910.
Benjamin, David A. *Competitive Tennis: A Guide for Parents and
  Young Players.* New York: Lippincott, 1979.

Blackburn, Lois H. *Handbook for Planning and Conducting Tennis Tournaments*. Princeton, New Jersey: United States Tennis Association, 1981.

Bourne, Charles R. *Lawn Tennis Score Book and Rules for Playing with Definitions of Terms*. New York: Charles R. Bourne, 1884.

Crawley, Alfred Ernest. *Lawn Tennis Umpire and Referee: What He Must Know, and What He Should Do*. London: Methuen and Company, 1923.

Dodgson, Charles Lutwidge. *Lawn Tennis Tournaments: The True Method of Assigning Prizes with a Proof of the Fallacy of the Present Method*. London: Macmillan and Company, 1883.

Greeley, Peg. *Tennis Charting: The Graphic Way*. Saratoga, California: Magoos Umbrella, 1981.

Hall, Valentine Gill. *Lawn Tennis in America*. New York: D.W. Granbery and Company, 1888.

Heller, Reed. *The Tennis Score Book*. N.p., n.d.

Hultgren, Barbara. *Ball Persons: A Trainer's Manual*. New York: United States Tennis Association, 1981.

Kelly, Julie, and Kirwan, Nancy. *Tennis League Handbook*. Hinsdale, Illinois: Finn Hall Enterprises, 1975.

Kraft, Eve, and Whiting, Eunice S. *A Handbook for Chairmen of Junior Tennis Tournaments: A Guide to the Planning and Direction of Junior Tournaments*. Princeton, New Jersey: United States Tennis Association, 1976.

Owens, Eleanor. *Tennis: Easy On—Easy Off*. New York: United States Tennis Association, 1975.

Parker, Dave. *What's the Score?* Parsonsburg, Maryland, 1979.

Pearce, Francis Henry. *Lawn Tennis Hints on Umpiring*. Oxford, England: Shakespeare Head Press, 1936.

Powell, Nick. *The Code*. Lynn, Massachusetts: H.O. Zimman, 1981.

Shertenlieb, Bill, and Sanders, Phronie. *Focus on Competition: A Tennis Manual*. Fort Lauderdale, Florida: Tennis Manual, 1980.

Snibbe, Robert (ed.). *Pro-Am Tennis Guide*. Maplewood, New Jersey: Hammond, 1982.

Stahr, Jack. *Tennis Umpire's Clinic Kit*. New York: United States Tennis Association, 1975.

United States Lawn Tennis Association. *Junior Year Book*. New York: United States Tennis Association.

———. *Umpires Manual and Rules of Lawn Tennis with Cases and Decisions*. New York: United States Lawn Tennis Association, 1951.

United States Tennis Association. *A Handbook for Junior Tennis*

Tournament Players. New York: United States Tennis Association, 1976.

————. *Directory of Tennis Programs for Seniors*. New York: United States Tennis Association, 1981.

————. *Directory of Tennis Programs for the Disabled*. New York: United States Tennis Association.

————. *United States College Tennis Guide*. New York: United States Tennis Association.

————. *USTA Score Book for Coaches*. New York: United States Tennis Association, 1977.

————. *USTA Umpires Handbook*. New York: United States Tennis Association.

United States Tennis Survey. *Official United States Tennis Tournament Directory*. Ann Arbor, Michigan: United States Tennis Survey, 1978.

Whittelsey, Joseph T. *Official Lawn Tennis Score Book*. Cambridge, Massachusetts: University Press, 1893.

4

Equipment, Facilities, and Travel

EQUIPMENT

The *Lawn Tennis Catalogue and Directions for Playing* in 1884 provided the first equipment advertising in a tennis book. D.W. Granbery and Company advertised prizes, rackets, balls, nets, posts, markers, shoes, presses, and covers for sale and also offered racket restringing. While periodicals have advertised tennis equipment and clothing and businesses have marketed their products since the origin of tennis, not until the 1970s were consumer guides, such as the *Complete Guide to Tennis*, available. This comprehensive work includes stroke making, strategies and tactics, an equipment guide, travel information, and a history of the major championships. Stephen Fiott focuses on *Tennis Equipment*, while equipment is the first aspect of tennis Rob McGregor and Stephen Devereux emphasize in *EEVeTeC, The McGregor Solution for Managing the Pains of Fitness*. Moira Duggan provides a comprehensive listing of equipment and supplies in *The Tennis Catalog: The Complete Guide to the Tennis Market Place*. In Duggan's well-illustrated book, she describes every imaginable item related to tennis and furnishes an approximate cost for each. In addition to the usual rackets, balls, shoes, and nets, she lists squeegees, air domes, tennis camps, energy aids, books, periodicals, films, and even tennis careers. Another helpful volume for tennis enthusiasts is *The Tennis Player's Handbook: A Buyer's Guide and Service Directory*. After offering suggestions for choosing the right equipment and tennis wear, this book provides information about courts, clubs, leagues, and lessons. It also recommends practice devices, physical and mental conditioning, and how to treat and avoid injuries. Photographs enhance the presentation of the above material as well as the discussions concerning tennis vacations, camps, clinics, and businesses.

Originally published in 1767 *The Art of the Tennis-Racquet-Maker and of Tennis* by Francois Garsault explains the entire process of making rackets. Its four plates show the stages and descriptions of this ancient art.

FACILITIES

The construction, maintenance, and financing of public and private tennis courts are vital to individuals, clubs, and communities. The 1908 *"Weather-Proof" Lawn Tennis* describes how to make hard courts for summer and winter play. In 1912 George Walsh explained the selection of location, kind of court, marking, backstop, and care in *Making a Tennis Court*. The Portland Cement Association promoted *Tennis Courts of Concrete, Tennis Every Day on Concrete Courts,* and *Reinforced Concrete Tennis Courts* in its 1916, 1917, and 1976 publications. *How to Build a Tennis Court* was available in 1927 as was *Care and Construction of Tennis Courts* by Oliver Campbell.

Alan Anderson explained *How to Build Your Own Tennis Court and Save Thousands of Dollars* in 1977. Anderson details the entire construction process from surveying to preparing the base and the porous or nonporous playing surface to maintaining the court. He provides appendixes of manufactures, suppliers, how to estimate costs, playing qualities of various surfaces, and how to calculate quantities. *How to Build Your Own Tennis Court* by Blackwell Duncan explains preparing the site, building the base, fencing, landscaping, and lighting in a well-illustrated format. Charles Neal includes all aspects of having a tennis facility in *Build Your Own Tennis Court: Construction, Subcontracting, Equipping, and Maintaining In-*

door and Outdoor Courts. Specifically he discusses cost esti-
mation, surface selection, court foundation, surface preparation,
installation of electricity, plumbing, and fencing, indoor struc-
tures, and court maintenance. A comprehensive summary of
court construction, maintenance and equipment needs for courts,
surface evaluation, and information about lighting comprises
Tennis Courts 1984 by the United States Tennis Association.
Other helpful works include *A Manual of Clay Tennis Court
Maintenance* by Michael Humphrey, *Let's Cure the Court
Crunch, Lighting Outdoor Tennis Courts*, the United States
Lawn Tennis Association's *Construction and Maintenance of
Tennis Courts, The Princeton Story: An Example of Community
Tennis Planning and Programming*, and James Bright's *The
Tennis Court Book.*

L.D. Cox and R.E. Owens discussed strategies for financially
supporting tennis courts in *Maintenance Costs of Public Tennis
Courts* in 1946. *A Manual for Financing Public Playing Facilities* explains how to sell the project to government officials and
to the community, how to conduct a feasibility study, how to
obtain federal, state, and local funding, and how to solve the
court crunch. Fifteen case studies illustrate the various ways
communities can fund court construction. *Financing Public
Tennis Courts* and *A Guide to Tennis Club Planning, Building
and Financing* offer other helpful suggestions. Arthur Gimmy
provides a management guide for tennis club or program administrators in *Tennis Clubs and Racquet Sport Projects: A
Guide to Appraisal, Market Analysis, Development, and Financing*. Gimmy explains the importance of supply and de-
mand, site selection, financing, and the appraisal process plus
furnishes eleven case studies.

TRAVEL

Finding a court at home, planning a tennis vacation, or arranging travel based on tennis court availability is easier today
than ever before. *The United States Tennis Club Registry* publishes the locations of clubs throughout the country. For future
collegians, the United States Tennis Association provides the

United States College Tennis Guide which indexes all the teams which provide athletic grants-in-aid for both men and women.

Four books focus on arranging upcoming travel around tennis: *Gilbert Richards' Tennis for Travelers* by Gilbert Richards, *The Tennis Lover's Travel Guide* by Sandra Friedman, *The Traveler's Guide to Tennis* by Barry Tarshis, and Dick Zeldin's *A Tennis Guide to the USA: Where to Play in the Most Traveled Cities*. Using information from club and facility questionnaires, Zeldin reports on 419 locations with over 3000 courts. He includes alphabetical listings of fifty cities giving addresses, number of courts, hours, rates, locations, and availability of equipment and instruction. Tarshis divides the country into seven regions, and then alphabetically within the states he lists facilities, fees, court assignment systems, instructional programs, accommodations, and site directions. Fifteen tennis travelers' quick tips on technique encourage players to follow their serves to the net, to run with their rackets back, and to hit through the ball.

Many tennis buffs plan their vacations in order to take advantage of facilities or select resorts specifically because of their tennis accommodations. *Curtis Casewit's Guide to Tennis Resorts* briefly lists the locations and facilities of resorts by state. *Tennis Resorts: A Guide to Sporting Vacations in the West* also by Curtis Casewit focuses on resorts in nine western regions, such as Palm Springs and Los Angeles and Nevada, Lake Tahoe, and Utah. Casewit describes motels, resorts, and tennis ranches in these locales while including how to get there, available facilities, and addresses. In addition to the typical information, Helen Rosenbaum in *Tennis Vacations* offers selection advice from leading professional players, a directory of tennis camps for kids, conditioning for a tennis holiday, tennis publications, camps for adults, and tournament vacations. *The Tennis Player's Vacation Guide* by Jerome Klein describes 107 sites in twenty-two states and twenty-one countries. Each citation includes number of courts, hours of play, names of teaching professionals, tournaments, climates, rates, nearby attractions, and family activities.

Nicholas Van Daalen looks at 130 resorts in *The International Tennis Guide: To Some of the Most Exciting Tennis Re-*

sorts in the World. Quality facilities, accommodations, and location are the keys for selection of the leading resorts in Bermuda, Canada, the Caribbean, England, Europe, Mexico, and the United States. Gilbert Richards in *Tennis for Travelers: The International Guide to Hotel, Motel, Resort, Park, and Other Tennis Courts Available to Travelers* lists over 5,000 court locations. While in each case the courts are open to the public, some charge fees or are available only when staying in hotels or resorts.

BIBLIOGRAPHY: EQUIPMENT

Complete Guide to Tennis. New York: New American Library, 1975.

Duggan, Moira. *The Tennis Catalog: The Complete Guide to the Tennis Market Place.* New York: Macmillan, 1978.

Fiott, Stephen. *Tennis Equipment.* Radnor, Pennsylvania: Chilton Book Company, 1978.

Garsault, Francois Alexandre Pierre de. *The Art of the Tennis-Racquet-Maker and of Tennis.* Baltimore: Racquet Sports Information Service, 1977.

Lawn Tennis Catalogue and Directions for Playing. New York: D.W. Granbery and Company, 1884.

McGregor, Rob Roy, and Devereux, Stephen E. *EEVeTeC, The McGregor Solution for Managing the Pains of Fitness.* Boston: Houghton, Mifflin and Company, 1982.

The Tennis Player's Handbook: A Buyer's Guide and Service Directory. Norwalk, Connecticut: Tennis Magazine, 1980.

BIBLIOGRAPHY: FACILITIES

Anderson, Alan. *How to Build Your Own Tennis Court and Save Thousands of Dollars.* New York: Dutton, 1977.

Bright, James L. *The Tennis Court Book.* Andover, Massachusetts: Andover Publishing Group, 1979.

Campbell, Oliver Samuel. *Care and Construction of Tennis Courts.* New York: American Sports Publishing Company, 1927.

Cox, L.D., and Owens, R.E. *Maintenance Costs of Public Tennis Courts.* New York State College of Forestry, 1946.

Duncan, S. Blackwell. *How to Build Your Own Tennis Court.* Blue Ridge Summit, Pennsylvania: Tab Books, 1979.

Financing Public Tennis Courts. Princeton, New Jersey: United States
     Tennis Association, 1979.

Gimmy, Arthur E. *Tennis Clubs and Racquet Sport Projects: A Guide
     to Appraisal, Market Analysis, Development, and Financing.*
     Chicago: American Institute of Real Estate Appraisers of the
     National Association of Realtors, 1978.

A Guide to Tennis Club Planning, Building and Financing. North
     Miami, Florida: Tennis Industry Magazine, 1979.

How to Build a Tennis Court. New York: American Sports Publishing
     Company, 1927.

Humphrey, Michael R. *A Manual of Clay Tennis Court Mainte-
     nance.*N.p., 1982.

Let's Cure the Court Crunch. Princeton, New Jersey: Peoria Tennis
     Association Facilities Committee, 1977.

Lighting Outdoor Tennis Courts. Princeton, New Jersey: United States
     Tennis Association, 1978.

A Manual for Financing Public Playing Facilities. Chicago: Tennis
     Foundation of North America, 1975.

Neal, Charles D. *Build Your Own Tennis Court: Construction, Sub-
     contracting, Equipping, and Maintaining Indoor and Outdoor
     Courts.* Radnor, Pennsylvania: Chilton Book Company, 1977.

Portland Cement Association. *Reinforced Concrete Tennis Courts.* Chi-
     cago: Portland Cement Association, 1976.

———. *Tennis Courts of Concrete.* Chicago: Portland Cement Asso-
     ciation 1916.

———. *Tennis Every Day on Concrete Courts.* Chicago: Portland Ce-
     ment Association, 1917.

*The Princeton Story: An Example of Community Tennis Planning and
     Programming.* New York: United States Tennis Association,
     n.d.

United States Lawn Tennis Association. *Construction and Mainte-
     nance of Tennis Courts.* New York: United States Lawn Tennis
     Association, n.d.

United States Tennis Association. *Tennis Courts 1984.* Princeton, New
     York: United States Tennis Association, 1984.

Walsh, George Ethelbert. *Making a Tennis Court.* New York: McBride,
     Nast and Company, 1912.

"Weather-Proof" Lawn Tennis. London: Amateur Sports Publishing
     Co., 1908.

BIBLIOGRAPHY: TRAVEL

Casewit, Curtis W. *Curtis Casewit's Guide to Tennis Resorts.* New
     York: Pilot Books, 1978.

———. *Tennis Resorts: A Guide to Sporting Vacations in the West.* San Francisco: Chronical Books, 1978.

Friedman, Sandra C. *The Tennis Lover's Travel Guide.* Washington, D.C.: Acropolis Books, 1978.

Klein, Jerome. *The Tennis Player's Vacation Guide.* New York: Interbook, 1974.

Richards, Gilbert. *Gilbert Richards' Tennis for Travelers.* Cincinnati: Gilbert Richards Industries, 1970.

———. *Tennis for Travelers: The International Guide to Hotel, Motel, Resort, Park, and Other Tennis Courts Available to Travelers.* Cincinnati: Gilbert Richards Industries, 1972.

Rosenbaum, Helen. *Tennis Vacations.* New York: Popular Lirary, 1977.

Tarshis, Barry, ed. *The Traveler's Guide to Tennis.* Norwalk, Connecticut: Tennis Magazine, 1976.

United States Tennis Association. *United States College Tennis Guide.* New York: United States Tennis Association.

United States Tennis Club Registry. Irvine, California: Tennis Club Registry, 1976.

Van Daalen, Nicholas. *The International Tennis Guide: To Some of the Most Exciting Tennis Resorts in the World.* New York: Scribner, 1974.

Zeldin, Dick. *A Tennis Guide to the USA: Where to Play in the Most Traveled Cities.* New York: Watts, 1980.

5

General Tennis Technique

When tennis was still a relatively unknown game, the first how-to-play books appeared in the United States and in England. This new game, one of several leisurely pastimes of the wealthy in the 1800s, soon surpassed the others in popularity. Today it is one of the popular lifetime racket sports of all ages and skill levels. The majority of the over 450 instructional books describe the basic strokes plus provide some tactics and strategies for match play, while others focus on building on the fundamentals to improve performance. This chapter examines the general technique books.

In 1874 Walter Wingfield in marketing his tennis equipment provided instructions in the basics in *The Major's Game of Lawn Tennis*. Robert Osborn in the 1880s described *Lawn Tennis, Its Players, and How to Play, with the Laws of the Game* while Herbert Wilberforce in *Lawn Tennis* included instructional hints as well as a chapter for women players by a Mrs. Hillyard. Wilfred Baddeley instructed in *Lawn Tennis* in 1895, as did Sarah Whittelsley in *A Manual of Lawn Tennis* in 1894. Julian Marshall's *Lawn Tennis with the Laws Adopted by the M.C.C. and A.E.C. and L.T.C. and Badminton* in 1879 provided both instruction and rules. Sometimes called the father of tennis in the United States, James Dwight explained the techniques of this new sport in *Lawn-Tennis* in 1886 and *Practical Lawn-*

Tennis in 1893. *Campbell's Lawn Tennis and the Way to Play It* by Oliver Campbell also described tennis and its techniques in 1891 as did *Lessons in Lawn Tennis: A New Method of Study and Practice for Acquiring a Good and Sound Style of Play* by Eustace Miles. Henry Slocum, a leading player of the time, described *Lawn Tennis in Our Own Country* including technique instruction in 1890, while Solomon Peile's *Lawn Tennis as a Game of Skill* (1885) provided technique instructions too.

Several books associate tennis with lawn games and racket sports. The first of these combines instructional hints about *Lawn Tennis, Badminton, Croquet, Troco, Racquets, Fives, Nurr and Spell, Bowling, Hurling, etc.* Julian Marshall, James Spoons, and Arnan Tait in *Tennis, Rackets, and Fives* described their favorite sports respectively in 1891. One year earlier *Tennis, Lawn Tennis, Rackets, and Fives* under John Heathcote's editorship included information on tennis by C. G. Heathcote, Lottie Dod, Herbert Wilberforce, H. F. Lawford, Spencer Gore, and Richard Sears. Eustace Miles instructed in *Racquets, Tennis, and Squash* in 1903. Paul Champ, et al., discussed *Lawn–Tennis, Golf, Croquet, Polo, Par MM* in 1911. F. De Bellet instructs on lawn tennis. Clarence Aberdare describes and illustrates playing techniques for *Rackets, Squash Rackets, Tennis, Fives and Badminton*. Riding, golf, and lawn tennis comprise the sports in Cecil Aldin's *Omnibus Book of Sports for Young and Old* with John Doeg and Allison Danzig explaining lawn tennis. Gordon Winter provides information about various playing techniques, the courts, equipment, and the rules for lawn tennis, badminton, squash, rugby fives, archery, croquet, and small lawn games, such as quoit tennis and rounders, in *Games for Court and Garden*. Allison Danzig focuses on tennis, rackets, and squash rackets in *The Racquet Game* while George Starke examines two sports in *Starke's Table and Lawn Tennis Technology*. *Enjoying Racquet Sports* in 1978, using more diagrams than text, furnishes the basics about facilities, equipment, basic strokes, and rules for tennis, badminton, squash, racquetball, paddle tennis, table tennis, platform tennis, and paddleball. Herbert FitzGibbon and Jeffrey Bairstow ask what is *The Complete Racquet Sports Player?* They categorize tennis as a game of steadiness, badminton as a game of deception and attrition, platform tennis as a cat and mouse game, squash as a fast and furious game, and racquetball as a simple power game. For each sport the authors discuss the grips, serves, longer and shorter strokes, strategies, equipment, and competition plus add some ideas for conditioning. Carol Morgenstern uses many photographs to teach the history, strokes, and strategies for six sports in *Playing the Racquets*. She also includes the rules for tennis, squash, racquetball, paddle tennis, platform tennis, and paddleball. Elinor Nickerson discusses technique, history, and equipment for court tennis, platform tennis, table tennis, racquets, squash racquets, racquetball, badminton, handball, playground racquet sports, and tennis in *Racquet Sports: An Illustrated Guide*.

George Agutter, head instructor at the West Side Tennis Club in Forest Hills, New York, explains and diagrams the forehand and backhand drives, serving, volleying, lobbing, footwork, tactics, and the cut strokes in *Develop Correct Tennis Form*. *Lawn Tennis for Public Courts Players* by A. J. Aitken in 1924 focuses on the knowledge that the 500,000 players in parks and on community courts need to learn. The basic strokes, ladies play, advanced strokes, tennis holidays, and tournament play are among the topics therein. Using pictures of the author in action, *How to Play Lawn Tennis* presents the basic strokes and how to play the game in 1920. Fred Alexander also gives hints about doubles play, conditioning, what to wear, and how to build and to keep a grass court. *Learn to Play Tennis*, an extensively illustrated tennis guide by James Allen, describes the basic strokes, scoring, etiquette, equipment, and a brief history of tennis. Reginald Applewhaite diagrams boys and girls executing the various strokes in *Play the Game Lawn Tennis*. In addition to the fundamental techniques for shots, he explains the topspin drive, drop volley, sliced drive, and chop shot while stressing the impact point when stroking.

Alfred Beamish explained the basic strokes of the game in the 1920s in *First Steps to Lawn Tennis* and *The Lawn Tennis Tip Book*. The author demonstrates the strokes in the first of these books. In *How to Improve Your Tennis* Mercer Beasley states that accuracy is the primary principle in tennis. Footwork, body position, and timing are components of accuracy which players should develop prior to hitting the various strokes. He also explains where balls should be hit, strategy, rules, and provides a tennis quiz. *Lawn Tennis Up-to-Date* by Powell Blackmore provides instruction in the basic shots, explains the selection process of the English Davis Cup teams, and includes six sections by other authors. Andre Gobert discusses strokes, tactics, and hard courts; F. M. B. Fisher evaluates style versus effort in tennis; George Stoddart describes players he knows; Lady Waverlee asks why not a ladies' Davis Cup; and Bill Tilden tells his impressions of tennis in England. George Beldam and Pembroke Vaile offer stroke instruction through *Great Lawn Tennis Players: Their Methods Illustrated*.

How to Play Tennis by James Burns initially in 1915 described the fundamentals and encouraged players to practice, force the pace, and reduce playing weaknesses. In London Alfred Crawley's *Lawn Tennis, Lawn Tennis Do's and Don'ts*, and *The Technique of Lawn Tennis Demonstrated by Cinematography* provide explanations and demonstrations of the strokes. He includes tactics in the first book and offers psychological hints in the second book. F. R. Burrow described *Lawn Tennis: The World-Game of Today* in 1922, *Lawn Tennis of Today: Its Strokes, Strategy, and Tactics* in 1924, and *Lawn Tennis: How to Succeed* in 1933. Strokes are the focus of the second book plus he discusses some tactics, the rules, and doubles play. *Tennis Made Easy* by Lloyd Budge, the brother of tennis champion Don Budge, explains timing, footwork and adjustments to ball height for ground strokes, the serve, supplementary strokes, court strategy, and position play. Four years later he authored *Lawn Tennis* which also focuses on techniques.

Geoffrey Clayton helped keep tennis interest high through his wartime (1946) publication *Introducing Tennis*. He provides advice on stroking, positioning, and tactics in this forty-five page book. Merritt Cutler relies heavily on diagrams of players to instruct in *Basic Tennis Illustrated*. He shows and briefly discusses the forehand, backhand, volley, three types of serves, return of serve, lob, smash, use of spin and slice, tactics, poaching, mixed doubles, women's play, and play on various courts. That same year Cutler authored *The Tennis Book*. Stanley Doust in *Lawn Tennis* uses photographs of thirty stars to demonstrate proper technique. He uses a large picture of the player, a brief biographical sketch, and a short instructional text in this book. *America's Tennis Book* by Curtis Casewit uses photographs throughout to show the strokes. He also discusses etiquette, rules and scoring, where to improve your game, playing competitively, tennis careers, and history. *Net Results: A Picture Book of Tennis Fundamentals* by Jane Donnalley uses mostly diagrams to teach the fundamental and specialty shots. David Litz's *A Photographic Guide to Tennis Fundamentals* teaches the basic strokes primarily through pictures. *Tennis Techniques Illustrated* by Wynn Mace uses diagrams to show the strokes, shot placement, and match strategy. Humorous artwork, cartoons, and photographs of the stars fill about half of Cornel Lumiere's basic instructional *The Book of Tennis: How to Play the Game*. Donald Megale and Bill Winkler use many photographs along with instructional hints in their mimeographed booklet *Tennis: Fundamentals and Basic Principles Illustrated*. *Tennis in Pictures* features the author Tom Okker in sequential instructional photographs of the strokes. Don Platt relies mostly on photographs to instruct in *Tennis: Playing a Winning Game with Don Platt*. Oscar Fraley's *How to Play Championship Tennis* show stars demonstrating proper shot execution.

Edward Dewhurst explained *The Science of Lawn Tennis* in 1910 by describing the strokes, match play, and psychology of tennis. After instructing in the basic and advanced strokes and tactics, *Lawn Tennis* by Leslie Godfree and Henry Wakelam provides information about governance and administration of tennis, umpiring, and line judging. Eli Epstein in *Tennis Cues* explains the basic strokes, practicing, playing, conditioning, and the rules. George Hughes offers three ways for *Improving Your Tennis*. These include learning the fundamentals, practicing with a purpose, and playing with a tactical plan. Former champion and noted coach Evelyn Dewhurst provides hints on how to play in *Lawn Tennis: May I Introduce You?* Kenneth Hughes provided *Helpful Advice on Lawn Tennis* in 1952. *Lawn Tennis* by John Hankinson uses fifty-one pages of text and forty-eight photographs to instruct in the basic strokes, methods of practice, how to watch a match, and court-craft. Using cartoons, action shots of players, and line drawings in addition to the text, Cecil Irvine explains *The Mechanics of Lawn Tennis*. In addition to the strokes, he discusses the effect the varying court surfaces have on the speed of the ball, cramps and tennis elbow, how to organize a tournament, how to construct a tennis court, and psychology in match play. In *How to Beat Better Tennis Players* Loring Fiske focuses on learning the fundamental shots.

Vic Braden's Tennis for the Future by Vic Braden and Bill Bruns describes in an entertaining way all the fundamental shots, plus strategy, the psychology of tennis, doubles play, and the importance of conditioning, practicing, and taking lessons. Ed Collins instructs in the fundamental shots, net play, opposing a net player, tactics, doubles, and psychology using text and cartoon illustrations in *Watch the Ball, Bend Your Knees, That'll be $20 Please!*

Clarence Jones offers comprehensive tennis instruction in seven books—*Manual of Instruction; Lawn Tennis; Tennis: How to Become a Champion; Your Book of Tennis; Match-Winning Tennis: Tactics, Temperament and Training; Improving Your Tennis: Strokes and Techniques;* and *Starting Tennis* with Angela Buxton. *Your Book of Tennis* focuses on the principles of strokes, practice, and competition, while *Improving Your Tennis: Strokes and Techniques* includes net play and defending it, use of spin, developing a winning attitude, training, and playing at the peaks. In *Match-Winning Tennis: Tactics, Temperament and Training* Jones suggests thinking of a tennis court as a battleground on which tactics are planned and where players use their abilities to best advantage.

In 1913 Raymond Little explained *Tennis Tactics* through discussion of the strokes, styles of play, and strategies. Beside the strokes *Gordon Lowe on Lawn Tennis* by Gordon Lowe suggests ideas for practice and match contests, court deportment, officiating, ladies' play, and junior events, and improving English players' performances. F. W. Last emphasizes sportsmanship, stroke development, practice, fitness, and reduction of errors in *How to Play Tennis*. *Learning Lawn Tennis* by Emlyn Jones builds upon practice of the basic strokes to develop a strong game. James Medlycott explains the basic strokes in

Tennis. Thomas Moss analyzes *Lawn Tennis: How to Discover and Correct Faults* by looking at stroke production, fundamental principles, and tactics. *Tennis Weaknesses and Remedies* by Paul Metzler discusses the basic shots and stresses playing your game, anticipating your opponent's shots, and employing tactics during matches. Rex Lardner humorously explains *Finding and Exploiting Your Opponent's Weaknesses.* Tactics he recommends are to attack the serve, to hit and move to the net, to care and feed a tired opponent, and to attack the left-hander.

Virginia Kraft in *Tennis Drills for Self-Improvement* uses over 100 photographs about technique to instruct average players. Using herself as an example, she recalls how she improved her game tremendously in only one season. She also offers hints in *Tennis Instruction for Fun and Competition. Sports Illustrated Tennis* by Doug MacCurdy and Shawn Tully stresses consistency, depth, pace, and spin when executing the strokes, fitness, practice, and positive thinking. Ruth Eddy and John LeBar use a basic instructional approach in *Learning Tennis Together.* In *Tennis: A Guide for the Developing Tennis Player* James Bryant comprehensively covers strokes, strategies, mental aspects, drills, and rules, plus he provides a self-appraisal checklist and a progressive breakdown of the skills in photographs. *Lifetime Treasury of Tested Tennis Tips: Secrets of Winning Play* examines all the strokes and furnishes 203 instructional tips plus extensive diagrams for reinforcing these principles. Among the tips William Murphy and Chester Murphy offer for ground strokes are "fling a frisbee to hit the backhand" and "steer the ball along a railroad track"; for serves: "watch your toss as you serve" and "change your stance when serving in the sun"; for volleys: "think backhand when at the net"; miscellaneous strokes: "be patient when attacking," "mix lobs with passing shots," and "outpsych your opponent by taking charge"; and for returnig the serve in doubles: "hit to the server's feet." Jack Groppel's *Principles of Tennis Techniques, Drills and Strategies* teaches all the shots while it emphasizes improving game strategy. Jack Groppel's knowledge of biomechanics and Arthur Shay's freeze-frame photography combine to offer a unique publication, *Optimal Tennis: The Freeze-Frame Photographic Approach to a Better Game.* They describe and show many variations in good basic mechanics of stroke production while applying their tips to players of all skill levels. In addition to basic concepts about stroking, *The Tennis Doctor: Everything You Always Wanted to Know about Tennis But Didn't Know Whom to Ask* by James Loomis discusses physical training, tennis injuries, drills and games, and answers to questions most frequently asked.

Arthur Myers writes about the history of tennis, the basic strokes, match play, doubles, and court construction in *The Complete Lawn Tennis Player* in 1908. Earlier in 1903 Myers describes *Lawn Tennis at Home and Abroad* while in 1930 he explains *Lawn Tennis—Its Principles and Practice—A Player's Guide to Modern Methods. Tennis without Tears* by Susan Noel contains stroke explanations plus information about doubles, match play, manners, and clothes. John Olliff's five books— *The Groundwork of Lawn Tennis, Olliff on Tennis, Lawn Tennis: The Complete Technique of Lawn Tennis Stroke Play, Lawn Tennis for Beginners,* and *Lawn Tennis: How to Succeed*—focus on stroke technique. In *Lawn Tennis: The Complete Technique of Lawn Tennis Stroke Play* and *Olliff on Tennis* he uses players as models of proper technique, while in the later book he features the leading players—the four best female and twenty best male players ever.

Jahial Paret first instructed on *How to Play Lawn Tennis* in 1902 by discussing the most important strokes and the styles and skills of the experts. In *Methods and Players of Modern Lawn Tennis* he teaches the fundamental shots, tactics, position play, ethics, and etiquette. Notable players at the time added their expert advice. *Mechanics of the Game of Lawn Tennis* offers instruction about stroke execution plus technique variations for women. He also describes *Lawn Tennis for Beginners, Psychology and Advanced Play of Lawn Tennis,* and *Everything You Need to Know about Lawn Tennis: How to Play the Game, Expert Instruction and Coaching of the World's Champions.* Norman Patterson's six instructional books— *Courtcraft: Lawn Tennis Tactics and Psychology, Lawn Tennis by Tyne and Wear, Lawn Tennis at School and After, How to Teach Lawn Tennis, The Elements of Lawn Tennis,* and *The Complete Lawn-Tennis Player*—also deal with playing technique. The last two of these books include information about sportsmanship, practice, how to improve play, umpiring, rules, and court craft. F. W. Payn described how to play in *Secrets of Lawn Tennis* in 1906, plus he also discusses training, diet and climate, varsity tennis, and lawn tennis in England. A year later Payn suggested *Tennis Topics and Tactics*.

The *Pro/Am Guide to Tennis*, borrowing extensively from David Lott's *Tennis Guide*, stresses the fundamental strokes; singles, doubles, and mixed doubles play for beginners, intermediates, juniors, seniors, women, and men; strategy; and instructional pointers such as concentration and confidence. Stanley Plagenhoef's *Fundamentals of Tennis*, Roy Petty's *Contemporary Tennis*, and H. Price's *Lawn Tennis, as It Is Played Today, Lawn Tennis,* and *Foulsham's How to Play Lawn Tennis, and Strokes Worth Practising* focus on the basic strokes. Beyond the basics Barry Pelton discusses shot placement, mental strategy, agility and quickness, court manners, and drills to measure improvement and achievement in *Tennis*.

Fundamentals and match play are the major topics in John Pollock's *Listening to Lacoste* as the outstanding player Rene Lacoste explains and demonstrates proper stroking technique. M.J.G. Ritchie in *The Text Book of Lawn Tennis* and *Lawn Tennis, the Modern Game*, and John Rendall in *Things That Matter in Lawn Tennis* and *Lawn Tennis: A Method of Acquiring Proficiency* similarly focus on the development of the fundamental skills. Rendall in this last book adds information about teaching children. Robert Scharff's *The Collier Quick and Easy Guide to Tennis* uses a large number of illustrations to show proper stroke execution and strategies. *How to Succeed at Tennis* by Peter Scholl and Nikki Schultz in *Tennis for Everyone* rely on photographs for over half of their presentation about the strokes. Scholl states six golden rules for success: make an effort, concentrate, watch the ball, hold the racket firmly, move, and play fairly. Using photographs and cartoons throughout, John Shingleton explains the basic fundamentals in *How to Increase Your Net Value: A Simplified Guide to Better Tennis*. He also discusses match preparation, tactics, strategies against lefties and when playing poorly, plus he advocates that the best way to improve your game is to practice. Cornel Lumiere uses the stars to show the strokes in *Better Tennis with the World's Best Players*. The stars demonstrate *Skills and Tactics of Tennis* to teach the shots, correction of stroke execution, court craft, positional play, practicing, the mental side of tennis, etiquette, and advice to parents.

The Playboy Book of Tennis: How to Play Winning Tennis ...and Everything Else You Forgot to Ask Your Pro by George Soules and Peter Range uses a question-answer approach to tell why you should play, how to find a court and a partner, the importance of taking lessons and going to a tennis camp in addition to the basic strokes. They also discuss finesse, the mental game, conditioning, injuries, etiquette, and the rules.

Stan Smith's Guide to Better Tennis, one of Stan Smith's (and Larry Sheehan's) five instructional books, examines mistakes then analyzes and corrects them. He recommends corrections for serves: into the net = toss the ball up and over; without power = add weight shift and wrist action; for returns of serve: poor percentage = adjust backswing to the speed of the serve; ground strokes: hitting into net = bend knees to the level of the shot; volley: hitting on the wood = watch the ball hit the strings; for overheads: mishitting = reduce size of strokes; for lobs: too short = practice targeting on the baseline. Nick Bollettieri's *Tennis Your Way* uses a lesson format similar to the approach he uses at his Tennis Academy to instruct in the basic shots. Bollettieri's successful teaching style includes explaining every aspect of a student's style of play using simple lessons and dialogue, suggesting changes only if the student understands and can patiently practice what is to be done, and building new abilities upon old skills.

Pembroke Vaile offers instructional guidance in three general tennis technique books. *Modern Lawn Tennis* in 1904 describes shots, ladies' play, doubles, practice hints, officiating, and leading players. In *The Strokes and Science of Lawn Tennis* he covers similar topics plus compares tennis as played in England, the United States, and Australia. Vaile also explains how to make and to keep a court and a synopsis of the laws of the game in *The Tennis Primer*.

Dave Snyder's *Tennis* uses a brief text and many illustrations to present the fundamentals of the game. R. F. Stroud in *Step-*

ping Stones to Better Tennis uses numbers one, two, and three as pointers to explain technique for all strokes. *The Game's the Same: Lawn Tennis in the World of Sport* by John Smyth explains the ingredients for tennis success and advocates that practice makes perfect. Charles Tuckey's *Lawn Tennis for Men*, an instructional work, is the only book which has males as the target audience. Several authors describe proper *Tennis Strokes and Strategies* by analyzing the champions' best strokes. Al Secunda's *Ultimate Tennis: The Pleasure Game* uses entertaining pictures to reinforce his three principles of practice: one action at a time, focus on producing the correct physical action, and ensure that the body is in a comfortable, relaxed state. He also emphasizes that players should feel good while learning and playing tennis. In *Lawn Tennis: Technique, Training, and Tactics* Douglas Gresham and A. E. Millman stress the importance of the eyes, feet, and hands in proper stroking, emphasize training and practice in order to improve performance, and discuss the principles of angles and positional play in singles and doubles.

Vincent Fotre explains *Why You Lose at Tennis* by examining types of opponents, court surfaces, how to exploit weaknesses, percentage tennis, partners as friends or foes, and tournament play. Charles LaRue discusses *The Thirty-Four Common Tennis Errors of the Million Players and the Remedies*. The most important problem is the wrong selection of degree of speed, twist, and close placement, while the two most harmful problems are too great zeal (pressing) and too great caution. His three positional errors include not keeping ready, improper footwork when stroking, and stooping with racket low when stroking. Among the other errors and their correction he mentions are not hitting winners, refusing to lob, and failure to play beside your partner in doubles. *Lessons in Tennis: A Textbook of the Game* reprints articles from *Country Life in America*. George Agutter explains how power comes from the forward swing of the racket, the proper grip to best control the ball, the importance of proper swinging motion, a good serve is an asset, and the importance of the ball toss on the serve.

Advantage Tennis: Racket Work, Tactics, and Logic by John Barnaby describes the basic strokes but emphasizes drills, half-court stroking, strategy and tactics, teaching and coaching, percentage tennis, and etiquette. Barnaby's *Ground Strokes in Match Play: Techniques, Tempo, and Winning Tactics* describes the essentiality of developing accurate and consistent forehands and backhands. While the fundamental strokes are the focus of Paul Douglas' *The Handbook of Tennis*, he encourages players to develop their own styles for every shot. He explains the strategies to use in singles and doubles, such as versus the net rusher or the baseline player, how and when to hit approach shots or to lob, and various formations. Incorporating a winning attitude, concentration, and fitness are also important according to Douglas. *Net Results: The Complete Tennis Handbook* by Rick Devereux builds upon the beginning, intermediate, and advanced shots by analyzing each thoroughly. For example, the serve is taught in three steps: toss and stance, hitting the ball, and complete motion. Match play theory and analysis provide insights into proper court positioning, shot placement, when to use spin, and differences in shot selection and strategies depending on the court surface. Vince Eldred takes an overall look at many facets of the game to explain how to play *Tennis without Mistakes*. Specifically, Eldred provides solutions to technique errors such as faulty footwork, pushing backhand strokes, poor serve tosses, and hitting shots too hard and too low. This comprehensive book also describes how to practice, recognition and use of spin, adjustments to playing surfaces, psychology, and tactics. *Extraordinary Tennis for the Ordinary Player* by Simon Ramo takes an amusing look at ordinary players attempting to play well in spite of the lack of practice. He recommends correction of cannonball first serves, easy second serves, following an easy serve to the net, and a backhand grip in serving. Positively he suggests where to stand, where to hit, proper net play, and reducing errors. Bob Harmon and Keith Monroe in *Use Your Head in Tennis* explain how to beat better players through ball control, anticipation, and stroke improvement.

Mitchell Charnley's *Play the Game: The Book of Sport* is a collection of articles about various sports from *The American Boy*. The two tennis pieces are Franklin Reck's "Take a Tip from the Stars" from his interview with George Agutter and

Charnley's "Tennis as Champions Play It" from an interview with Henri Cochet. *Selected Tennis and Badminton Articles* by the American Association for Health, Physical Education, and Recreation includes articles about theory, stroke production, strategy, and evaluations. Charles Hierons' *Lawn Tennis, How to Learn: A Simple Instructive Treatise* includes technique suggestions from C. P. Dixon, J. C. Parke, A. E. Beamish, Dorothea Lambert-Chambers, and Ethel Larcombe. Hierons also instructs in *Lawn Tennis: How to Become a Good Player* and *Lawn Tennis: How to Improve Your Game.*

Several companies publish activity series books about tennis for college students which consistently include stroke technique, strategies, rules, equipment, drills, and skill evaluations. Among these are *Tennis* by Jack Douglass, *Tennis* by Robert Gensemer, *Tennis, Anyone?* by Dick Gould, *Tennis Handbook* by Billie Herzog, *Tennis* by Joan Johnson and Paul Xanthos, *Tennis* by Elaine Mason, Kenneth Walts, and Mary Mott, *Tennis Everyone* by Clancy Moore and M. B. Chafin, *Tennis* by Wayne Pearce and Janice Pearce, *Tennis* by Barry Pelton, and *Tennis* by Don Sebolt.

General instructional books include Alec Doyle's *How to Improve Your Tennis*, John Crooke's *Better Tennis*, William Bockus' *Checklist for Better Tennis*, Denis Foster's *Improve Your Tennis*, Bernard Forer's *A New Practical Tennis Book: Strokes, Strategy, and Successful Play*, Dewayne Johnson's *Tennis*, Stephen Kessler and Jack Barth's *Tennis, Anyone?*, Rex Lardner's *The Complete Guide to Tennis*, Harry Leighton's *How to Improve Your Tennis* and *Tennis*, A. M. Lethbridge's *Tennis for All: Simple and Comprehensive Instructions*, Robert Lukin's *A Treatise on Tennis*, T. Mabbitt's *Tennis, Mastering Your Tennis Strokes*, John Moore's *Lawn Tennis*, J. C. Parke's *How to Play Lawn Tennis*, A. S. Pier's *Lawn Tennis*, Jack Pollard's *Advantage Receiver*, Tom Ravensdale's *Tennis*, Maxwell Robertson's the *LTA Book of the Game*, Bill Shertenlieb and Phronie Sander's *Focus on Competition: A Tennis Manual*, Harold Smith's *How to Improve Your Tennis*, James Sullivan's *How to Play Lawn Tennis: Containing Practical Instruction from an Expert*, G. H. Travell's *Courtcraft and Tactics in Lawn Tennis*, Ben Varn and H. Jungle's *Stairsteps to Successful Tennis, World*

Tennis' The Book of Tennis: How to Play the Game, Charles Young's *Winning Weekend Tennis,* Craig Wilson's *How to Improve your Tennis: Style, Strategy, and Analysis,* Jack Roberts' *So You're Going to Take Tennis Seriously,* Bill Wright's *Aerobic Tennis,* and Shep Campbell's *Quick Tips from the ABC Tennis Spot.* Bill Lenz in *Unisex Tennis* explains the physical, mental, and emotional differences between male and female players, the learning needs of each, and the basic strokes.

Stephen Merrihew edits several annual books in which the leading players instruct. These include *Lawn Tennis Manual, Lawn Tennis as Played by the Champions, How to Play Lawn Tennis, How Lawn Tennis Is Played, Lawn Tennis Illustrated, Lawn Tennis Manual,* and *Lawn Tennis Up-to-Date.* Robert Hynson coedits the last three.

BIBLIOGRAPHY

Aberdare, Clarence Napier Bruce, ed. *Rackets, Squash Rackets, Tennis, Fives and Badminton.* Philadelphia: J. B. Lippincott Company, 1933.

Agutter, George. *Develop Correct Tennis Form.* New York: Reader Mail, 1940.

————. *Lessons in Tennis: A Textbook of the Game.* New York: American Sports Publishing Company, 1929.

Aitken, A. J. *Lawn Tennis for Public Courts Players.* London: Methuen and Company, 1924.

Aldin, Cecil Charles Windsor, ed. *Ominibus Book of Sports for Young and Old.* New York: Coward-McCann, 1937.

Alexander, Frederick B. *How to Play Lawn Tennis.* New York: American Sports Publishing Company, 1914.

Allen, James. *Learn to Play Tennis.* Chicago: Rand McNally, 1968.

American Association for Health, Physical Education, and Recreation. *Selected Tennis and Badminton Articles.* Washington, D.C.: American Association for Health, Physical Education, and Recreation, 1970.

Applewhaite, Reginald Hanson. *Play the Game Lawn Tennis.* London: Educational Productions, 1956.

Baddeley, Wilfred. *Lawn Tennis.* London: G. Routledge and Sons, 1895.

Barnaby, John M. *Advantage Tennis: Racket Work, Tactics, and Logic.* Boston: Allyn and Bacon, 1975.

————[Jack]. *Ground Strokes in Match Play: Techniques, Tempo, and Winning Tactics*. Garden City, New York: Doubleday and Company, 1978.

Beamish, Alfred Ernest. *First Steps to Lawn Tennis*. Boston: Small, Maynard and Company, 1922.

————. *The Lawn Tennis Tip Book*. London: Mills and Boon, 1923.

Beasley, Mercer. *How to Improve Your Tennis*. New York: Home Institute, 1939.

Beldam, George W., and Vaile, Pembroke Arnold. *Great Lawn Tennis Players: Their Methods Illustrated*. London: Macmillan and Company, 1905.

Blackmore, S. Powell. *Lawn Tennis Up-to-Date*. London: Methuen and Company, 1921.

Bockus, H. William. *Checklist for Better Tennis*. Garden City, New York: Doubleday, 1973.

Bollettieri, Nick. *Tennis Your Way*. North Palm Beach, Florida: Athletic Institute, 1982.

Braden, Vic, and Bruns, Bill. *Vic Braden's Tennis for the Future*. Boston: Little, Brown, 1977.

Bryant, James E. *Tennis: A Guide for the Developing Tennis Player*. Englewood, Colorado: Morton Publishing Company, 1984.

Budge, Lloyd. *Lawn Tennis*. London: N. Kaye, 1949.

————. *Tennis Made Easy*. New York: A. S. Barnes, 1945.

Burns, James. *How to Play Tennis*. New York: Outing Publishing Company, 1915.

Burrow, F. R. *Lawn Tennis: How to Succeed*. London: Evans Brothers, 1933.

————. *Lawn Tennis: The World-Game of Today*. London: Hodder and Stoughton, 1922.

————. *Lawn Tennis of Today: Its Strokes, Strategy, and Tactics*. New York: Frederick A. Stokes Company, 1924.

Campell, Oliver Samuel. *Campbell's Lawn Tennis and the Way to Play It*. New York: Street and Smith, 1891.

Campbell, Shep. *Quick Tips from the ABC Tennis Spot*. Norwalk, Connecticut: Tennis Magazine, 1981.

Casewit, Curtis W. *America's Tennis Book*. New York: Scribner, 1975.

Champ, Paul, et al. *Lawn-Tennis, Golf, Croquet, Polo, Par MM*. Paris: Bibliotheque Larousse, 1911.

Charnley, Mitchell Vaughn, ed. *Play the Game: The Book of Sport*. New York: The Viking Press, 1931.

Clayton, Geoffrey. *Introducing Tennis*. Sussex, England: John Crowther, 1946.

Collins, Ed. *Watch the Ball, Bend Your Knees, That'll be $20 Please!* Ottawa, Illinois: Caroline House Books, 1977.

Crawley, Alfred Ernest. *Lawn Tennis.* London: Methuen and Company, 1919.

———. *Lawn Tennis Do's and Don'ts.* New York: Robert M. McBride and Company, 1923.

———. *The Technique of Lawn Tennis Demonstrated by Cinematography.* London: Methuen and Company, 1923.

Crooke, John. *Better Tennis.* New Rochelle, New York: Sportshelf, 1976.

Cutler, Merritt Dana. *Basic Tennis Illustrated.* New York: Dover Publications, 1967.

———. *The Tennis Book.* New York: McGraw-Hill, 1967.

Danzig, Allison. *The Racquet Game.* New York: The Macmillan Company, 1930.

Devereux, Rick. *Net Results: The Complete Tennis Handbook.* Boston: Pathfinder Publications, 1974.

Dewhurst, Edward Bury. *The Science of Lawn Tennis.* Philadelphia: Innes and Sons, 1910.

Dewhurst, Evelyn. *Lawn Tennis: May I Introduce You?* London: Pitman, 1949.

Donnalley, Mary Jane. *Net Results: A Picture Book of Tennis Fundamentals.* New York: Pageant Press, 1961.

Douglas, Paul. *The Handbook of Tennis.* New York: Alfred A. Knopf, 1983.

Douglass, Jack. *Tennis.* Dubuque, Iowa: Kendall/Hunt Publishing Company, 1977.

Doust, Stanley N. *Lawn Tennis.* London: Rockliff Publishing Corporation, 1947.

Doyle, Alec Varenne. *How to Improve Your Tennis.* Sydney: Angus and Robertson, 1935.

Dwight, James. *Lawn-Tennis.* Boston: Wright and Ditson, 1886.

———. *Practical Lawn-Tennis.* New York: Harper and Brothers, 1893.

Eddy, Ruth, and LeBar, John. *Learning Tennis Together.* West Point, New York: Leisure Press, 1982.

Eldred, Vince. *Tennis without Mistakes.* New York: Putnam, 1975.

Enjoying Racquet Sports. New York: Paddington Press, 1978.

Epstein, Eli. *Tennis Cues.* Ferndale, New York: Grossinger Tennis Club, 1943.

Fiske, Loring. *How to Beat Better Tennis Players.* Garden City, New York: Doubleday, 1970.

FitzGibbon, Herbert S., II, and Bairstow, Jeffrey N. *The Complete Racquet Sports Player.* New York: Simon and Schuster, 1979.

Forer, Bernard. *A New Practical Tennis Book: Strokes, Strategy, and Successful Play*. New York: Vantage Press, 1974.

Foster, Denis. *Improve Your Tennis*. London: Findon Publications, 1950.

Fotre, Vincent. *Why You Lose at Tennis*. New York: Barnes and Noble Books, 1973.

Fraley, Oscar. *How to Play Championship Tennis*. New York: A. A. Wyn, 1954.

Gautschi, Marcel. *Tennis, Playing, Training, and Winning*. New York: Arco Publishing Company, 1979.

Gensemer, Robert E. *Tennis*. Philadelphia: Saunders, 1982.

Godfree, Leslie Allison, and Wakelam, Henry Blythe Thornhill. *Lawn Tennis*. Philadelphia: David McKay Company, 1937.

Gould, Dick. *Tennis, Anyone?* Palo Alto, California: Mayfield Publishing Company, 1978.

Gresham, Douglas William, and Millman, A. E. *Lawn Tennis: Technique, Training, and Tactics*. London: Bell, 1953.

Groppel, Jack L. *Principles of Tennis Techniques, Drills and Strategies*. Champaign, Illinois: Stipes, 1980.

Groppel, Jack L., and Shay, Arthur. *Optimal Tennis: The Freeze-Frame Photographic Approach to a Better Game*. Chicago: Contemporary Books, 1983.

Hankinson, John Trevor. *Lawn Tennis*. London: Allen and Unwin, 1951.

Harmon, Bob, and Monroe, Keith. *Use Your Head in Tennis*. New York: Thomas Y. Crowell, 1977.

Heathcote, John Moyer, ed. *Tennis, Lawn Tennis, Rackets, and Fives*. London: Longmans, Green, and Company, 1890.

Herzog, Billie Jean. *Tennis Handbook*. Dubuque, Iowa: Kendall/Hunt Publishing Company, 1978.

Hierons, Charles. *Lawn Tennis: How to Become a Good Player*. Country Life, 1923.

——. *Lawn Tennis: How to Improve Your Game*. London: Ward, Lock, 1925.

——. *Lawn Tennis, How to Learn: A Simple Instructive Treatise*. London: Ward, Lock and Company, 1919.

Hughes, George Patrick. *Improving Your Tennis*. London: Faber and Faber, 1947.

Hughes, Kenneth. *Helpful Advice on Lawn Tennis*. Teignmourth: T. H. Aggett, 1952.

Irvine, Cecil Victor. *The Mechanics of Lawn Tennis*. Salisbury, Rhodesia: Irvine, 1968.

Johnson, Dewayne J. *Tennis*. New York: American Press, 1980.

Johnson, Joan D., and Xanthos, Paul J. *Tennis*. Dubuque, Iowa: William C. Brown Company, 1981.

Jones, Clarence Medlycott. *Improving Your Tennis: Strokes and Techniques*. London: Faber and Faber, 1973.

———. *Lawn Tennis*. London: Arco Publications, 1961.

———. *Manual of Instruction*. Middlesex, England: British Lawn Tennis, 1947.

———. *Match-Winning Tennis: Tactics, Temperament and Training*. London: Faber and Faber, 1971.

———. *Tennis: How to Become a Champion*. London: Faber and Faber, 1968.

———. *Your Book of Tennis*. London: Faber and Faber, 1970.

Jones, Clarence Medlycott, and Buxton, Angela. *Starting Tennis*. London: Ward, Lock, 1975.

Jones, Emlyn Barley. *Learning Lawn Tennis*. London: G. Bell, 1960.

Kessler, Stephen, and Barth, Jack. *Tennis, Anyone?* New York: Simon and Schuster, 1984.

Kraft, Virginia, *Tennis Drills for Self-Improvement*. Garden City, New York: Doubleday, 1978.

———. *Tennis Instruction for Fun and Competition*. New York: Grosset and Dunlap, 1976.

Lardner, Rex. *The Complete Guide to Tennis*. New York: Cornerstone Library, 1979.

———. *Finding and Exploiting Your Opponent's Weaknesses*. Garden City, New York: Doubleday, 1976.

LaRue, Charles. *The Thirty-Four Common Tennis Errors of the Million Players and the Remedies*. New York: American Sports Publishers, 1916.

Last, Frederick W. *How to Play Tennis*. London: Thorsons, 1949.

Lawn Tennis, Badminton, Croquet, Troco, Racquets, Fives, Nurr and Spell, Bowling, Hurling, etc. London: Ward, Lock and Company, 1883.

Leighton, Harry. *How to Improve Your Tennis*. Chicago: Athletic Institute, 1953.

———. *Tennis*. New York: Sterling Publishing Company, 1962.

Lenz, Bill. *Unisex Tennis*. Port Washington, New York: Kennikat Press, 1977.

Lethbridge, A. M. *Tennis for All: Simple and Comprehensive Instructions*. New York: Universal Publications, 1939.

Little, Raymond Demorest. *Tennis Tactics*. New York: Outing Publishing Company, 1913.

Litz, David. *A Photographic Guide to Tennis Fundamentals*. New York: Arco Publishing Company, 1977.

Loomis, James C. *The Tennis Doctor: Everything You Always Wanted to Know about Tennis But Didn't Know Whom to Ask*. New York: Vantage, 1983.

Lott, David, ed. *Tennis Guide*. Maplewood, New Jersey: Hammond, 1981.

Lowe, Francis Gordon. *Gordon Lowe on Lawn Tennis*. London: Hutchinson and Company, 1924.

Lukin, Robert. *A Treatise on Tennis*. London: Rodwell and Martin, 1922.

Lumiere, Cornel. *Better Tennis with the World's Best Players*. London: Eyre and Spottiswoode, 1963.

————. *The Book of Tennis: How to Play the Game*. New York: Grosset and Dunlap, 1970.

Mabbitt, T. *Tennis: Mastering Your Tennis Strokes*. London: Collins, 1979.

MacCurdy, Doug, and Tully, Shawn. *Sports Illustrated Tennis*. New York: Lippincott and Crowell, 1980.

Mace, Wynn. *Tennis Techniques Illustrated*. New York: Ronald Press, 1958.

Marshall, Julian. *Lawn Tennis with the Laws Adopted by the M.C.C. and A.E.C. and L.T.C. and Badminton*. New York: C.F.A. Hinrichs, 1879.

Marshall, Julian, Spoons, James, and Tait, J. A. Arnan. *Tennis, Rackets, and Fives*. New York: F. A. Stokes and Company, 1891.

Mason, R. Elaine, Walts, Kenneth, and Mott, Mary L. *Tennis*. Boston: Allyn and Bacon, 1974.

Mastering Your Tennis Strokes. London: Collier-Macmillan, 1977.

Medlycott, James. *Tennis*. London: Macmillan, 1975.

Megale, Donald, and Winkler, Bill. *Tennis: Fundamentals and Basic Principles Illustrated*. Corvallis, Oregon: Oregon State University, 1967.

Merrihew, Stephen Wallis, ed. *How Lawn Tennis Is Played*. New York: American Lawn Tennis, 1937.

————. *How to Play Lawn Tennis*. New York: American Lawn Tennis, 1936.

————. *Lawn Tennis as Played by the Champions*. New York: American Lawn Tennis, 1935.

————. *Lawn Tennis Manual*. New York: American Lawn Tennis, 1933.

Merrihew, Stephen Wallis, and Hynson, Robert C., eds. *Lawn Tennis Illustrated*. New York: American Lawn Tennis, 1938.

————. *Lawn Tennis Up-to-Date*. New York: American Lawn Tennis, 1940.

Metzler, Paul. *Fine Points of Tennis*. New York: Sterling Publishing Company, 1978.

————. *Tennis Weaknesses and Remedies*. New York: Sterling Publishing Company, 1973.

Miles, Eustace. *Lessons in Lawn Tennis: A New Method of Study and Practice for Acquiring a Good and Sound Style of Play*. London: Gill, 1899.

————. *Racquets, Tennis, and Squash*. New York: D. Appleton and Company, 1903.

Moore, Clancy, and Chafin, M. B. *Tennis Everyone*. Winston-Salem, North Carolina: Hunter Publishing Company, 1981.

Moore, John Ambrose. *Lawn Tennis*. London: Weidenfeld and Nicolson, 1963.

Morgenstern, Carol. *Playing the Racquets*. New York: Delta Books, 1980.

Moss, Thomas. *Lawn Tennis: How to Discover and Correct Faults*. Croydon, England: Link House, 1936.

Murphy, William E., and Murphy, Chester W. *Lifetime Treasury of Tested Tennis Tips: Secrets of Winning Play*. West Nyack, New York: Parker Publishing Company, 1978.

Myers, Arthur Wallis. *The Complete Lawn Tennis Player*. Philadelphia: George W. Jacobs and Company, 1908.

————. *Lawn Tennis at Home and Abroad*. London: G. Newnes, 1903.

————. *Lawn Tennis—Its Principles and Practice—A Player's Guide to Modern Methods*. Philadelphia: J. B. Lippincott, 1930.

Nickerson, Elinor. *Racquet Sports: An Illustrated Guide*. Jefferson, North Carolina: McFarland and Company, Publishers, 1982.

Noel, Susan. *Tennis without Tears*. London: Hutchinson's Library of Sports and Pastimes, 1947.

Okker, Tom. *Tennis in Pictures*. New York: Sterling Publishing Company, 1975.

Olliff, John Sheldon. *The Groundwork of Lawn Tennis*. London: Methuen and Company, 1934.

————. *Lawn Tennis: The Complete Technique of Lawn Tennis Stroke Play*. London: Pitman, 1950.

————. *Lawn Tennis for Beginners*. London: W. and G. Foyle, 1951.

————. *Lawn Tennis: How to Succeed*. London: Evans Brothers, 1951.

————. *Olliff on Tennis*. London: Eyre and Spottiswoode, 1948.

Osborn, Robert Durie. *Lawn Tennis, Its Players, and How to Play, with the Laws of the Game*. London: Strahan and Company, 1881.

Paret, Jahial Parmly. *Everything You Need to Know about Lawn Tennis: How to Play the Game, Expert Instruction and Coaching of the World's Champions*. New York: American Lawn Tennis, 1934.

———. *How to Play Lawn Tennis*. New York: American Sports Publishing Company, 1902.

———. *Lawn Tennis for Beginners*. New York: Macmillan Company, 1916.

———. *Mechanics of the Game of Lawn Tennis*. New York: American Lawn Tennis, 1926.

———. *Methods and Players of Modern Lawn Tennis*. New York: American Lawn Tennis, 1915.

———. *Psychology and Advanced Play of Lawn Tennis*. New York: American Lawn Tennis, 1927.

Parke, J. C. *How to Play Lawn Tennis*. London: Ewart, Seymour and Company, 1920.

Patterson, Norman Hills. *The Complete Lawn-Tennis Player*. London: Adam and Charles Black, 1948.

———. *Courtcraft: Lawn Tennis Tactics and Psychology*. London: Eyre and Spottiswoode, 1934.

———. *The Elements of Lawn Tennis*. London: Faber and Faber, 1950.

———. *How to Teach Lawn Tennis*. London: Methuen, 1947.

———. *Lawn Tennis at School and After*. London: Methuen, 1939.

———. *Lawn Tennis by Tyne and Wear*. Newcastle-on-Tyne, 1921.

Payn, F. W. *Secrets of Lawn Tennis*. London: L. U. Gill, 1906.

———. *Tennis Topics and Tactics*. London: Upcott Gill, 1907.

Pearce, Wayne, and Pearce, Janice. *Tennis*. Englewood Cliffs, New Jersey: Prentice-Hall, 1971.

Peile, Solomon Charles Frederick. *Lawn Tennis as a Game of Skill*. London: William Blackwood and Sons, 1885.

Pelton, Barry C. *Tennis*. Santa Monica, California: Goodyear Publishing Company, 1980.

Petty, Roy. *Contemporary Tennis*. Chicago: Contemporary Books, 1978.

Pier, A. S. *Lawn Tennis*. Boston: Houghton, 1907.

Plagenhoef, Stanley. *Fundamentals of Tennis*. Englewood Cliffs, New Jersey: Prentice-Hall, 1970.

Platt, Don. *Tennis: Playing a Winning Game with Don Platt*. New York: McGraw-Hill Ryerson, 1977.

Pollard, Jack. *Advantage Receiver*. London: Frederick Muller, 1960.

Pollock, John. *Listening to Lacoste*. London: Mills & Boon, 1926.

Price, H. *Foulsham's How to Play Lawn Tennis, and Strokes Worth Practising*. London: Foulsham, 1930.

———. *Lawn Tennis*. British Sports Publishing Company, 1930.

———. *Lawn Tennis, as It Is Played Today*. New York: Spalding's Athletic Library, 1924.

Pro/Am Guide to Tennis. Maplewood, New Jersey: Hammond, 1982.

Ramo, Simon. *Extraordinary Tennis for the Ordinary Player*. New York: Crown Publishers, 1977.

Ravensdale, Tom. *Tennis*. Leicester, England: Knight Books, 1977.

Rendall, John Charles Shuttleworth. *Lawn Tennis: A Method of Acquiring Proficiency*. London: Cassell and Company, 1926.

———. *Things That Matter in Lawn Tennis*. London: Besant and Company, 1930.

Ritchie, M. J. G. *Lawn Tennis, the Modern Game*. London: Athletic Publications, 1928.

———. *The Text Book of Lawn Tennis*. London: Ewart, Seymour and Company, 1915.

Roberts, Jack. *So You're Going to Take Tennis Seriously*. New York: Workman Publishing, 1974.

Robertson, Maxwell. *LTA Book of the Game*. London: Max Parrish, 1957.

Scharff, Robert. *The Collier Quick and Easy Guide to Tennis*. New York: Collier Books, 1962.

Scholl, Peter. *How to Succeed at Tennis*. New York: Sterling Publishing Company, 1982.

Schultz, Nikki. *Tennis for Everyone*. New York: Grosset and Dunlap, 1975.

Sebolt, Don R. *Tennis*. Dubuque, Iowa: Kendall/Hunt Publishing Company, 1974.

Secunda, Al. *Ultimate Tennis: The Pleasure Game*. Englewood Cliffs, New Jersey: Prentice-Hall, 1984.

Shertenlieb, Bill, and Sanders, Phronie. *Focus on Competition: A Tennis Manual*. Fort Lauderdale, Florida: Tennis Manual, 1980.

Shingleton, John D. *How to Increase Your Net Value: A Simplified Guide to Better Tennis*. New York: Winchester Press, 1975.

Skills and Tactics of Tennis. New York: Arco Publishing Company, 1980.

Slocum, Henry Warner. *Lawn Tennis in Our Own Country*. New York: A. G. Spalding and Brothers, 1890.

Smith, Harold Leslie. *How to Improve Your Tennis*. London: Athletic Publications, 1951.

Smith, Stan, and Sheehan, Larry. *Stan Smith's Guide to Better Tennis*. New York: Grosset and Dunlap, 1975.

Smyth, John George. *The Game's the Same: Lawn Tennis in the World of Sport*. London: Cassell, 1957.

Snyder, Dave. *Tennis*. North Palm Beach, Florida: Athletic Institute, 1971.

Soules, George, and Range, Peter Ross. *The Playboy Book of Tennis: How to Play Winning Tennis . . . and Everything Else You Forgot to Ask Your Pro*. New York: Playboy Press, 1981.

Starke, George Alexander. *Starke's Table and Lawn Tennis Technology*. London: G. A. Starke, 1960.

Stroud, R. F. *Stepping Stones to Better Tennis*. N.p. 1952.

Sullivan, James Edward. *How to Play Lawn Tennis: Containing Practical Instruction from an Expert*. New York: American Sports Publishing Company, 1911.

Tennis. Charleston, South Carolina: Tennis Services Company, 1974.

Tennis Strokes and Strategies. New York: Simon and Schuster, 1975.

Travell, G. H. *Courtcraft and Tactics in Lawn Tennis*. London: Link House, 1934.

Tuckey, Charles Raymond Darys. *Lawn Tennis for Men*. New York: M. S. Mill Company, 1937.

Vaile, Pembroke Arnold. *Modern Lawn Tennis*. London: W. Heinemann, 1904.

———. *The Strokes and Science of Lawn Tennis*. London: British Sports Publishing Company, 1906.

———. *The Tennis Primer*. New York: American Sports Publishing Company, 1915.

Varn, Ben, and Jungle, H. *Stairsteps to Successful Tennis*. Charleston, South Carolina: Tennis Services Company, 1974.

Whittelsey, Sarah Scovill. *A Manual of Lawn Tennis*. London: Butterick Publishing Company, 1894.

Wilberforce, Herbert William Wrangham. *Lawn Tennis*. London: George Bell and Sons, 1889.

Wilson, Craig R. *How to Improve Your Tennis: Style, Strategy, and Analysis*. South Brunswick, New Jersey: A. S. Barnes, 1974.

Wingfield, Walter C. *The Major's Game of Lawn Tennis*. London: n.p., 1874.

Winter, Gordon. *Games for Court and Garden*. London: Pilot Press, 1947.

World Tennis. *The Book of Tennis: How to Play the Game*. New York: Grosset and Dunlap, 1965.

Wright, Bill. *Aerobic Tennis*. Bolinas, California: Shelter Publications, 1983.

Young, Charles R. *Winning Weekend Tennis*. Detroit: Harlo Press, 1981.

6

Tennis Techniques for Various Skill Levels and Specific Groups

Many of the books about tennis technique focus on specific groups or approaches. This chapter will discuss books written for beginners to advanced players and includes those volumes which explain particular strokes and drills. Singles and doubles play and instruction to groups, in schools, or for teachers are other specialized topics. Women, children, and older adults must be among the special tennis populations, based on the availability of books targeting players in these categories.

Paul Metzler explains equipment, stroke techniques, terminology, and rules in *Getting Started in Tennis*. Fourteen books name beginners as their target population for instruction starting with George Wright's *Lawn Tennis: Revised Units to Beginners* in 1911. Wright's later work, *Lawn Tennis for Beginners*, discusses and illustrates the strokes plus includes information about how to build and to mark a court; tournament play; ways to overcome nervousness, to avoid worry, and to conserve energy; and the importance of playing the score. Jahial Paret's *Lawn Tennis for Beginners* stresses the basic shots yet adds hints for using chop and cut strokes, the twist serve, and corrections for technique errors. *Beginners Guide to Winning Tennis* by Helen Jacobs provides instruction about the fundamental shots, position play, spin, timing, and strategy. She furnishes ten lessons for juniors, such as swing your body weight on every stroke, learn how to conserve energy, and a double fault is a tennis crime. In *Beginning Tennis: For the "Love" of Tennis* Ballard Moore explains the strokes, scoring, and strategy plus provides practice drills, photographs, and skill checklists to allow the reader to self-instruct. Rex Lardner includes the rules, strokes, tactics, match preparation strategies, and special advice for young female players on how to beat a left-handed opponent, on how to use the wind and sun to your advantage, and on playing on various court surfaces in *The Complete Beginner's Guide to Tennis*. Other works for beginning players include *Tennis for Beginners*, a children's book, by Lud Duroska, *Beginning Tennis* by Peter Everett and Virginia Dumas, *Tennis for Beginners* by H. A. Murray, *Tennis for Beginners* by William Murphy and Chester Murphy, and *Lawn Tennis for Beginners* by John Olliff. Gloria Payne's *A Tennis Manual for Beginning and Intermediate Players* teaches the forehand, backhand, and serve as well as variety strokes, such as the slice serve, approach shots, volley, lob, and overhead. Harry Fogleman's *Tennis for the Beginner and the Average Player* and Eustace Miles' *Lawn Tennis Lessons for Beginners and Others* also focus on developing proper stroke technique. In *Tennis and You* William DeGroot uses photographs extensively to instruct beginners in the basic strokes and strategies.

Optic Yellow Fever by Steve Van Kanegan offers advice to novice players just taking up tennis. Fred Pons in addition to teaching the strokes suggests ways to improve in *Tennis Made (Somewhat) Easier*. Beginning players learn about common mistakes plus Pons stresses concentration in executing strokes correctly and constant practice. The Lawn Tennis Association in England offers instructions to beginners in its *Start Lawn Tennis with Dan Maskell, the LTA Training Manager* through photographs of players and technique hints from Dan Maskell, George Allan, and Lew Hoad.

Advantage Tennis Anyone by Harry Meng includes strokes and strategies for beginning, intermediate, and advanced players. *Preparing for Tennis in the 1980s* is a reprint of articles from the *Journal of Physical Education, Recreation and Dance* in 1979 about techniques for players at the intermediate level and above. Robert Gensemer's *Intermediate Tennis* is directed toward the player who wants to improve. He explains effective technique, hitting decisive ground strokes, spin and power for the serve, tactics and strategies, the mental game, practice, conditioning, equipment, and rule interpretations. He illustrates technique, placement, and strategies in photographs and diagrams. Chester Bowers stresses the fundamentals in his book *Advanced Tennis*. Jack Groppel in *Tennis for Advanced Players: And Those Who Would Like to Be* explains the quest for a perfect game by examining footwork, control versus power, ball spin, ultimate weapons of the serve and overhead, and handling continuous emergencies during matches. The *Fine Points of Tennis* by Paul Metzler includes match temperament, selection and execution of shots when playing the various styles—net game, all-court, and baseline—and what to expect in a match. Metzler in *Advanced Tennis* uses diagrams and photographs extensively to emphasize advanced stroke technique, footwork, watching the ball, and doubles play. Rico Ellwanger explains and illustrates the beginning shots (forehand, backhand, and serve), advanced strokes (volley and overhead), and shots used by tournament players (half volley, lob, volley lob, drop, chop, drop volley, and use of slice and topspin). In *Tennis, Up to Tournament Standards* he also stresses conditioning and tactics. *John Zwieg's Courtside Companion: A Tennis Workbook for the Serious Player* by Richard Isaacs uses sequences of photographs to teach every shot while describing each, too. In addition this book suggests how to practice, drills, and winning tips so players can develop their abilities maximally. Chester Murphy advocates the importance of players' concentrating on their technique and tactics in practice in *Tennis for Thinking Players*. Through a careful application of the mind to tennis, serious players can improve their performances and avoid choking according to Murphy. His *Advanced Tennis* includes information about stroke development, strategies, drills, and conditioning.

Every stroke is the subject of at least one book. Jack Barnaby stresses proper technique and practice of ground strokes for players of all skill levels in *Ground Strokes in Match Play: Techniques, Tempo, and Winning Tactics*. Pembroke Vaile focuses on the principles of backhand shots including the drive, chop, lob, drop, and volley in *The Backhand Book*. In *Tennis Know-How: The Forehand, Backhand and Service* John Hopman focuses on the three basic strokes. Peter Talbert and Lew Fishman in *Secrets of a Winning Serve and Return* explain the importance of the technique and the strategy of the serve. Photographs display for the novice the stance, footwork, toss, and swing for hitting flat, spin, and twist serves. They also discuss the return of serve as does Sterling Lord in *Returning the Serve Intelligently*. Lord in describing the potential of this aspect of the game tells about placement, second serve returns, and doubles' returns. Peter Schwed explains and illustrates the stance, rhythm, grip, toss, backswing, and contact of flat, slice, and twist serves in *The Serve and the Overhead Smash*. For the overhead he focuses on positioning, whether to hit the ball before or after it bounces, backhand technique, hitting on the run, and the stroke's use in doubles. In *The Serve: Key to Winning Tennis* Tony Trabert and Jim Hook break the serve into preparatory measures: grip, hold (ball), decisions, target, position at the baseline, and stance; preliminary motions: respiration, lean, ball bounce, ball fingering, and recovery; and propelling actions: lift (ball), swing-strike-swing, stride, and finish. *Tennis/It Serves You Right* by Eric Nicol and Dave More also looks at this important stroke. Play an aggressive style of tennis says John Kenfield and George Janes in *The Volley and the Half Volley: The Attacking Game* while Sidney Summerfield recommends a new teaching strategy in *Tennis: Learn to Volley First*. Kenfield and Janes explain the volley position; how to hit high, low, forehand, and backhand volleys; the backhand syndrome; and advocates use of the half volley when situations prevent use of a volley. He also stresses practicing, quickness drills, and developing attacking attitudes. *Lobbing into the Sun* by Harry Hopman includes the ethics and tactics for use of this shot plus information about serving, doubles play, and the ladies' game.

Tennis drills are the focus of books such as William Murphy's *Complete Book of Championship Drills*, Gary Sailes' *Championship Tennis Drills for Advanced Players and Coaches*, and Sharon Petro's *The Tennis Drill Book*. Gary Bodenmiller's *Drills for Skills* includes offensive and defensive drills while Pat Yeomans' *Ten Tests for Better Tennis* also provides skill tests. Robert Greene relies heavily on photographs to demonstrate his *Tennis Drills: On- and Off-Court Drills and Exercises for Beginners, Intermediates, Tournament Players, and Teaching Professionals*. Steven Kraft provides the number of players required, the purpose, an explanation, and a diagram of each of his *Tennis Drills for Self-Improvement*. Drills for ground strokes and volleys using shots hit down-the-line and cross-court comprise his three rhythms, three patterns emphasis. He also includes drills for lobs, approach shots, serves, returns of serve, singles and doubles pepper drills, and conditioning. John Fox and Elizabeth Vasil explain and diagram tennis lead-up games and drills for students, teachers, and coaches in *When Do We Get to Play, Coach?*

In *Tactics in Women's Singles, Doubles, and Mixed Doubles* Rex Lardner explains offensive and defensive strategies to use in each. Bill Tilden in his general book *Singles and Doubles* looks at tennis from a champion player's perspective. In addition to brief suggestions on how to play singles and doubles, he discusses history, junior tennis, psychology, personalities, and common errors. As a successor to their earlier books about *The Game of Singles in Tennis* and *The Game of Doubles in Tennis*, Bill Talbert and Bruce Old focus on tactics as more important than strokes, style, and stamina in *Tennis Tactics: Singles and Doubles*. After explaining the shots, they examine net play, such as volleying, positioning, getting to the net, shot placement, and poaching; baseline play; and studying famous players to improve one's game tactically.

Paul Metzler diagrams and explains formations such as one up and one back and both players back when serving and when receiving, the net game, positioning depending on the shot, and what shot to hit in various situations in *Tennis Doubles: Tactics and Formations*. He also explains how to deal with a left-handed opponent, a weak partner, and an aggressive net player plus how to lob aggressively and to force opponents to retreat from the net. Stan Smith, Bob Lutz, and Larry Sheehan explain the principles, shifting roles, and special approaches for *Modern Tennis Doubles*. For tailoring strokes to doubles play, they recommend serving with spin at 3/4 speed, returning back-hands with chip shots, stepping into more volleys, and using more lobs and overheads. They state that balance, movement as a team, helping one's partner, outplaying opponents, and getting the edge through conditioning are the keys to successful doubles play. *Winning Tennis Doubles*, a heavily illustrated book by Cynthia Doerner, Peter Doerner, and Dan Ozier, provides advice for the server, the offensive net player, the receiver, and the defensive net player while furnishing tips on tactics and tips for special situations. Bob Harmon explains how to *Use Your Head in Doubles*. French player Francoise Durr explains various tactics such as the use of the alley, poaching, anticipation, and communication in *Doubles Strategy: A Creative and Psychological Approach to Tennis*. *How to Play Winning Doubles* by George Lott and Jeffrey Bairstow uses diagrams and some discussion to teach the basic strokes and to emphasize doubles as a thinking player's game. Their six axioms for better doubles are a) use the whole court; b) look before you hit; c) plan your moves in advance; d) look at your court through your opponents' eyes; e) don't get set in your ways; and f) make the best use of your partner.

Allegra Charles focuses on strategies, concentration, conditioning, practice, gameswomanship, and how to develop winning habits in *How to Win at Ladies Doubles*. This volume also instructs in the basic strokes, positioning, percentage tennis, and psychology of winning plus explains how women's doubles differ from men's. Excellent doubles players Clarke Graebner and Carol Graebner in *Mixed Doubles Tennis* and Billie Jean King, Fred Stolle, and Greg Hoffman in *How to Play Mixed Doubles* share their expertise and the strategies they find succcessful. King, Stolle, and Hoffman discuss the physical and psychological complexities of mixed doubles, court strategies, playing tactics, stroke techniques, and compatibility of partnerships. They also explain how to play better and have more fun, how to recognize each player's weaknesses, and how to cover the court. Geoffrey Godbey and Frank Guadagnolo introduce the rules for a new dimension in tennis play in *Triples: A New Tennis Game*. Advantages include ease of learning since there is not as much ground to cover, alleviation of crowding on courts, teamwork, and fun, plus it is adaptable to fast-paced strategies and exchanges.

In order to play tennis singles, doubles, or triples, many take group or private lessons from teaching professionals, attend clinics and camps, and read books. In *Lawn Tennis: Group Teaching* Thomas Moss briefly explains how to teach the basic shots. To the principle of proper stroke production, Moss adds strategies and tactics in *Lawn Tennis for Teachers and Players*. Group instructional ideas about organization and how best to teach the strokes and tactics to camp, school, and college classes comprises *Tennis Organized for Group Instruction* by Dorothy Randle and Marjorie Hillas and *Group Instruction in Tennis and Badminton* by Harry Edgren and Gilmer Robinson. The American Association for Health, Physical Education and Recreation furnishes organizational guidelines, teaching hints, games, and drills in its *Tennis Group Instruction* as does the United States Tennis Association in *Teaching Tennis to Groups*. Tom Meinhardt and Jim Brown in conjunction with these two organizations in 1984 included strokes, skill progressions, rules, customs, courtesies, playing the game, sample unit plans, written and skill tests, teaching aids, safety, facilities, equipment, and tournament play in *Tennis: Group Instruction II*. *Tennis: A Manual for Teachers with Materials—Methods—Programs for Group Instruction* by Marjorie Hillas and John LeFevre provides organizational techniques, teaching hints, lead-up games, skill tests, rules, and strategies as well as stroke production.

Tennis Instructor's Guide by the Athletic Institute and *Ideas for Tennis Instruction* by the American Association of Health, Physical Education and Recreation include drills, organizational tips, and skill tests. Jim Brown's *Tennis: Teaching, Coaching, and Directing Programs* through instruction about strokes, strategies, and drills provides a guide to tennis teaching and administration. He explains how to give private and class lessons to various age groups. *Tennis, Strokes, Strategy, and Programs* also by Brown relates the fundamental skills to teaching, coaching, and the psychological aspects of the game. He furnishes numerous drills, too. *Teaching Tennis* by Rick Chavez and Lois Nieder helps prepare teachers of tennis. It includes information about facilities and equipment, class organization, instructional techniques for all skill levels, strategies, evaluation measures, coaching, and rules. Lesson planning guides and group formations for instruction are the focus of Eve Kraft and John Conroy's *The Tennis Teacher's Guide: Group Instruction and Team Coaching*. John Kenfield gives in-depth instruction about how to best teach the strokes and strategies in *Teaching and Coaching Tennis*. Don Leary provides information for *The Teaching Tennis Pro* while Paul Xanthos furnishes a *Handbook for Organization and Conduct of Tennis Clinics and Teacher Training Workshops* and *Tennis, A Pictorial Guide for Teachers*. William Jacobs explains the clinic procedures the USLTA uses in *Tennis, Builder of Citizenship: The Psychology and Technique of the Game as Taught in the Tennis Clinic*. Selected articles about the social, psychological, and physical characteristics of tennis players, stroke mechanics, and the organization and administration of school competition comprise *What Research Tells the Coach about Tennis* by Marvin Gray. *Teaching of Tennis, for Schools and Recreational Programs* by Eloise Jaeger and Harry Leighton instructs in the basic strokes plus adds lead-up games, skills tests, tips for high school players, practice patterns, and teaching aids. Helen Driver explains various instructional techniques in *Tennis for Teachers*, and *Tennis Self-Instructor: A Student's Handbook* offers advice to players. Charlotte Stewart explains *Tennis Type Games: An Experimetal Unit for High School Girls*. Harcourt Roy discusses the basic strokes, reminders for teachers, practice drills, and fitness activities in *Tennis for Schools*. Harold Smith discusses *Lawn Tennis Coaching*.

Evelyn Dewhurst explains how to teach and what to teach by emphasizing proper stroke execution, anticipation, use of spin, and match play tactics in *Lawn Tennis Guaranteed: How to Teach and Play It*. Dewhurst later provides *A Handbook for Coaching Lawn Tennis*. Eleanor Tennant's highly successful instructional techniques comprise *Play Tennis the "Teach" Tennant Way*. Chester Murphy and William Murphy describe the many variations in teaching methods in *Tennis for the Player, Teacher, and Coach*, yet they advocate instructing through progressions using the hand, then a paddle, and finally the racket. They explain the mechanics of beginning, intermediate, and advanced shots, strategies for singles and doubles, psychological aspects, coaching, team practice, and conditioning. Gundars Tilmanis in *Advanced Tennis for Coaches, Teachers, and Players*, using pictures of the greatest players and neophytes, introduces the basic strokes using a group teaching approach. This comprehensive work includes practical tactics for singles and doubles, systematic ways to keep students actively learning, biomechanical principles in tennis, coaching methodology, class control and discipline, beginners' activities, and physical fitness training for advanced players. Bruce Elliott and Rob Kilderry in *The Art and Science of Tennis* provide hints about stroke production and strategy but also discuss sport psychology, training, player evaluation, junior development, administration, and equipment design. They provide advice on coaching and teaching tennis and give unit outlines for various age groups and levels of players.

Wimbledon champion Dorothea Lambert-Chambers provided the first instructional book specifically for women in 1912. In *Lawn Tennis for Ladies* she discusses athletics for young females, how to improve through practice, match and tournament play, equipment, clothing, training, and tournament management. Molla Bjurstedt and Samuel Crowther in *Tennis for Women* and Mary Hardwick in *Lawn Tennis for Women* use their tennis experience and expertise to instruct women. Lou Anderson in *Tennis for Women, with Special Reference to the Training of Teachers* explains the basic strokes, suggests lessons and testing measures, and briefly mentions match play. Alfred Beamish and W. G. Beamish also instruct females in *Lawn Tennis for Ladies*.

Inside Tennis for Women describes how to execute all the strokes and how to implement them in singles, doubles, and mixed doubles play. Leslie Hunt also provides practice drills and insights into the mental game of tennis. Rex Lardner emphasizes tactics, stroke varieties, practice, how to hit rally winners, and doubles formations in *Tactics in Women's Singles, Doubles, and Mixed Doubles*. *Tennis for Women* by Ford Hovis includes stroke analysis and demonstrations by the following players: Wendy Overton, backhand; Valerie Ziegenfuss, forehand; Leslie Hunt, serve and return of serve; Karen Krantzche, overhead; Rosemary Casals, volley; Kerry Melville, lob and drop shot; Nancy Gunter, court strategy; Betty Stove, doubles; Francoise Durr, mixed doubles; and Kerry Harris, physical fitness and equipment.

The majority of the books written for children instruct them in the basic strokes. A full discussion of these works appears in Chapter 11. The initial teachers that many children have for tennis are their parents. Thus, Chester Murphy offers *A Parent's Guide to Teaching Kids to Play*; Carol Kleinman suggests that *You Can Teach Your Child Tennis: A 30-Day Guide to Tennis Readiness*; and Bob Huang and Arthur Shay explain the process for *Teaching Your Child Tennis*. In *Teaching Children Tennis the Vic Braden Way* Vic Braden and Bill Bruns discuss age differences, getting started, maintaining interest, teaching children who have little ability or excellent potential, the elements of good teaching, handling positive and negative attitudes, planning, goal setting, proper stroking technique, and sample lessons. Former player Julie Anthony and teaching pro Nick Bollettieri combine their expertise in *A Winning Combination*, written for parents who want to teach their children the how and when of tennis. They emphasize mental and physical health, conditioning and nutrition, equipment, hiring coaches, sportsmanship, and tournaments.

Since tennis is a popular lifetime sport and many people want to learn, several books provide instruction for older beginners. Jim Montgomery explains fitness, practice techniques, motivational hints, and precautions in *Tennis for the Mature Adult*. Peter Burwash and John Tullius attempt to teach their readers how to become their own coach by understanding tennis. *Peter Burwash's Tennis for Life* states that tennis is a game of emergencies which results in not-so-perfect strokes that collapse under the pressure of a match. They recommend how and where to hit the ball in various situations, what to do when your game falls apart, finding a superior player's weakness, and exploiting vulnerabilities. Henry Cummings describes *Tennis as a Hobby*.

Jason Morton, Seymour Russell, and Clyde Burleson suggest that senior players develop mental toughness regardless of their playing skills in *Winning Tennis after Forty*. They explain how to polish your best shots and develop your own classic style, strategies for tournament competition, warm-up and warm-down exercises, getting the most from a tennis week vacation, practice drills, match strategies, how to select a pro, and learning how to win. Through stroke and strategy instruction and photographs Pancho Gonzales and Jeffrey Bairstow offer classic hints in *Tennis Begins at Forty: A Guide for All Players Who Don't Have Wrists of Steel or a Cannonball Serve, Don't Always Rush the Net or Have a Devastating Overhead, But Want to Win*. Tennis is for relaxation, exercise, competition, or all three according to *Prime Time Tennis: Tennis for Players over Forty*. Reminiscences of tennis personalities and politics flavor Vic Seixas and Joel Cohen's book that includes comparisons of current playing styles with those in the 1950s and advice on warm-up exercises, court etiquette, psychology, playing on various court surfaces, and picking doubles partners. Alvin Bunis and Roger Williams initially help players assess their abilities from beginner to retread to late bloomer to social player. *Tennis with the Grand Masters: How to Play Winning Tennis in the Prime of Life* explains five keys to seniors' success in singles and doubles, shoring up stroke execution, tactics, doubles play, using your head, and conditioning.

Bradley Parks, chairman of the National Foundation of Wheelchair Tennis, explains coaching and teaching techniques in *Tennis in a Wheelchair*. He explains the basic strokes, racket movement, wheelchair mobility, advanced movement shots, and how to play approach shots, lobs, and high balls.

The Six Insidious Traps of College Tennis and How to Avoid Them! by Gordon Hull assesses players' failure to know enough about the school, the tennis program, the team, and the coach, failure to put a scholarship in proper perspective, and failure to graduate in four years. Insights from players stress the essentiality of knowing yourself and making the most of college visits while several coaches make candid suggestions about what to look for, what to expect, and the importance of academics.

BIBLIOGRAPHY

American Association for Health, Physical Education, and Recreation. *Ideas for Tennis Instruction*. Washington, D.C.: American Association for Health, Physical Education, and Recreation, 1967.

————. *Tennis Group Instruction*. Washington, D.C.: American Association for Health, Physical Education, and Recreation, 1972.

Anderson, Lou Eastwood. *Tennis for Women, with Special Reference to the Training of Teachers*. New York: A.S. Barnes and Company, 1926.

Anthony, Julie, and Bollettieri, Nick. *A Winning Combination*. New York: Charles Scribner's and Sons, 1980.

Athletic Institute. *Tennis Instructor's Guide*. Chicago: Athletic Institute, 1958.

Barnaby, Jack. *Ground Strokes in Match Play: Techniques, Tempo, and Winning Tactics*. Garden City, New York: Doubleday and Company, 1978.

Beamish, Alfred Ernest, and Beamish, W. G. *Lawn Tennis for Ladies*. Boston: Small, Maynard and Company, 1924.

Bjurstedt, Molla, and Crowther, Samuel. *Tennis for Women*. New York: Doubleday, Page and Company, 1916.

Bodenmiller, Gary. *Drills for Skills*. New York: United States Tennis Association, 1980.

Bowers, Chester. *Advanced Tennis*. New York: Macmillan, 1940.

Braden, Vic, and Bruns, Bill. *Teaching Children Tennis the Vic Braden Way*. Boston: Little, Brown, 1980.

Brown, Jim. *Tennis, Strokes, Strategy, and Programs*. Englewood Cliffs, New Jersey: Prentice-Hall, 1980.

————. *Tennis: Teaching, Coaching, and Directing Programs*. Englewood Cliffs, New Jersey: Prentice-Hall, 1976.

Bunis, Alvin, and Williams, Roger. *Tennis with the Grand Masters: How to Play Winning Tennis in the Prime of Life*. Norwalk, Connecticut: Tennis Magazine, 1983.

Burwash, Peter, and Tullius, John. *Peter Burwash's Tennis for Life*. New York: New York Times Book Company, 1981.

Charles, Allegra. *How to Win at Ladies Doubles*. New York: Arco Publishing Company, 1975.

Chavez, Rick, and Nieder, Lois Smith. *Teaching Tennis*. Minneapolis: Burgess Publishing Company, 1982.

Cummings, Henry I. *Tennis as a Hobby*. New York: Harper and Brothers, 1940.

DeGroot, William L. *Tennis and You*. Englewood, Colorado: Morton Publishing Company, 1984.

Dewhurst, Evelyn. *A Handbook for Coaching Lawn Tennis*. London: Dewpool School of Lawn Tennis, 1966.

———. *Lawn Tennis Guaranteed: How to Teach and Play It*. London: Pitman, 1939.

Doerner, Cynthia, Doerner, Peter, and Ozier, Dan. *Winning Tennis Doubles*. Chicago: Contemporary Books, 1978.

Driver, Helen Irene. *Tennis for Teachers*. Philadelphia: W. B. Saunders, 1936.

———. *Tennis Self-Instructor: A Student's Handbook*. Madison, Wisconsin: Monona Driver Book Company, 1953.

Duroska, Lud. *Tennis for Beginners*. New York: Grosset and Dunlap, 1975.

Durr, Francoise. *Doubles Strategy: A Creative and Psychological Approach to Tennis*. New York: David McKay Company, 1978.

Edgren, Harry Daniel, and Robinson, Gilmer G. *Group Instruction in Tennis and Badminton*. New York: A. S. Barnes and Company, 1939.

Elliott, Bruce, and Kilderry, Rob. *The Art and Science of Tennis*. Philadelphia: Saunders, 1983.

Ellwanger, Rico. *Tennis, Up to Tournament Standards*. Boston: Charles River Reprints, 1976.

Everett, Peter, and Dumas, Virginia. *Beginning Tennis*. Belmont, California: Wadsworth Publishing Company, 1962.

Fogleman, Harry. *Tennis for the Beginner and the Average Player*. Portsmouth, Ohio: Johnson Publishing Company, 1937.

Fox, John, and Vasil, Elizabeth. *When Do We Get to Play, Coach?* Glassboro, New Jersey, 1976.

Gensemer, Robert. *Intermediate Tennis*. Englewood, Colorado: Morton Publishing Company, 1985.

Godbey, Geoffrey, and Guadagnolo, Frank. *Triples: A New Tennis Game*. State College, Pennsylvania: Venture Publishing Company, 1980.

Gonzales, Pancho, and Bairstow, Jeffrey. *Tennis Begins at Forty: A Guide for All Players Who Don't Have Wrists of Steel or a Cannonball Serve, Don't Always Rush the Net or Have a Devastating Overhead, But Want to Win*. New York: Dial Press, 1976.

Graebner, Clarke, and Graebner, Carol. *Mixed Doubles Tennis*. New York: McGraw-Hill, 1973.

Gray, Marvin R., ed. *What Research Tells the Coach about Tennis*. Washington, D.C.: American Alliance for Health, Physical Education and Recreation, 1974.

Greene, Robert Ford. *Tennis Drills: On- and Off-Court Drills and Exercises for Beginners, Intermediates, Tournament Players, and Teaching Professionals*. New York: Hawthorn Books, 1976.

76 The Literature of Tennis

Groppel, Jack L. *Tennis for Advanced Players: And Those Who Would Like to Be*. Champaign, Illinois: Human Kinetics Publishers, 1984.

Hardwick, Mary. *Lawn Tennis for Women*. New York: M.S. Mill Company, 1937.

Harmon, Bob. *Use Your Head in Doubles*. New York: Scribner, 1979.

Hillas, Marjorie, and LeFevre, John R. *Tennis: A Manual for Teachers with Materials—Methods—Programs for Group Instruction*. Dubuque, Iowa: William C. Brown Company, 1955.

Hopman, Harry. *Lobbing into the Sun*. Indianapolis: Bobbs-Merrill Company, 1975.

Hopman, John. *Tennis Know-How: The Forehand, Backhand and Service*. Artarmon, New South Wales, 1958.

Hovis, Ford, ed. *Tennis for Women*. Garden City, New York: Doubleday, 1980.

Huang, Bob, and Shay, Arthur. *Teaching Your Child Tennis*. Chicago: Contemporary Books, 1979.

Hull, Gordon. *The Six Insidious Traps of College Tennis and How to Avoid Them!* Mineola, New York: Goodworth Publishers, 1979.

Hunt, Leslie. *Inside Tennis for Women*. Chicago: Contemporary Books, 1978.

Isaacs, Richard S. *John Zwieg's Courtside Companion: A Tennis Workbook for the Serious Player*. San Francisco: Chronicle Books, 1973.

Jacobs, Helen. *Beginners Guide to Winning Tennis*. North Hollywood, California: Wilshire Book Company, 1961.

Jacobs, William Plumer. *Tennis, Builder of Citizenship: The Psychology and Technique of the Game as Taught in the Tennis Clinic*. Clinton, South Carolina: Jacobs Press, 1941.

Jaeger, Eloise M., and Leighton, Harry. *Teaching of Tennis, for Schools and Recreational Programs*. Minneapolis: Burgess Publishing Company, 1963.

Kenfield, John F. *Teaching and Coaching Tennis*. Dubuque, Iowa: William C. Brown Company, 1976.

Kenfield, John F., and Janes, George. *The Volley and the Half Volley: The Attacking Game*. Garden City, New York: Doubleday, 1978.

King, Billie Jean, Stolle, Fred, and Hoffman, Greg. *How to Play Mixed Doubles*. New York: Simon and Schuster, 1980.

Kleinman, Carol. *You Can Teach Your Child Tennis: A 30–Day Guide to Tennis Readiness*. New York: Popular Library, 1979.

Kraft, Eve. *The Tennis Workbook: Unit I*. New York: United States Tennis Association, 1980.

Kraft, Eve, and Conroy, John. *The Tennis Teacher's Guide: Group Instruction and Team Coaching*. New York: United States Tennis Association, 1980.

——. *The Tennis Workbook: Unit II*. New York: United States Tennis Association, 1982.

Kraft, Steven. *Tennis Drills for Self-Improvement*. Garden City, New York: Doubleday, 1978.

Lambert-Chambers, Dorothea Douglass. *Lawn Tennis for Ladies*. New York: Outing Publishing Company, 1912.

Lardner, Rex. *The Complete Beginner's Guide to Tennis*. Garden City, New York: Doubleday, 1967.

——. *Tactics in Women's Singles, Doubles, and Mixed Doubles*. Garden City, New York: Doubleday, 1975.

Lawn Tennis Association. *Start Lawn Tennis with Dan Maskell, the LTA Training Manager*. London: Allen and Unwin, 1963.

Leary, Don. *The Teaching Tennis Pro*. New York: Pinnacle Books, 1979.

Lord, Sterling. *Returning the Serve Intelligently*. Garden City, New York: Doubleday, 1976.

Lott, George, and Bairstow, Jeffrey. *How to Play Winning Doubles*. Norwalk, Connecticut: Tennis Magazine, 1979.

Meinhardt, Tom, and Brown, Jim. *Tennis: Group Instruction II*. Washington, D.C.: American Alliance for Health, Physical Education, Recreation, and Dance and United States Tennis Association, 1984.

Meng, Harry G. *Advantage Tennis Anyone*. Dubuque, Iowa: Kendall/Hunt Publishing Company, 1979.

Metzler, Paul. *Advanced Tennis*. New York: Sterling Publishing Company, 1972.

——. *Fine Points of Tennis*. New York: Sterling Publishing Company, 1978.

——. *Getting Started in Tennis*. New York: Sterling Publishing Company, 1972.

——. *Tennis Doubles: Tactics and Formations*. New York: Sterling Publishing Company, 1975.

Miles, Eustace. *Lawn Tennis Lessons for Beginners and Others*. Norwich: London and Norwich Press, 1925.

Montgomery, Jim. *Tennis for the Mature Adult*. Jackson, Mississippi: Hunter's Mountain Tennis Corporation, 1979.

Moore, Ballard J. *Beginning Tennis: For the "Love" of Tennis*. Dubuque, Iowa: Kendall/Hunt Publishing Company, 1976.

Morton, Jason, Russell, Seymour, and Burleson, Clyde. *Winning Ten-*

nis after Forty. Englewood Cliffs, New Jersey: Prentice-Hall, 1980.

Moss, Thomas. *Lawn Tennis for Teachers and Players*. London: G. Allen and Unwin, 1949.

————. *Lawn Tennis: Group Teaching*. New Rochelle, New York: SportShelf, 1960.

Murphy, Chester W. *Advanced Tennis*. Dubuque, Iowa: William C. Brown Company, 1982.

————. *A Parent's Guide to Teaching Kids to Play*. West Point, New York: Leisure Press, 1982.

————. *Tennis for Thinking Players*. West Point, New York: Leisure Press, 1982.

Murphy, Chester W., and Murphy, William E. *Tennis for the Player, Teacher, and Coach*. Philadelphia: Saunders, 1975.

Murphy, William E. *Complete Book of Championship Drills*. West Nyack, New York: Parker Publishing Company, 1975.

Murphy, William E. and Murphy, Chester W. *Tennis for Beginners*. New York: Ronald Press Company, 1958.

Murray, H. A. *Tennis for Beginners*. North Hollywood, California: Wilshire, 1974.

Nicol, Eric, and More, Dave. *Tennis/It Serves You Right*. Edmonton, Alberta: Hurtig Publishers, 1984.

Olliff, John Sheldon. *Lawn Tennis for Beginners*. London: W. and G. Foyle, 1951.

Paret, Jahial Parmly. *Lawn Tennis for Beginners*. New York: Macmillan Company, 1916.

Parks, Bradley A. *Tennis in a Wheelchair*. N.p., n.d.

Payne, Gloria. *A Tennis Manual for Beginning and Intermediate Players*. Dubuque, Iowa: Kendall/Hunt Publishing Company, 1982.

Petro, Sharon. *The Tennis Drill Book*. West Point, New York: Leisure Press, 1984.

Pons, Fred. *Tennis Made (Somewhat) Easier*. New York: Exposition Press, 1973.

Preparing for Tennis in the 1980s. New York: United States Tennis Association, 1979.

Randle, Dorothy, and Hillas, Marjorie. *Tennis Organized for Group Instruction*. New York: A.S. Barnes, 1932.

Roy, Harcourt. *Tennis for Schools*. London: Pelham Books, 1974.

Sailes, Gary A. *Championship Tennis Drills for Advanced Players and Coaches*. Chicago: Chicago State University, 1984.

Schwed, Peter. *The Serve and the Overhead Smash*. Garden City, New York: Doubleday, 1976.

Seixas, Vic, and Cohen, Joel. *Prime Time Tennis: Tennis for Players over Forty*. New York: Scribner, 1983.

Sheehan, Larry, ed. *Mastering Your Tennis Strokes*. New York: Atheneum, 1976.

Smith, Harold Leslie. *Lawn Tennis Coaching*. London: Physical Education Association, 1960.

Smith, Stan, Lutz, Bob, and Sheehan, Larry. *Modern Tennis Doubles*. New York: Atheneum/SMI, 1975.

Stewart, Charlotte. *Tennis Type Games: An Experimental Unit for High School Girls*. Washington, D.C.: American Association for Health, Physical Education, and Recreation, 1939.

Summerfield, Sidney C. *Tennis: Learn to Volley First*. New York: Vantage Press, 1970.

Talbert, Peter, and Fishman, Lew. *Secrets of a Winning Serve and Return*. Englewood Cliffs, New Jersey: Prentice-Hall, 1977.

Talbert, William F., and Old, Bruce S. *The Game of Doubles in Tennis*. Philadelphia: Lippincott, 1977.

———. *The Game of Singles in Tennis*. Philadelphia: Lippincott, 1977.

———. *Tennis Tactics: Singles and Doubles*. New York: Harper and Row, 1983.

Teaching Tennis to Groups. New York: United States Tennis Association, 1974.

Tennant, Eleanor. *Play Tennis the "Teach" Tennant Way*. London: Evening News, 1952.

Tennis Self-Instructor, A Student's Handbook. Madison, Wisconsin: Monona Driver Book Company, 1973.

Tilden, William Tatem. *Singles and Doubles*. New York: George H. Doran Company, 1923.

Tilmanis, Gundars A. *Advanced Tennis for Coaches, Teachers, and Players*. Philadelphia: Lea and Febiger, 1975.

Trabert, Tony, and Hook, Jim. *The Serve: Key to Winning Tennis*. New York: Dodd, Mead and Company, 1984.

Vaile, Pembroke Arnold. *The Backhand Book*. Chicago: T. E. Wilson, 1918.

Van Kanegan, Steve. *Optic Yellow Fever*. Los Alamitos, California: S. V. Wingit Press, 1984.

Wright, George. *Lawn Tennis for Beginners*. Boston: Wright and Ditson, 1928.

———. *Lawn Tennis: Revised Units to Beginners*. Boston: Wright and Ditson, 1911.

Xanthos, Paul J. *Handbook for Organization and Conduct of Tennis Clinics and Teacher Training Workshops*. New York: United States Tennis Association, 1981.

————. *Tennis: A Pictorial Guide for Teachers*. Encino, California: Paul J. Xanthos Enterprises, 1963.

Yeomans, Pat. *Ten Tests for Better Tennis*. New York: United States Tennis Association, 1981.

7

Players and Teaching Professionals Instruct

Players and individuals who teach as a vocation can provide additional insights into how they personally or through their students develop stroke expertise and successful strategy. Explanations of unique systems or instructional approaches offer readers success, if they incorporate specific techniques and skills into their games. In this chapter the first group of books utilizes the instructions and demonstrations of players and teaching professionals, while in the second players' writings are the focus. Finally, systems or various methods for learning tennis are the focus.

Jim Leighton's *Inside Tennis: Techniques of Winning* includes strokes and strategies for beginning, intermediate, and advanced players. Teaching professionals Bill Murphy, Pauline Betz Addie, Welby Van Horn, Wayne Sabin, Chet Murphy, Bill Luffer, and Dennis Van der Meer contribute articles on the forehand, the backhand, the serve, volley, the smash, tactics, drills and play situations, percentage tennis, and the rhythm approach respectively. Jack Pollard draws together players' instructional comments and demonstrations in *Lawn Tennis: The Australian Way*. Charlie Pasarell on the serve, Tom Okker with the forehand, Arthur Ashe on the serve, Tony Roche with the volley, and Harold Solomon on the lob explain and illustrate in Arthur Ashe and Larry Sheehan's *Mastering Your Tennis*

Strokes. Tennis Handbook by Chester Murphy and William
Murphy contains fifty-nine sections about technique written
by former champions, such as Don Budge, Fred Perry, Bill
Talbert, Jack Kramer, Tony Trabert, and Alice Marble, and
many teaching pros. Tennis fundamentals plus nine articles
comprise *Lawn Tennis Manual of Instruction.* Among these
brief essays are Ted Schroeder on volleying, Jack Kramer on
ground strokes, Don Budge on psychology and strategy, and
Alice Marble on the value of sage counsel. *Championship Tennis by the Experts, How to Play Championship Tennis* by Paul
Assaiante includes instructional articles by leading teachers
such as Vic Braden, Fred Stolle, Dennis Van der Meer, and
Chet Murphy.

Alan Trengrove in 1964 published *The Art of Tennis* and
How to Play Tennis the Professional Way which use leading
players to explain and to demonstrate tennis strokes and strategies. The later book includes the following: backhand, Ken
Rosewall; forehand, Andres Gimeno; serve, Pancho Gonzales;
volley, Lew Hoad; advantage left-hander, Rob Laver; delicate
touch, Ken Rosewall; competitiveness, Pancho Segura; lob, Lew
Hoad; doubles strategy, Tony Trabert; conditioning, temperament and equipment, Frank Sedgman; winning tennis after
fifty, Don Budge; and the complete lawn tennis player, Tony
Trabert. Following his edited *Lawn Tennis Manual* in 1933,
Stephen Merrihew again used players and teachers to explain
How Lawn Tennis Is Played. Don Budge explains the mechanics of ground strokes, serves, and volleys; Fred Perry offers tips
on the forehand and serve; Adrian Quist describes the merits
of net play; Bill Tilden discusses the all-court game; and Henri
Cochet emphasizes strategy in match play and court tactics
and the theory of angles. Stephen Merrihew and Robert Hynson
use a similar format in *Lawn Tennis Up-to-Date.* In *Instant
Tennis Lessons* and *More Instant Tennis Lessons* edited by Robert La Marche teaching professionals share their expertise about
serves, ground strokes, volleys, lobs, overheads, serve returns,
singles tactics, and doubles tactics. Both books contain technique tips which include one to three paragraphs of explanation
plus illustrations and are reprints from *Tennis Magazine. Winning Tennis: Strokes and Strategies of the World's Top Pros*

Analyzed by Dick Stockton and Wendy Overton by Bob Gillen uses the most effective strokes of players according to a *Tennis USA* poll. Each skill includes a technique description, photographs of the stars executing the stroke, and an analysis of the stroke. For example, John Conroy explains how to execute the backhand, Jimmy Connors and Evonne Goolagong demonstrate, and Dick Stockton and Wendy Overton analyze their techniques. Barry Meadow for singles and Jack Barnaby for doubles explain tactics and playing techniques in this book.

The Nestle Books of Tennis, *Match Point, Game, Set and Match* and *Points for Victory*, the latter two by David Young, include historical, biographical, fitness, and technique articles by players, writers, and teaching pros. In *Match Point*, Martin Mulligan discusses how sports films help young Australian players while George Worthington explains purposeful practice. Clarence Jones focuses on tournament play in the second book, and Dan Maskell describes the qualities of a champion in the last volume. *Tennis A Professional Guide* by the United States Professional Tennis Association, comprehensively covers every aspect of tennis. Among the chapters written by different authors are those on specialty shots by Chet Murphy and Jack Barnaby, doubles tactics and strategy by Rod Laver and Roy Emerson, junior tennis by Nick Bollettieri, and choosing a pro and a tennis camp by Mike Eikenberry.

Over fifty players from the United States and other countries offer tennis instruction. Illustrative of Bill Tilden's thirteen books are *Lawn Tennis for Club Players* and *Tennis for the Junior Player, the Club Player, the Expert* which focus on the basic strokes. *The Common Sense of Lawn Tennis* adds some fine points for playing and watching tennis while *How to Play Better Tennis* emphasizes tactics, how to exploit weaknesses, how to pressure opponents, and concentration. In *The Art of Lawn Tennis* he teaches the basics and explains match play, fitness, and the growth of the game. Tilden's other books are *Better Tennis for the Club Player, The Expert, "The Kid": A Tennis Lesson, Tennis A to Z, Singles and Doubles,* and *Match Play and the Spin of the Ball* (with Stephen Merrihew). Helen Jacobs, who became an author after finishing her tennis career, offers five basic techniques books: *Beginners Guide to Winning*

Tennis, Tennis, Improve Your Tennis, Modern Tennis, and *Tennis.* Mary Browne draws from her years as a player and a teaching professional to instruct in *Top-Flite Tennis, Streamline Tennis,* and *Design for Tennis.* Billie Jean King shows her technique for all shots and for doubles play as well as providing practice and conditioning hints in *Tennis to Win* with Kim Chapin. She and Joe Hyams use a question-response approach in *Billie Jean King's Secrets of Winning Tennis* to teach the basic strokes and strategies. With Reginald Brace she explains how to *Play Better Tennis.* King, partner Fred Stolle, and Greg Hoffman use their playing expertise to explain *How to Play Mixed Doubles.* Pauline Betz Addie provides instruction in the basic fundamentals in *Tennis for Everyone, with Official USLTA Rules* and *Tennis with or without a Partner: Top Tennis Training Tips for Tennis Buffs of All Ages and All Abilities.* Clarke Graebner and Carol Graebner share their successful tennis partnership in *Mixed Doubles Tennis.* Leslie Hunt and several other players explain proper stroke technique in *Inside Tennis for Women* as does Wendy Overton in *Tennis for Women.* Maureen Connolly draws from her outstanding career to instruct in *Championship Tennis, Forehand Drive,* (with Tom Gwynne), and *Power Tennis.* In the third of these she explains strokes, strategies, clothing, equipment, and the basic rules, plus includes chapters explaining how she learned to play and what tennis means to her. Hazel Wightman, Helen Wills, and Barbara Gordon also offer ways to improve play in their books *Better Tennis, Tennis,* and *Improving Your Tennis Game* respectively. Gordon uses a dialogue between herself as the teacher and her student in this first-aid book for tennis. Molla Bjurstedt and Samuel Crowther examine the fundamentals in *Tennis for Women.* Ethel Sutton Bruce and Bert Bruce describe and illustrate the form, rhythmical timing, body balance, and technique in stroke production, plus discuss etiquette and strategy in *Tennis Fundamentals and Timing.* Sarah Palfrey's *Tennis for Anyone!* explains how tennis is adaptable to any player's abilities, describes the basic strokes, and discusses tactics, sportsmanship, and the rules. Sarah Palfrey Cooke also offers technique instructions in *Winning Tennis and How to Play It.*

Martina Navratilova and Mary Carillo explain strokes, strategies, and training in *Tennis My Way*.

Following the lead of James Dwight in *Lawn-Tennis* (1886)
and *Practical Lawn-Tennis* (1893) and Henry Slocum's *Lawn
Tennis in Our Country* (1890), other male players in the United
States share their expertise. Bill Talbert's eight instructional
books include *Sports Illustrated Tennis* and *Tennis Strokes and
Strategies* which discuss the basics. The first of these focuses
on the forehand, backhand, net play, and the volley as fundamental strokes for singles, doubles formations and move-
ments, and mixed doubles strategies. Talbert and Bruce Old
explain stroke development and match play skills in *The Game
of Doubles in Tennis, The Game of Singles in Tennis, Stroke
Production in the Game of Tennis*, and the successor to these
three *Tennis Tactics: Singles and Doubles*. Talbert and Gordon
Greer explain how to overcome common faults, how to hit the
basic shots and employ proper tactics, the rules, play after forty,
and family tennis in *Bill Talbert's Weekend Tennis: How to
Have Fun and Win at the Same Time*. Stan Smith, a champion
many times, states *It's More Than Just a Game* in his brief
inspirational book. Smith and partner Bob Lutz with Larry
Sheehan explain their successful strokes and strategies in *Modern Tennis Doubles*. Smith and Larry Sheehan describe, analyze, and correct common mistakes made when improperly
executing the strokes in *Stan Smith's Guide to Better Tennis*.
They also combine to explain *Stan Smith's Six Tennis Basics*
which include relaxing on the court, getting ready, getting the
racket back, keeping your eye on the ball, hitting out in front,
and following through. *Inside Tennis* by Smith and Tom Valentine instructs in the basic shots using photographs of Smith.

Pancho Gonzales and Dick Hawk explain the fundamental
strokes in *Tennis* as do Gonzales and Joe Hyams in *Winning
Tactics for Weekend Singles*. This later book uses a question-
answer format. *Tennis Begins at Forty: A Guide for All Players
Who Don't Have Wrists of Steel or a Cannonball Serve, Don't
Always Rush the Net or Have a Devastating Overhead, But Want
to Win* by Gonzales and Jeffrey Bairstow explains the basic
shots and tactics to senior players. Ellsworth Vines uses unique

instructional approaches in two of his four books. In *Tennis Simplified for Everybody* he explains the fundamental principles in an illustrated series of questions and answers. With Gene Vier in *Tennis: Myth and Method* he reflects on the methods of the top ten male players since Don Budge in addition to discussing stroke techniques, strategies, and tactics. According to Vines in *How to Play Better Tennis*, the most important rule in tennis is keep your eyes on the ball. He also instructs in *Ellsworth Vines' Quick Way to Better Tennis: A Practical Book on Tennis for Men and Women.*

Maurice McLoughlin combines an overview of his special matches with information about equipment, clothing, court conditions, the strokes, doubles, women's tennis, and training practices in *Tennis as I Play It*. Jack Kramer and Larry Sheehan discuss ground stroke fundamentals, serving, tactics, mental preparation, and how to compete against different opponents in *How to Play Your Best Tennis All the Time*. Kramer explains stroke technique, tactics, temperament, and practice in *How to Win at Tennis*. *Arthur Ashe's Tennis Clinic* illustrates and briefly describes the basic strokes, advanced shotmaking, tactics, and training in these reprints from Arthur Ashe's series in *Tennis Magazine*. Ashe and Larry Sheehan emphasize proper technique in *Mastering Your Tennis Strokes*. Tony Trabert and Joe Hyams explain the fundamental strokes and strategies to the occasional player in *Winning Tactics for Weekend Tennis*. *The Serve: Key to Winning Tennis* by Trabert and Jim Hook emphasizes the progressive steps in learning the serve and its importance to tennis performance. In *Tennis: How to Play, How to Win* also by Trabert, several outstanding male players explain and demonstrate tennis fundamentals. Instructions are for the forehand, backhand, serve and return, volley, overhead, lob, approach shot, drop, half volley, singles and doubles strategy, play versus left-handers, and conditioning and practicing. Other players who offer instruction include Don Budge in *Budge on Tennis*, Vic Seixas and Joel Cohen in *Prime Time Tennis: Tennis for Players over Forty*, Charlie Pasarell in *Mastering Your Tennis Strokes*, Dick Stockton in *Winning Tennis*, John Doeg and Allison Danzig in *Elements of Lawn Tennis* and *Lawn Tennis*, and John Patty in *Tennis My Way*. Dennis Ralston and

Barry Tarshis stress setting goals and priorities, learning the fundamentals, and conditioning in *Six Weeks to a Better Level of Tennis*. George Wright instructs in *Lawn Tennis for Beginners*, *Lawn Tennis: Revised Units to Beginners*, and *Rules of Lawn Tennis, with a Description of Important Strokes*.

French champion Suzanne Lenglen's *Lawn Tennis, the Game of Nations* and *Tennis by Simple Exercises* with Margaret Morris describe the basic strokes. Francoise Durr emphasizes a thinking game in *Doubles Strategy: A Creative and Psychological Approach to Tennis*. Several English women offer instructional hints, such as Kathleen McKane in *Lawn Tennis: How to Improve Your Game*, Dorothea Lambert-Chambers in *Lawn Tennis for Ladies*, Kitty Godfree in *Lawn Tennis Simplified*, and *Playing Tennis* by Sue Barker. Betty Nuthall in *Learning Lawn Tennis* demonstrates and describes the strokes as she does in *Learning Tennis*. Angela Buxton in *Tackle Lawn Tennis This Way* describes the strokes, physical and mental fitness, tournament play, tactics, advanced play, and psychology. Clarence Jones and Buxton offer similar advice in *Starting Tennis*. *Modern Lawn Tennis* by Dorothy Round offers tips on technique, tournament play, and practice. Mary Hardwick's *Lawn Tennis, Lawn Tennis for Women*, and *Lawn Tennis: How to Master the Strokes* provide instructions on stroke development.

French male star Jean Lacoste explains his winning technique in *Tennis, Lacoste on Tennis*, and *How to Play Tennis*. Henri Cochet in *The Art of Tennis* seeks to raise the average playing standards of French players through his explanations of the strokes, strategies, tactics, placing the ball, learning how to win, doubles, and common sense play. Reginald Doherty and Hugh Doherty instruct in the strokes, singles and doubles match play, and practice in *R.F. and H.L. Doherty on Lawn Tennis*. English player Tony Mottram stresses the basic strokes and strategies in his six technique books: *Improve Your Tennis, Play Better Tennis, Quick Way to Better Tennis, Skills and Tactics of Tennis, Tackle Tennis*, and *Modern Lawn Tennis*. With Joy Mottram he explains common errors, practicing, percentage placement, and match preparation in the later volume. She and Stanley Doust also describe *Lawn Tennis: How to Master the Strokes*. Other English male stars who provide tennis instruc-

tion include Bunny Austin in *Lawn Tennis Bits and Pieces* and
Lawn Tennis Made Easy by the Austin-Caulfeild System, Alfred
Beamish in *First Steps to Lawn Tennis, The Lawn Tennis Tip
Book*, and *Lawn Tennis for Ladies* with W. G. Beamish, Gra-
ham Houston and Bobby Wilson in *Lawn Tennis*, and Fred Perry
in *Perry on Tennis: Expert Advice for All on Lawn Tennis*. Mike
Davies from Wales discusses strokes, net play, strategy, dou-
bles, the ladies' game, and court behavior in *Lawn Tennis*. Owen
Davidson in *Tackle Lawn Tennis This Way* discusses the basic
strokes, the net game, court craft, and doubles. In *Lawn Tennis:
How to Become a Champion* Mark Cox explains the strokes, percentage tennis, doubles play, and training.

*Pancho Segura's Championship Strategy: How to Play Win-
ning Tennis* by Pancho Segura and Gladys Heldman includes
conditioning advice, stroke technique instructions, suggestions
for playing the mental game, and doubles strategies. *Ivan
Lendl's Power Tennis* by Eugene Scott and Ivan Lendl and Tom
Okker's *Tennis in Pictures* rely heavily on photographs to instruct in the basic strokes. New Zealander Anthony Wilding
teaches tennis in *On the Court and Off*. Australian stars who
share their playing expertise include Neale Fraser in *Successful Tennis*, Frank Sedgman in *How to Play Tennis* plus Ken
Rosewall, John Newcombe, Roy Emerson, and Rod Laver. Sedgman in *Tennis Fundamentals* focuses on the forehand, backhand, and serve plus adds some insights about net play, tactics,
and doubles. *Frank Sedgman's Winning Tennis: The Australian Way to a Better Game* stresses power and control as the
formula for championship tennis. He explains how to study
opponents' games, the importance and technique of all the
strokes, tactics, and doubles play. *Play Tennis with Rosewall:
The Little Master and His Method* by Rosewall and John Barrett
combines stroke instructions and strategies with some biographical information about Rosewall. John Newcombe in *Bedside Tennis* and he, Angie Newcombe, and Clarence Mabry in
The Family Tennis Book describe the basic strokes. In the latter
book the Newcombe family demonstrates the strokes and playing the game. Rod Laver explains tennis through his six technique books including *How to Play Championship Tennis* and
How to Play Winning Tennis with Jack Pollard, *Rod Laver's*

Tennis Digest with Bud Collins, *228 Tennis Tips*, and *Australia's Rod Laver Grand Slam Champion Tennis: Serve, Forehand, Backhand, Smash*. *Tennis for the Bloody Fun of It* written with Roy Emerson and Barry Tarshis provides information about camps, etiquette, the basic and not-so-basic shots, spins, the thinking game, concentration, doubles strategy, practice drills, and conditioning.

Numerous systems and specialized approaches for teaching tennis strokes exist, such as *Hitting Blind: The New Visual Approach to Winning Tennis* by Harold Stein and Bernie Slatt; Jack Groppel and Arthur Shay's *Optimal Tennis*, a biomechanical analysis of strokes; Eleanor Tennant's *Play Tennis the "Teach" Tennant Way*; and *Cannonball Tennis* by Mike Sangster and John Ballantine. DeWitt Willis in *Learn to Play Tennis at Home* stresses the use of rhythmetonics to learn and to perfect tennis techniques and to fix them in your memory. *Vic Braden's Tennis for the Future* by Vic Braden and Bill Bruns describes the stroke fundamentals, serves, returns, and use of spins through pictures and text. They emphasize developing confidence through drills and practice under pressure as well as strategy and tennis psychology. Glenn Bassett and Terry Galanoy discuss ground strokes, serves, net play, footwork, court positioning, practice techniques, and strategies for *Tennis: The Bassett System*. Court, ball, and opponent awareness, eye-hand coordination, triple vision, getting in shape, eating right, and common-sense tennis in addition to the fundamentals of strokes and strategies comprise *Peter Burwash's Tennis for Life* by Peter Burwash and John Tullius. *Tennis Clinic: Play the TennisAmerica Way* by Dennis Van der Meer and Murray Olderman describes the technique Van der Meer uses at his Tennis University. This book includes the strokes, tactics, rationale, and descriptions of his successful system. Mercer Beasley in *How to Play Tennis: The Beasley System of Tennis Instruction* discusses accuracy, hitting, timing, and the pivot for the basic strokes. He includes information about court positioning, zoning, training, exercises, and match play.

Nine rules for motion economy are a key for Dick Bradlee's *Instant Tennis: A New Approach Based on the Coordination, Rhythm and Timing of Champions*. In addition to the basic strokes, he points out fifty things to remember in tennis. *Pattern Play Tennis* emphasizes the use of repeated patterns to improve one's play. In this book Spencer Brent analyzes every stroke and reconstructs each from the basics to refinements as they relate to different patterns so that players can reason out stroke problems based on the mastery of patterns. Jack Arkinstall teaches the use of phonetic, smooth-sounding words or numbers to emphasize the effect of smoothness when stroking in *The Arkinstall Tennis Rhythm Method*. In describing the strokes and their rhythm he stresses slowly saying backswing, smooth/lean, and forward swing. *Lawn Tennis Made Easy by the Austin-Caulfeild System* by Bunny Austin uses a method of teaching stroke production by means of suggestion and comparison. Timing, stroke execution, practice, training, and tactics are a part of this system. Charles LaRue in *The "French" Revolution in "American" Tennis* states that French players succeed because they prefer the vertical face racket use and prefer to pickup over hitting a backcourt shot. Using the concept of "whirl-cause," LaRue explains the importance of the racket angle in stroking and describes the tennis "egg" for hitting the ball earlier.

Stroke analysis and strategies are central to Jack Lowe's *Winning with Percentage Tennis: An Expert's Guide to Smart Court Strategy*. Arthur Shay analyzes errors such as unorthodox grips, hitting the ball too close to your body, flicking the wrist, lazy legs, lollipop serves, and late contact and offers remedies in *40 Common Errors in Tennis and How to Correct Them*. Craig Wilson in *Total Health Tennis: A Lifestyle Approach* emphasizes visualization as a technique for improving stroking technique. Joel Brecheen provides technique explanations and instructions for learning the forehand, backhand, overhead, serve, and volley by executing each in one count using the whole body in *Count One! To Top Tennis Technique*. The basic premise in this system is that tennis is a body game. He also provides advanced strategies and tips to coaches. He instructs in a similar manner is *Tennis Made Easy*.

Jim Brown in *Tennis without Lessons* advocates using a teach-yourself approach by providing information for beginning and intermediate players about strokes, strategies, and practices.

Anthony Annariono and Charles Smith explain the fundamentals in their *Tennis: Individualized Instructional Program*
as does Smith in *An Individualized Instructional Approach to
Tennis. Ed Faulkner's Tennis: How to Play It, How to Teach It*
by Edwin Faulkner and Frederick Weymuller suggests how to
teach yourself tennis using photographs, charts about stroking
trouble spots, and drills. The strokes are the focus of Frederick
Creek's *Teach Yourself Lawn Tennis*. Helen Driver provides a
step-by-step learning process for all the strokes in *Tennis Self-
Instructor: A Student's Handbook*. The basics of what, where,
and how, the practicing of strokes, match tactics, and winning
strategies from Vic Seixas, Stan Smith, Billie Jean King, Tony
Trabert, Julie Anthony, Roy Emerson, and Ron Holmberg comprise Robert La Marche's *Teach Yourself Tennis! Solo Tennis*
uses a backboard as the key to teaching tennis to yourself by
Virginia Yale and Morey Lewis. They explain how to develop
proper stroke form, how to correct bad habits, how to sharpen
your tennis intellect, and how to become more fit and agile,
plus they describe how to build a tennis backboard.

Peter Schwed asks if play is different against left-handed
players and examines all aspects of the game to answer this
query. In *Sinister Tennis: How to Play against and with Left-
Handers* he discusses lefties as singles opponents, as doubles
opponents, and as doubles partners. *Two-Handed Tennis: How
to Play a Winner's Game* by Jeffrey McCullough looks at the
phenomenon of stroking the ball using two hands. He reviews
the past history of the two-handed craze, explains the strengths
of this stroke (greater power, control, and versatility), describes
the technique for hitting two-handed ground strokes and volleys, and adds advice on playing a two-handed opponent.

BIBLIOGRAPHY

Addie, Pauline Betz. *Tennis for Everyone, with Official USLTA Rules.*
Washington, D.C.: Acropolis Books, 1973.
———. *Tennis with or without a Partner: Top Tennis Training Tips
for Tennis Buffs of All Ages and All Abilities.* Washington, D.C.:
Acropolis Books, 1978.
Annariono, Anthony, and Smith, Charles. *Tennis: Individualized In-*

structional Program. Englewood Cliffs, New Jersey: Prentice-Hall, 1973.

Arkinstall, Jack. *The Arkinstall Tennis Rhythm Method.* New York: Vantage Press, 1967.

Ashe, Arthur. *Arthur Ashe's Tennis Clinic.* Norwalk, Connecticut: Golf Digest/Tennis, 1981.

Ashe, Arthur, and Sheehan, Larry. *Mastering Your Tennis Strokes.* New York: Atheneum/SMI, 1976.

Assaiante, Paul, ed. *Championship Tennis by the Experts, How to Play Championship Tennis.* West Point, New York: Leisure Press, 1981.

Austin, Henry Wilfred. *Lawn Tennis Bits and Pieces.* London: S. Low, Marston and Company, 1930.

――――. *Lawn Tennis Made Easy by the Austin-Caulfeild System.* London: Methuen and Company, 1935.

Barker, Sue. *Playing Tennis.* London: Batsford, 1979.

Bassett, Glenn, and Galanoy, Terry. *Tennis: The Bassett System.* Chicago: Contemporary Books, 1977.

Beamish, Alfred Ernest. *First Steps to Lawn Tennis.* Boston: Small, Maynard and Company, 1922.

――――. *The Lawn Tennis Tip Book.* London: Mills and Boon, 1923.

Beamish, Alfred Ernest, and Beamish, W.G. *Lawn Tennis for Ladies.* Boston: Small, Maynard and Company, 1924.

Beasley, Mercer. *How to Play Tennis: The Beasley System of Tennis Instruction.* New York: Garden City Publishing Company, 1933.

Bjurstedt, Molla, and Crowther, Samuel. *Tennis for Women.* New York: Doubleday, Page and Company, 1916.

Braden, Vic, and Bruns, Bill. *Vic Braden's Tennis for the Future.* Boston: Little, Brown, 1977.

Bradlee, Dick. *Instant Tennis: A New Approach Based on the Coordination, Rhythm and Timing of Champions.* New York: Devin-Adair Company, 1974.

Brecheen, Joel. *Count One! To Top Tennis Technique.* Tucson, Arizona: Palo Verde Publishing Company, 1969.

――――. *Tennis Made Easy.* North Hollywood, California: Wilshire, 1971.

Brent, R. Spencer. *Pattern Play Tennis.,* Garden City, New York: Doubleday, 1974.

Brown, Jim. *Tennis without Lessons.* Englewood Cliffs, New Jersey: Prentice-Hall, 1977.

Browne, Mary Kendall. *Design for Tennis.* New York: A. S. Barnes, 1949.

————. *Streamline Tennis*. New York: American Sports Publishing Company, 1940.

————. *Top-Flite Tennis*. New York: American Sports Publishing Company, 1928.

Bruce, Ethel Sutton, and Bruce, Bert O. *Tennis Fundamentals and Timing*. New York: Prentice-Hall, 1938.

Budge, John Donald. *Budge on Tennis*. New York: Prentice-Hall, 1939.

Burwash, Peter, and Tullius, John. *Peter Burwash's Tennis for Life*. New York: New York Times Book Company, 1981.

Buxton, Angela. *Tackle Lawn Tennis This Way*. London: Stanley Paul, 1958.

Cochet, Henri. *The Art of Tennis*. New York: Hillman-Cure, 1937.

Connolly, Maureen. *Championship Tennis*. London: F. Mueller, 1954.

————. *Power Tennis*. New York: A. S. Barnes, 1954.

Connolly, Maureen Catherine, and Gwynne, Tom. *Forehand Drive*. London: MacGibbon and Kee, 1957.

Cooke, Sarah Palfrey. *Winning Tennis and How to Play It*. Garden City, New York: Doubleday, 1946.

Cox, Mark. *Lawn Tennis: How to Become a Champion*. London: W. Luscombe, 1975.

Creek, Frederick Norman Smith. *Teach Yourself Lawn Tennis*. London: English Universities Press, 1952.

Davidson, Owen. *Tackle Lawn Tennis This Way*. London: Stanley Paul, 1970.

Davies, Mike. *Lawn Tennis*. New York: Arc Books, 1963.

Doeg, John Hope, and Danzig, Allison. *Elements of Lawn Tennis*. New York: Coward-McCann, 1931.

————. *Lawn Tennis*. London: Eyre and Spottiswoode, 1932.

Doherty, Reginald Frank, and Doherty, Hugh Lawrence. *R. F. and H. L. Doherty on Lawn Tennis*. New York: Baker and Taylor Company, 1903.

Driver, Helen Irene. *Tennis Self-Instructor: A Student's Handbook*. Madison, Wisconsin: Monona Driver Book Company, 1953.

Durr, Francoise. *Doubles Strategy: A Creative and Psychological Approach to Tennis*. New York: David McKay Company, 1978.

Dwight, James. *Lawn-Tennis*. Boston: Wright and Ditson, 1886.

————. *Practical Lawn-Tennis*. New York: Harper and Brothers, 1893.

Faulkner, Edwin J., and Weymuller, Frederick. *Ed Faulkner's Tennis: How to Play it, How to Teach It*. New York: Dial Press, 1970.

Fraser, Neale. *Successful Tennis*. North Hollywood, California: Wilshire, 1977.

Gillen, Bob, ed. *Winning Tennis: Strokes and Strategies of the World's*

Top Pros Analyzed by Dick Stockton and Wendy Overton. Radnor, Pennsylvania: Chilton Book Company, 1978.

Godfree, Kitty. *Lawn Tennis Simplified.* London: T. Butterworth, 1929.

Gonzales, Pancho, and Bairstow, Jeffrey. *Tennis Begins at Forty: A Guide for All Players Who Don't Have Wrists of Steel or a Cannonball Serve, Don't Always Rush the Net or Have a Devastating Overhead, But Want to Win.* New York: Dial Press, 1976.

Gonzales, Pancho, and Hawk, Dick. *Tennis.* New York: Fleet Publishing Corporation, 1962.

Gonzales, Pancho, and Hyams, Joe. *Winning Tactics for Weekend Singles.* New York: Holt, Rinehart and Winston, 1974.

Gordon, Barbara Breit. *Improving Your Tennis Game.* New York: Hawthorn Books, 1973.

Graebner, Clarke, and Graebner, Carol. *Mixed Doubles Tennis.* New York: McGraw-Hill, 1973.

Groppel, Jack L., and Shay, Arthur. *Optimal Tennis.* Chicago: Contemporary Books, 1983.

Hardwick, Mary. *Lawn Tennis.* London: Blackie and Son, 1937.

———. *Lawn Tennis for Women.* New York: M. S. Mill Company, 1937.

———. *Lawn Tennis: How to Master the Strokes.* London: Foulsham's Sports Library, 1938.

Houston, Graham John, and Wilson, Bobby. *Lawn Tennis.* London: W. Foulsham and Company, 1964.

Hunt, Leslie. *Inside Tennis for Women.* Chicago: Contemporary Books, 1978.

Jacobs, Helen Hull. *Beginners Guide to Winning Tennis.* North Hollywood, California: Wilshire Book Company, 1961.

———. *Improve Your Tennis.* London: Methuen and Company, 1936.

———. *Modern Tennis.* Indianapolis: Bobbs-Merrill Company, 1933.

———. *Tennis.* New York: A. S. Barnes, 1941.

———. *Tennis.* New York: Ronald Press, 1941.

Jones, Clarence Medlycott, and Buxton, Angela. *Starting Tennis.* London: Ward Lock, 1975.

King, Billie Jean, and Brace, Reginald. *Play Better Tennis.* New York: Smith Publishing, 1981.

King, Billie Jean, and Chapin, Kim. *Tennis to Win.* New York: Harper and Row, 1970.

King, Billie Jean, and Hyams, Joe. *Billie Jean King's Secrets of Winning Tennis.* New York: Holt, Rinehart and Winston, 1974.

King, Billie Jean, Stolle, Fred, and Hoffman, Greg. *How to Play Mixed Doubles.* New York: Simon and Schuster, 1980.

Kramer, John Albert. *How to Win at Tennis*. Chicago: Ziff-Davis Publishing Company, 1949.

Kramer, John Albert, and Sheehan, Larry. *How to Play Your Best Tennis All the Time*. New York: Atheneum/SMI, 1977.

Lacoste, Jean Rene. *How to Play Tennis*. London: E. J. Barrow and Company, 1930.

———. *Lacoste on Tennis*. New York: W. Morrow and Company, 1928.

———. *Tennis*. Paris: Grasset, 1928.

La Marche, Robert J. *Instant Tennis Lessons*. Norwalk, Connecticut. Golf Digest/Tennis, 1978.

———. *More Instant Tennis Lessons*. Norwalk, Connecticut: Golf Digest/Tennis, 1984.

———, ed. *Teach Yourself Tennis!* Norwalk, Connecticut: Golf Digest/Tennis, 1980.

Lambert-Chambers, Dorothea Douglass. *Lawn Tennis for Ladies*. New York: Outing Publishing Company, 1912.

LaRue, Charles. *The "French" Revolution in "American" Tennis*. New York: Charles LaRue, 1927.

Laver, Rodney George. *Australia's Rod Laver Grand Slam Champion Tennis: Serve, Forehand, Backhand, Smash*. Australia: Thumbflix International Pty, 1970.

———. *228 Tennis Tips*. Northfield, Illinois: DBI Books, 1977.

Laver, Rodney George, and Collins, Bud, eds. *Rod Laver's Tennis Digest*. Chicago: Follett Publishing Company, 1973.

Laver, Rodney George, Emerson, Roy, and Tarshis, Barry. *Tennis for the Bloody Fun of It*. New York: Quadrangle/New York Times Book Company, 1976.

Laver, Rodney George, and Pollard, Jack. *How to Play Championship Tennis*. New York: Macmillan, 1965.

———. *How to Play Winning Tennis*. London: Mayflower, 1970.

Lawn Tennis Manual of Instruction. Middlesex, England: British Lawn Tennis, 1947.

Leighton, Jim. *Inside Tennis: Techniques of Winning*. Englewood Cliffs, New Jersey: Prentice-Hall, 1977.

Lenglen, Suzanne. *Lawn Tennis, the Game of Nations*. London: G. G. Harrap and Company, 1925.

Lenglen, Suzanne, and Morris, Margaret. *Tennis by Simple Exercises*. London: W. Heinemann, 1937.

Lowe, Jack. *Winning with Percentage Tennis: An Expert's Guide to Smart Court Strategy*. Amelia Island, Florida, 1974.

Match Point: The Nestle Book of Tennis No. 1 London: Stanley Paul, 1963.

McCullough, Jeffrey F. *Two-Handed Tennis: How to Play a Winner's Game*. New York: M. Evans and Company, 1984.

McKane, Kathleen. *Lawn Tennis: How to Improve Your Game*. London: Ward, Lock and Company, 1925.

McLoughlin, Maurice Evans. *Tennis as I Play It*. New York: George H. Doran Company, 1915.

Merrihew, Stephen Wallis, ed. *How Lawn Tennis Is Played*. New York: American Lawn Tennis, Inc., 1937.

———. *Lawn Tennis Manual*. New York: American Lawn Tennis, 1933.

Merrihew, Stephen Wallis, and Hynson, Robert C., eds. *Lawn Tennis Up-to-Date*. New York: American Lawn Tennis, 1940.

Mottram, Anthony. *Improve Your Tennis*. Baltimore: Penguin Books, 1966.

———. *Play Better Tennis*. New York: Arco Publishing Company, 1971.

———. *Quick Way to Better Tennis*. Kent, England: Le Roye, 1952.

———. *Skills and Tactics of Tennis*. New York: Arco Publishing, 1980.

———. *Tackle Tennis*. London: Stanley Paul, 1975.

Mottram, Anthony, and Mottram, Joy. *Modern Lawn Tennis*. London: N. Kaye, 1957.

Mottram, Joy, and Doust, Stanley N. *Lawn Tennis: How to Master the Strokes*. London: W. Foulsham and Co., 1952.

Murphy, Chester W., and Murphy, William E. *Tennis Handbook*. New York: The Ronald Press, 1962.

Navratilova, Martina, and Carillo, Mary. *Tennis My Way*. New York: Charles Scribner's Sons, 1983.

Newcombe, John. *Bedside Tennis*. New York: St. Martin, 1983.

Newcombe, John, Newcombe, Angie, and Mabry, Clarence. *The Family Tennis Book*. London: Angus and Robertson, 1975.

Nuthall, Betty. *Learning Lawn Tennis*. London: Herbert Jenkins,1928.

———. *Learning Tennis*. New York: Duffield and Green, 1928.

Okker, Tom Samuel. *Tennis in Pictures*. New York: Sterling Publishing Company, 1975.

Overton, Wendy. *Tennis for Women*. London: Angus and Robertson, 1975.

Palfrey, Sarah. *Tennis for Anyone!* New York: Cornerstone Library, 1980.

Pasarell, Charlie. *Mastering Your Tennis Strokes*. New York: Atheneum, 1976.

Patty, John Edward. *Tennis My Way*. London: Hutchinson, 1951.

Perry, Frederick John. *Perry on Tennis: Expert Advice for All on Lawn Tennis*. London: Hutchinson and Company, 1936.

Pollard, Jack, ed. *Lawn Tennis: The Australian Way.* New York: Drake Publishers, 1973.

Ralston, Dennis, and Tarshis, Barry. *Six Weeks to a Better Level of Tennis.* New York: Simon and Schuster, 1977.

Rosewall, Ken R., and Barrett, John. *Play Tennis with Rosewall: The Little Master and His Method.* London: Queen Anne Press, 1975.

Round, Dorothy. *Modern Lawn Tennis.* London: G. Newnes, 1935.

Sangster, Mike, and Ballantine, John. *Cannonball Tennis.* London: A. Barker, 1965.

Schwed, Peter. *Sinister Tennis: How to Play against and with Left-Handers.* Garden City, New York: Doubleday, 1975.

Scott, Eugene, and Lendl, Ivan. *Ivan Lendl's Power Tennis.* New York: Simon and Schuster, 1983.

Sedgman, Frank. *Frank Sedgman's Winning Tennis: The Australian Way to a Better Game.* New York: Prentice-Hall, 1954.

———. *How to Play Tennis.* Gloscester, England: Pollard Publishing Company, 1972.

———. *Tennis Fundamentals.* Sydney: Reed, 1978.

Segura, Pancho, and Heldman, Gladys. *Pancho Segura's Championship Strategy: How to Play Winning Tennis.* New York: McGraw Hill, 1976.

Seixas, Vic, and Cohen, Joel. *Prime Time Tennis: Tennis for Players over Forty.* New York: Scribner, 1983.

Shay, Arthur. *40 Common Errors in Tennis and How to Correct Them.* Chicago: Contemporary Books, 1978.

Slocum, Henry Warner. *Lawn Tennis in Our Own Country.* New York: A. G. Spalding and Brothers, 1890.

Smith, Charles. *An Individualized Instructional Approach to Tennis.* Dubuque, Iowa: Kendall/Hunt Publishing Company, 1981.

Smith, Stan. *It's More Than Just a Game.* Old Tappan, New Jersey: F. H. Revell Company, 1977.

Smith, Stan, Lutz, Bob, and Sheehan, Larry. *Modern Tennis Doubles.* New York: Atheneum/SMI, 1975.

Smith, Stan, and Sheehan, Larry. *Stan Smith's Guide to Better Tennis.* New York: Grosset and Dunlap, 1975.

———. *Stan Smith's Six Tennis Basics.* New York: Atheneum, 1974.

Smith, Stan, and Valentine, Tom. *Inside Tennis.* Chicago, Regnery, 1974.

Stein, Harold, and Slatt, Bernie. *Hitting Blind: The New Visual Approach to Winning Tennis.* New York: Beaufort Books, 1981.

Stockton, Dick. *Winning Tennis.* Radnor, Pennsylvania: Chilton Book Company, 1978.

Talbert, William F. *Sports Illustrated Tennis*. Philadelphia: Lippincott, 1972.

———. *Tennis Strokes and Strategies*. New York: Simon and Schuster, 1975.

Talbert, William F., and Greer, Gordon. *Bill Talbert's Weekend Tennis: How to Have Fun and Win at the Same Time*. Garden City, New York: Doubleday, 1970.

Talbert, William F., and Old, Bruce S. *The Game of Doubles in Tennis*. Philadelphia: Lippincott, 1977.

———. *The Game of Singles in Tennis*. Philadelphia: Lippincott, 1977.

———. *Stroke Production in the Game of Tennis*. Philadelphia: Lippincott, 1971.

———. *Tennis Tactics: Singles and Doubles*. New York: Harper and Row, 1983.

Tennant, Eleanor. *Play the "Teach" Tennant Way*. London: Evening News, 1952.

Tilden, William Tatem. *The Art of Lawn Tennis*. London: Methuen and Company, 1920.

———. *Better Tennis for the Club Player*. New York: American Sports Publishing Company, 1923.

———. *The Common Sense of Lawn Tennis*. London: Methuen, 1924.

———. *The Expert*. New York: American Sports Publishing Company, 1923.

———. *How to Play Better Tennis*. New York: Cornerstone Library, 1950.

———. *"The Kid": A Tennis Lesson*. New York: American Sports Publishing Company, 1921.

———. *Lawn Tennis for Club Players*. London: Methuen and Company, 1922.

———. *Singles and Doubles*. New York: George H. Doran Company, 1923.

———. *Tennis A to Z*. London: Gollancy, 1950.

———. *Tennis for the Junior Player, the Club Player, the Expert*. New York: American Sports Publishing Company, 1926.

Tilden, William Tatem, and Merrihew, Stephen Wallis. *Match Play and the Spin of the Ball*. New York: American Sports Publishing Company, 1925.

Trabert, Tony. *Tennis: How to Play, How to Win*. Norwalk, Connecticut: Tennis Magazine, 1978.

Trabert, Tony, and Hook, Jim. *The Serve: Key to Winning Tennis*. New York: Dodd, Mead and Company, 1984.

Trabert, Tony, and Hyams, Joe. *Winning Tactics for Weekend Tennis*. New York: Holt, Rinehart and Winston, 1972.

Trengrove, Alan, ed. *The Art of Tennis*. London: Hodder, 1964.

———. *How to Play Tennis the Professional Way*. New York: Simon and Schuster, 1964.

United States Professional Tennis Association. *Tennis: A Professional Guide*. Tokyo: Kodansha International, 1984.

Van der Meer, Dennis, and Olderman, Murray. *Tennis Clinic: Play the TennisAmerica Way*. New York: Hawthorn Books, 1974.

Vines, Ellsworth. *Ellsworth Vines' Quick Way to Better Tennis: a Practical Book on Tennis for Men and Women*. New York: Sundial, 1939.

———. *How to Play Better Tennis*. Drexel Hill, Pennsylvania: Bell Publishing Company, 1938.

———. *Tennis Simplified for Everybody*. New York: American Sports Publishing Company, 1933.

Vines, Ellsworth, and Vier, Gene. *Tennis: Myth and Method*. New York: Viking Press, 1978.

Wightman, Hazel Hotchkiss. *Better Tennis*. Boston: Houghton Mifflin Company, 1933.

Wilding, Anthony F. *On the Court and Off*. Garden City, New York: Doubleday, Page and Company, 1913.

Willis, DeWitt. *Learn to Play Tennis at Home*. New York: McGraw-Hill, 1976.

Wills, Helen. *Tennis*. New York: Charles Scribner's Sons, 1928.

Wilson, Craig R. *Total Health Tennis: A Lifestyle Approach*. Ardmore, Pennsylvania: Whitmore Publishing Company, 1979.

Wright, George. *Lawn Tennis for Beginners*. Boston: Wright and Ditson, 1928.

———. *Lawn Tennis: Revised Units to Beginners*. Boston: Wright and Ditson, 1911.

———. *Rules of Lawn Tennis, with a Description of Important Strokes*. Boston: Wright and Ditson, 1932.

Yale, Virginia, and Lewis, Morey. *Solo Tennis*. New York: Drake, 1976.

Young, David. *Game, Set and Match: The Nestle Book of Tennis No. 2*. London: Stanley Paul, 1964.

———. *Points for Victory: The Nestle Book of Tennis No. 3*. London: Stanley Paul, 1965.

8

Health and Fitness in Tennis

Authors of technique books frequently mention or discuss conditioning, but not until the 1970s did books deal specifically with this vital aspect of the game. Yet, Martina Navratilova's *Tennis My Way* with Mary Carillo explains how her dedication to a training and conditioning program helps her dominate women's tennis.

Marcel Gautschi explains the importance of both physical and mental conditioning in *Tennis Playing, Training and Winning*. General exercise and conditioning programs include Craig Wilson's *Total Health Tennis: A Lifestyle Approach, The Winning Ingredient in Tennis* by Henry Hines and Carol Morgenstern, and *Bathroom Tennis* by Alan Boltin. Briefly in sixty-four pages, Boltin describes home exercises and provides four wall charts to aid in fitness development.

Dick and Ann Gould explain how to develop strength and aerobic fitness plus proper stretching techniques for individuals and teams in *Conditioning for Tennis: A Guide for Players and Coaches*. *Conditioning for Tennis: The Cal Way* with B. Manning decribes Bill Wright's system of conditioning tennis players. Connie Haynes, Eve Kraft, and John Conroy offer eight-week conditioning programs for adults, high school and elementary students, and advanced players in *Speed, Strength, and Stamina: Conditioning for Tennis*.

Aerobic Tennis by Bill Wright focuses on using the whole body in every aspect of tennis and on letting the body loose to run, stretch, and sweat in order to get a good aerobic workout. He emphasizes stretching and fitness drills, work-outs on and off the court, running using proper technique, weight training, aerobic dancing, and circuit training to enhance cardiovascular fitness. Related directly to conditioning, Connie Haynes and Steven Kraft stress the basics of good nutrition as they relate to improvement in performances in *The Tennis Player's Diet: A Guide to Better Nutrition on and off the Court*. A. Bolliger's *Get Fit for Tennis: Practical Advice for Every Tennis Player* provides comprehensive coverage of all aspects of health and fitness. Bolliger discusses pre-competition and day of competition meals, vitamins, salt, minerals, fluid replacement, sleep, and drugs. He also describes sports medicine rules for competitors, recuperative measures, nervousness, and injuries.

Another group of health and fitness books explains injuries and their prevention and care. Kenneth Campbell describes *Playing Tennis When It Hurts. EEVeTeC: The McGregor Solution for Managing the Pains of Fitness* offers a self-help system for preventing and eliminating pain. In this book Rob McGregor and Stephen Devereux discuss equipment, the environment, velocity, technique, and conditioning. Michael Nacinovich and John Anthony explain prevention and rehabilitation exercises in *The Tennis and Racquetball Players Self-Guide to Injuryfree Fun: How to Avoid and Treat Tennis Elbow and Other Court Injuries*. They describe and diagram the exercises in their program which will reduce susceptability to tennis elbow.

Beckett Howorth and Fred Bender provide *A Doctor's Answer to Tennis Elbow: How to Cure It, How to Prevent It*. After explaining how the arm works and its vulnerability, they describe home treatment to cure the malady. They encourage selecting the proper equipment, correct stroking, and preventive physical conditioning but discount as fads and fancies the use of copper bracelets, acupuncture, and bands and braces. George Dintiman, Robert Davis, John Myers, and George Borden comprehensively cover health and fitness in *Doctor Tennis: A Complete Guide to Conditioning and Injury Prevention for All Ages*.

After determining conditioning status, they recommend through discussion and charts ways to improve strength, stroke power, and court speed. They explain how to stay healthy and injury free and how by selecting the right foods you can eat your way to success. *The Doctor's Guide to Better Tennis and Health* edited by Claude Frazier includes twenty-two chapters by medical doctors and others on topics such as back strain, Achilles tendon rupture, arthritis, playing tennis while pregnant, eye injuries, tennis elbow, ankle injuries, and sunburn. *Sports Injuries: An Aid to Prevention and Treatment*, Steven Levisohn and Harvey Simon's *Tennis Medic: Conditioning, Sports Medicine and Total Fitness for Every Player*, and Pat Croce's *Tennis Player's Guide to Sports Medicine* are recent books which offer helpful advice on prevention and care of injuries and on fitness.

BIBLIOGRAPHY

Bolliger, A. *Get Fit for Tennis: Practical Advice for Every Tennis Player*. London: Michael Joseph, 1982.

Boltin, Alan S. *Bathroom Tennis*. New York: Ballantine Books, 1978.

Campbell, Kenneth Gordon. *Playing Tennis When It Hurts*. Millbrae, California: Celestial Arts, 1976.

Croce, Pat. *Tennis Player's Guide to Sports Medicine*. West Point, New York: Leisure Press, 1984.

Dintiman, George B., et al. *Doctor Tennis: A Complete Guide to Conditioning and Injury Prevention for All Ages*. Richmond, Virginia: Champion Athletic Publishing Company, 1980.

Frazier, Claude Albee, ed. *The Doctors' Guide to Better Tennis and Health*. New York: Funk and Wagnalls, 1974.

Gautschi, Marcel. *Tennis Playing, Training and Winning*. New York: Arco Publishing Company, 1979.

Gould, Dick, and Gould, Ann. *Conditioning for Tennis: A Guide for Players and Coaches*. West Point, New York: Leisure Press, 1982.

Haynes, Connie, Kraft, Eve, and Conroy, John. *Speed, Strength, and Stamina: Conditioning for Tennis*. Garden City, New York: Doubleday, 1975.

Haynes, Connie, and Kraft, Steven. *The Tennis Player's Diet: A Guide to Better Nutrition on and off the Court*. Garden City, New York: Doubleday, 1978.

Hines, Henry, and Morgenstern, Carol. *The Winning Ingredient in Tennis*. New York: Dutton, 1977.

Howorth, M. Beckett, and Bender, Fred. *A Doctor's Answer to Tennis Elbow: How to Cure It, How to Prevent It*. New York: Chelsea House Publishers, 1977.

Levisohn, Steven R., and Simon, Harvey B. *Tennis Medic: Conditioning, Sports Medicine and Total Fitness for Every Player*. St. Louis, Missouri: C.V. Mosby, 1984.

McGregor, Rob Ray, and Devereux, Stephen E. *EEVeTeC: The McGregor Solution for Managing the Pains of Fitness*. Boston: Houghton, Mifflin and Company, 1982.

Nacinovich, Michael J., and Anthony, John. *The Tennis and Racquetball Players Self-Guide to Injuryfree Fun: How to Avoid and Treat Tennis Elbow and Other Court Injuries*. Paradise Valley, Arizona: Phoenix Books, 1980.

Navratilova, Martina, and Carillo, Mary. *Tennis My Way*. New York: Scribners, 1983.

Sports Injuries: An Aid to Prevention and Treatment. American College of Sports Medicine, American Orthopaedic Society for Sports Medicine, and Sports Medicine Committee of the United States Tennis Association, New York: United States Tennis Association, 1982.

Wilson, Craig, *Total Health Tennis: A Lifestyle Approach*. Ardmore, Pennsylania: Whitmore Publishing Company, 1979.

Wright, Bill. *Aerobic Tennis*. Bolinas, California: Shelter Publications, 1983.

Wright, Bill, and Manning, B. *Conditioning for Tennis: The Cal Way*. West Point, New York: Leisure Press, 1983.

9

Psychological Aspects of Tennis

Today, serve-and-volley specialists, steady baseliners, and all-court players rely extensively on psychological strategies to overcome the competitive pressures of the professional circuits as well as to combat a hacker's negative feedback after a miss-hit. Rather than a leisurely game of the country club set or an amateur sports pastime of a few elite players, serious tennis players of all levels of ability now take a dramatically different approach to tennis by employing psychological ploys to win.

Most early tennis books about technique mention playing tactics and strategies only in passing. Three exceptions are Jahial Paret's *Psychology and Advanced Play of Lawn Tennis* (1927), John Rendall's *Things That Matter in Lawn Tennis* (1930), and Norman Patterson's *Courtcraft: Lawn Tennis Tactics and Psychology* (1934). Paret discusses the element of surprise, when to play defensively and when to attack, the psychology of the volleyer, center court theory, anticipation, psychology of serving, temperature, and psychology of doubles. In his book for advanced players Rendall gives advice on judging the ball's flight, tactics, how often to play, having character in tennis, and nerves. Patterson's focus is on tactics in singles and doubles plus he includes information about match play, practice, and the rules. In 1968 Richard Fish devotes an entire book to *The Anatomy and Psychology of Tennis*. After introducing the basic strokes *Use Your Head in Tennis* by Bob Harmon and Keith Monroe discusses outsmarting opponents, dealing with partners in doubles, enlarging one's stroke arsenal, adjusting to play against left-handers or on different courts, and unwritten laws. In *Use Your Head in Doubles* Bob Harmon explains how it pays to deceive, how to utilize lobs to win, how to win the crucial points, how to use secret signals, how to capture the momentum, plus how to adjust one's game to short balls, against lobs, or versus a lefty. According to Bill Talbert and Bruce Old, tactics are more important than strokes, style, and stamina. In *Tennis Tactics: Singles and Doubles* they advocate studying famous players to improve one's skill, understanding, and strategies. For baseline play they recommend forcing the action and using passing shots, while they also suggest getting to the net whenever possible and then strategically placing volleys and overheads. Francoise Durr, a former French star, explains the popularity of doubles through her dicsussion of the importance of the alleys, the building blocks for doubles, and strategies, such as how and when to poach. *Doubles Strategy: A Creative and Psychological Approach to Tennis* also stresses the importance of anticipation and communication.

The mental side of the game is also important for children according to Billie Jean King and Greg Hoffman in *Tennis Love: A Parents' Guide to the Sport* and Jim Fannin and John Mullin in *Tennis and Kids: The Family Connection*. King and Hoffman's book with illustrations by Charles Schulz discusses the importance of sports, good, bad, and obnoxious parents, the tennis basics, the mental game of tennis including concentration, singles and doubles strategies, the emotional game, motivation, temperament, and sportsmanship. Fannin and Mullin question parents about what they are asking kids to do as they emphasize the American credo of one-upmanship. Instead, they advocate SCORE—self-discipline, concentration, optimism, relaxation, and enjoyment. To accomplish SCORE they explain what parents can do and provide, basic strokes, practice drills, and lessons. They try to get parents to objectively assess what place tennis should have in a child's life. William Jacobs in 1941 described the importance of the mental aspects of the game in *Tennis, Builder of Citizenship: The Psychology and Technique of the Game as Taught in the Tennis Clinic*. He reports that the United States Lawn Tennis Association's tennis clinics at Lake Erie College in Ohio and in St. Petersburg, Florida, teach technique, strategy, match play, and thinking in playing while emphasizing physical, moral, social, and spiritual development.

Jack Lowe explains *Winning with Percentage Tennis: An Expert's Guide to Smart Court Strategy*. After discussing the various stroke techniques, he explains how to play percentage singles and doubles, how to counter opponents' varying playing styles, and how to play against left-handed opponents. Lowe furnishes strategies for percentage serves, returns of serve, and baseline play. *Tennis Tactics: Match Play Strategies That Get Immediate Winning Results* by Robert Greene includes tips about how to make tennis fun and rewarding, how to analyze an opponent's strengths and weaknesses, which tactics to use against various shots and versus the weather, how to concentrate, and how to build confidence. In an outline format using key points, descriptions, and questions, Marcel Gautschi presents *Tennis Playing, Training and Winning*. He stresses physical and mental preparation and explains how to play nine different types of opponents. *Covering the Court* according to Edward Chase is the most important factor for winning. In addition to explaining and diagramming court coverage in singles and doubles, Chase describes pre-match preparation, match play, the use of fakes and spins, playing to the score, and the use of angles and depth on shots. *Tennis My Way* by Martina Navratilova and Mary Carillo provides playing tactics and strategies including maximizing your strengths while exploiting your opponent's weaknesses, court positioning, and combating little or lots of pace. Champion Navratilova also emphasizes the mental side of tennis such as concentration, having a positive attitude, the killer instinct, handling wins and losses, guts, and sportsmanship.

The numerous books written between Timothy Gallwey's *The Inner Game of Tennis* (1974) and Scott Ford's *Design B: How to Play Tennis in the Zone* (1984) demonstrate the popularity of trying to explain the mental side of the game while maximizing one's play. Gallwey's analysis of tennis, a dramatic departure from the traditional technique- and practice-oriented approach to improved performance, results in his advocacy of strategies for quieting the mind, letting it happen, and inner-game learning. Two years later in *Inner Tennis: Playing the Game* Gallwey expands on his earlier premise of letting your game happen by emphasizing leaving your mind and relying on your senses, body awareness, self-image, and the will to win. Ford, a teaching professional, revises his instructional approach to tennis by advocating looking for and hitting the ball at the touchpoint. He describes and diagrams the way to zone in on this point of contact using an invisible shield. He also discusses the visual, physical, and cognitive patterns, the challenge of zoning, using the contact zone, and serving in the zone. In seeming contrast to Gallwey's and Ford's approaches, highly successful University of California at Berkeley tennis coach Chet Murphy argues that the best players must think carefully about their tactics, strategies, and stroke technique in practice and pre-competition in order to properly prepare themselves for the stresses of match play. Written for those with advanced skills, *Tennis for Thinking Players* stresses integrating the mind and the body for improvement in tactics and technique and even includes suggestions for alleviating choking.

Josef Brabenec in *Tennis: The Decision-Making Sport* emphasizes never hurrying between points since this is a time to relax, to concentrate, and to reduce your errors to become a better player. In addition to instructions about stroke mechanics, Brabenec tells the importances of concentration, anticipation, momentum, and mental and physical exercises. *Tennis Is an Unnatural Act* by Thomas Winnett and Marion Fay, *Psyching Up for Tennis* by Jack Leedy and Mort Malkin, and *Mind over Tennis* by James Loehr and Dennis Van der Meer stress the importance of the mental side of tennis. Motivation, anxiety, concentration, fitness, and situational creativity help a player psych up according to Leedy and Malkin. They humorously describe the differences between mental and physical preparation, stresses and strains, and hackers and stars; yet they emphasize that since feelings can adversely affect performance, players must control their emotions.

Cecilia Martinez and Harold Geist explain how *Tennis Psychology* is important, such as gamesmanship in the use of on- and off-court distractions, and how and when to use shots most effectively and strategically. In *Mastering the Art of Winning Tennis: The Psychology behind Successful Strategy* several authors in Claude Frazier's compilation tell how to win by using your head. Topics include the art of gamesmanship, mind over matter (the key to success), winning and losing tendencies in tennis, how to pull yourself out of a slump, the choke and how to fight it, emotionalized tennis (psychology of the game), the real love game of mixed doubles, mastering the art of stroke control, relaxation, why you want to win, and tennis and the game of life.

Barry Tarshis' *Tennis and the Mind* uses winning formulas from leading players to show the importance of controlling the mind and emotions and concentrating. *Love and Hate on the Tennis Court: How Hidden Emotions Affect Your Game* by Stanley Cath, Alvin Kahn, and Nathan Cobb similarly stresses that emotions critically affect performances. Case histories of players illustrate how to recognize and to take advantage of various personality characteristics of opponents. Each chapter contains a net profit section which explains how to improve one's game in ways never previously considered. The book also explains the lure of tennis, playing patty-cakers, reluctant smashers, and even cheaters, doubles troubles, and handling the backhand. Allen Fox and Richard Evans use top professionals as examples of mental preparation in *If I'm the Better Player, Why Can't I Win?* They discuss how to sharpen your game, the fear of losing, shattering your opponent's mental armor, (how to use psychology and to counter it), the psychodynamics of doubles, and how to avoid psychological pitfalls. Psychologist Walter Luszki in *Psych Yourself to Better Tennis* reprints several of his articles from *World Tennis, Athletic Journal*, and other periodicals plus adds some additional hints about psychological aspects of tennis. He explains the ego aspects of the game, such as concentration, distractions, deception, and psychological warfare. He also advocates controlling one's emotions and thinking while playing.

Psychodynamic Tennis: You, Your Opponent, and Other Obstacles to Perfection by Ethan Gologor topically addresses sports and shrinks, rational therapy, the best offense is a good defense, the emotions, masochism, individual personality types, risk taking, and self-fulfilling prophecies in order to emphasize that the use of psychology can improve performance. Barrie Richmond states that understanding your emotions is the key to the integration of the mind and the body in *Total Tennis: The Mind-Body Method*. The body practices, drills, and conditions while use of the intellect to really learn tennis is more essential. Champions Billie Jean King, Bjorn Borg, Jimmy Connors, Chris Evert-Lloyd, Martina Navratilova, Tracy Austin, and John McEnroe illustate the importance of mind-body integration. Craig Wilson stresses more than just the mind in *Tennis, beyond the Inner Game* and *Total Health Tennis: A Lifestyle Approach*. In his second book Wilson describes the philosophy of a total health lifestyle and its private motivation as well as explains tennis technique for adults at the beginning level of play. Approximately half of this volume stresses visualization in stroke production for children, as it relates to health. Donald Burkett's purpose in writing *Peaking through Tennis: A Mind/Body Guide to Peak Performances* is to get players to become totally centered. Integration of one's emotional, social, intellectual, and physical characteristics results in a totally centered player. The inside job emotionally includes a positive self-image, control of tension and agitation, and concentration while social awareness of one's impact on others leads to productive behavior such as sportsmanship. Intellectually players utilize proper strokes and strategies thereby reducing errors. Flexibility, fluidity, and endurance contribute to the physical component. According to the text and the cartoon-like graphics, the removal of the barriers to these four parts of one's game results in peaking. Taking psychological strategies one step farther, Walter Luszki explains the importance of mental toughness, determination, concentration, anxiety, control, momentum, and psychological warfare in *Winning Tennis through Mental Toughness*. Based on the latest research, Linda Bunker and Robert Rotella summarized the status of tennis psychology in 1982 in *Mind, Set and Match: Using Your Head to Play Better Tennis*. They recommend building confidence, attentional focus to overcome distractions, concentration, relieving anxiety and muscular tension, and enjoyment to develop a successful mental game plan.

Tennis by Machiavelli (1984), Simon Ramo's literal translation into English of a sixteenth-century Niccolo Machiavelli manuscript, discusses cunning and deception, strategies for ordinary play, and how to win at tennis. Although originally written for court tennis, the discussions of poaching, teamwork, use of ruses and covert influences on opponents, and the use of conversation during matches are remarkable in their potential use in tennis today.

BIBLIOGRAPHY

Brabenec, Josef. *Tennis: The Decision-Making Sport*. North Vancouver, British Columbia: Hancock House, 1980.

Bunker, Linda K., and Rotella, Robert J. *Mind, Set and Match: Using Your Head to Play Better Tennis*. Englewood Cliffs, New Jersey: Prentice-Hall, 1982.

Burkett, Donald. *Peaking through Tennis: A Mind/Body Guide to Peak Performances*. Champaign, Illinois: WaterPark Press, 1979.

Cath, Stanley H., Kahn, Alvin, and Cobb, Nathan. *Love and Hate on the Tennis Court: How Hidden Emotions Affect Your Game*. New York: Scribner, 1977.

Chase, Edward Tinsley. *Covering the Court*. Garden City, New York: Doubleday, 1976.

Durr, Francoise. *Doubles Strategy: A Creative and Psychological Approach to Tennis*. New York: David McKay Company, 1978.

Fannin, Jim, and Mullin, John. *Tennis and Kids: The Family Connection*. Garden City, New York: Doubleday, 1979.

Fish, Richard Alan. *The Anatomy and Psychology of Tennis*. London: Maybank Press, 1968.

Ford, Scott. *Design B: How to Play Tennis in the Zone*. South Bend, Indiana: Icarus, 1984.

Fox, Allen, and Evans, Richard. *If I'm the Better Player, Why Can't I Win?* Norwalk, Connecticut: Tennis Magazine, 1979.

Frazier, Claude Albee, ed. *Mastering the Art of Winning Tennis: The*

Psychology behind Successful Strategy. New York: Pagurian Press, 1974.

Gallwey, W. Timothy. *The Inner Game of Tennis*. New York: Random House, 1974.

————. *Inner Tennis: Playing the Game*. New York: Random House, 1976.

Gautschi, Marcel. *Tennis Playing, Training and Winning*. New York: Arco Publishing Company, 1979.

Gologor, Ethan. *Psychodynamic Tennis: You, Your Opponent, and Other Obstacles to Perfection*. New York: Morrow, 1979.

Greene, Robert Ford. *Tennis Tactics: Match Play Strategies That Get Immediate Winning Results*. New York: Putnam, 1978.

Harmon, Bob. *Use Your Head in Doubles*. New York: Scribner, 1979.

Harmon, Bob, and Monroe, Keith. *Use Your Head in Tennis*. New York: Thomas Y. Crowell, 1977.

Jacobs, William Plumer. *Tennis, Builder of Citizenship: The Psychology and Technique of the Game as Taught in the Tennis Clinic*. Clinton, South Carolina: Jacobs Press, 1941.

King, Billie Jean, and Hoffman, Greg. *Tennis Love: A Parents' Guide to the Sport*. New York: Macmillan, 1978.

Leedy, Jack J., and Malkin, Mort. *Psyching Up for Tennis*. New York: Basic Books, 1977.

Loehr, James E., and Van der Meer, Dennis. *Mind over Tennis*. Norwalk, Connecticut: Tennis Magazine, 1982.

Lowe, Jack. *Winning with Percentage Tennis: An Expert's Guide to Smart Court Strategy*. Amelia Island, Florida, 1974.

Luszki, Walter A. *Psych Yourself to Better Tennis*. North Hollywood, California: Wilshire, 1971.

————. *Winning Tennis through Mental Toughness*. New York: Everest House, 1982.

Martinez, Cecilia A., and Geist, Harold. *Tennis Psychology*. Chicago: Nelson-Hall, 1976.

Murphy, Chester W. *Tennis for Thinking Players*. West Point, New York: Leisure Press, 1982.

Navratilova, Martina, and Carillo, Mary. *Tennis My Way*. New York: Scribners, 1983.

Paret, Jahial Parmly. *Psychology and Advanced Play of Lawn Tennis*. New York: American Lawn Tennis, 1927.

Patterson, Norman Hills. *Courtcraft: Lawn Tennis Tactics and Psychology*. London: Eyre and Spottiswoode, 1934.

Ramo, Simon. *Tennis by Machiavelli*. New York: Rawson Associates, 1984.

Rendall, John Charles Shuttleworth. *Things That Matter in Lawn Tennis.* London: Besant and Company, 1930.

Richmond, M. Barrie. *Total Tennis: The Mind-Body Method.* New York: Macmillan, 1980.

Talbert, William F., and Old, Bruce S. *Tennis Tactics: Singles and Doubles.* New York: Harper and Row Publishers, 1983.

Tarshis, Barry. *Tennis and the Mind.* New York: Atheneum/SMI, 1977.

Wilson, Craig R. *Tennis, beyond the Inner Game.* New York: Drake Publishers, 1977.

————. *Total Health Tennis: A Lifestyle Approach.* Ardmore, Pennsylvania: Whitmore Publishing Company, 1979.

Winnett, Thomas, and Fay, Marion. *Tennis Is an Unnatural Act.* Berkeley, California: Wilderness Press, 1977.

10

Biography

Over one hundred tennis books, besides the more than fifty written for children, partially or completely describe one or numerous players' lives. Of this number, seventy are biographies about individual players and fifty-seven of these are autobiographies. These works focus on individual player's achievements and to varying degrees include family backgrounds, developmental years in tennis, influential people and events, and other unique occurrences in the player's life and career. Other books either sketch the careers of several players, combine biographies with technique instructions, or show tennis players' tournament achievements through a history of the game.

Hazel Wightman in *Better Tennis* combines brief sketches of her life with instructional information. In *Fifteen-Thirty: The Story of a Tennis Player* Helen Wills tells of her career successes as a baseline artist. Wearing her sun visor trademark and displaying a stoic demeanor, Wills dominated women's tennis in the late 1920s and 1930s. Helen Jacobs, a frequent opponent of Helen Wills, recounts her life story in *Beyond the Game: An Autobiography*. She highlights her introduction of shorts into world-class tennis and her personal financial struggles in the amateur sport of tennis. Doris Hart describes her struggles with physical problems and the psychological obstacle of repeated second-place finishes in *Tennis with Hart*. Pauline Betz Addie traces her early life and years as a leading amateur player in *Wings on My Tennis Shoes*. The first black to win the United States Championship, Althea Gibson, tells of her struggles in life and in tennis in *I Always Wanted to Be Somebody*. She describes her life on the streets of Harlem, her American Tennis Association championships, and her successful 1957 season as well as acknowledges those individuals who befriended her and gave her a chance in the elite sport of tennis. Billie Jean King and Kim Chapin combined to write her first biography, *Billie Jean*, in 1974. In it King details her early family years and the struggles of a girl from a middle-class family competing in the world of tennis. She candidly relates the ups and downs of her tennis career, including her promotion of the women's professional tennis circuit. Eight years later a second *Billie Jean*, written by King and Frank Deford, repeats a good deal of the earlier information plus candidly discusses her homosexual affair. *Chrissie: My Own Story* by Chris Evert-Lloyd and Neil Amdur, describes Lloyd's private, personal life as well as her championship achievements. Renee Richards tells about her early life as a male, her struggles for sexual identity, and her new life as a female player in *Second Serve*. Maureen Connolly in *Forehand Drive* briefly describes why she took up tennis and how she developed into a champion.

Arthur Ashe in three books, *Advantage Ashe, Arthur Ashe: Portrait in Motion* with Frank Deford and *Off the Court* with Neil Amdur, describes the various stages of his career. The second of these is a diary of his career from Wimbledon 1973 through Wimbledon 1974. He includes personal insights, comments on the tennis circuit, and portrays some of the leading players. The third book begins with the surgery following his heart attack and reflects on his early tennis opportunities, his family, his college years, and his tennis career. He discusses the apartheid practices in South Africa and his attempts to effect changes in this policy. Bobby Riggs has written two autobiographies, *Tennis Is My Racket* and *Court Hustler* with George McGann. In his first autobiography Riggs tells about his rise to the top of amateur tennis and his professional career. He then profiles other players including Jack Kramer, Don

Budge, Bill Tilden, Fred Perry, Ellsworth Vines, and Pancho Gonzales. In the third section of this book he gives tips on how to play better tennis. The second book recounts his life and amateur tennis championships yet focuses on his hustling endeavors in golf and tennis climaxing with his defeat of Margaret Court on Mother's Day in 1973. Other male champions from the United States write about their careers including Gardnar Mulloy in *The Will to Win: An Inside View of the World of Tennis* and *Advantage Striker*, Don Budge in *Don Budge: A Tennis Memoir*, Ellsworth Vines in *Tennis: Myth and Method*, and John Patty in *Tennis My Way*. Patty includes technique instructions with his look at tennis in southern California and in the European and United States tournaments.

Marty Riessen and Richard Evans tell about Riessen's career as he deals with the mental pressure of elite tennis competition in *Match Point: A Candid View of Life on the International Tennis Circuit*. They describe amateurism, his becoming a professional player, challenges of the tour, other players, and the European tennis circuit. Bill Tilden's first autobiography, *Me—the Handicap* in 1929, looks at his early tennis development, professionalism, and political issues in tennis. He also introduces other tennis personalities. In *Aces, Places, and Faults* Tilden again portrays his early tennis career but also includes information about ladies' tennis, tennis countries, professional tennis, famous people outside tennis, his artistic activities, and brief instructions about tennis technique. He later described his tennis career in *My Story, A Champion's Memoirs*. Bill Talbert joins with John Sharnik to write *Playing for Life: Billy Talbert's Story*. Talbert explains overcoming his diabetic condition and his family's poor economic status to become a successful player and a Davis Cup captain. *The Game: My 40 Years in Tennis* by Jack Kramer and Frank Deford traces Kramer's early years at the Los Angeles Tennis Club through his amateur and professional careers in tennis. He emphasizes his father's influence, acknowledges the importance of learning percentage tennis from Cliff Roche, and states his opposition to equal prize money for women.

Rod Laver in *The Education of a Tennis Player* analyzes his 1969 Grand Slam victories in addition to giving his family background. He also includes twenty-five lessons about stroke technique and strategy. Among the other players who wrote autobiographies are Englishmen Bunny Austin in *A Mixed Double*, (with Phyllis Konstam), Francis Burrow in *My Tournaments*, Dinny Pails in *Set Points: My Tennis Story*, and Bobby Wilson in *My Side of the Net*, plus *Tennis Rebel* by Mike Davies from Wales, Frenchman Henri Cochet in *Tennis* with Jacques Feuillet, Czechoslovakian Jaroslav Drobny in *Champion in Exile*, Ecuador's Pancho Gonzales in *Man with a Racket*, Dutchman Tom Okker in *Tennis Met Tom*, and Australian Lew Hoad in *My Game* and *The Lew Hoad Story* both with Jack Pollard. Sweden's Bjorn Borg tells of his early life and family influences, his coach's role, and his tennis achievements through age twenty-four in *The Bjorn Borg Story*, while also commenting on his major rivals and including their remarks about him. He also demonstrates and explains the proper technique for the various strokes. A later book, *Bjorn Borg: My Life and Game*, written with Eugene Scott, emphasizes his successful playing theories in his ten best matches.

Neale Fraser and Ian McDonald describe Fraser's "bridesmaid" career in *Power Tennis*. They also include information about Margaret Smith, Fraser's family, and technique hints for beginners. *Play Tennis with Rosewall: The Little Master and His Method* by Ken Rosewall and John Barrett briefly describes Rosewall's youth, explains stroke technique and tactics, discusses some of his career highlights, and portrays some of his friends and rivals. Mike Sangster and John Ballantine in *Cannonball Tennis* include tips on technique throughout the story of Sangster's early years and career successes. English champion Fred Perry describes his tennis career in three autobiographies. In *My Story* he tells about his early years, his greatest year in 1934, the world's ten best male and female players, plus he gives some tennis instructions. *Perry on Tennis: Expert Advice for All on Lawn Tennis*, while providing some playing fundamentals, discusses his tennis championships, his early years, Davis Cup play, the professional game, and other stars. In *Fred Perry: An Autobiography* (1984) this most recent Englishman to win at Wimbledon provides an anecdotal look at his career.

Five English women emphasize their tennis achievements and their early years in their autobiographies such as Angela Mortimer in *My Waiting Game*. Sue Barker describes her life as a pro in addition to technique and tactical instructions in *Playing Tennis*. Dorothea Lambert-Chambers in *Lawn Tennis for Ladies* includes some personal reminiscences plus provides descriptions of nine players' most memorable matches. Christine Truman in *Tennis Today* describes her life, the rewards of tennis, the world game, information about Wimbledon, Davis Cup, and Wightman Cup play, and her most memorable matches. Ann Jones in *A Game to Love* focuses on her 1969 Wimbledon championship. Similarly, Virginia Wade and Mary Lou Wallace emphasize Wade's 1977 win at Wimbledon in *Courting Triumph*. They both candidly describe the ups and downs of their involvement in the world of tennis, while Wade also reveals how she struggled to develop the will to win. Australians Margaret Court in two books, *The Margaret Smith Story* with Donald Lawrence and *Court on Court, a Life in Tennis* with George McGann, and Evonne Goolagong and Bud Collins in *Evonne! On the Move* recount these two stars' early years in tennis through their career successes. In Court's second book she expresses her concern about amateurism, the changes in tennis because of professionalism, and prize money; she also describes her boredom with tennis, retirement, marriage, comeback, family, and the match with Bobby Riggs. Goolagong's early years, her mentor and coach Vic Edwards, her admiration of Margaret Court, her first Wimbledon, and her 1972 Wimbledon victory are the focal points of her autobiography.

Biographies of other players include *Captain Anthony Wilding* by Arthur Myers, *Jean Borotra, The Bounding Basque: His Life of Work and Play* by John Smyth, *Nastase Superstar* by Gilles Delamarre, *Bjorn Borg* by Bjorn Hellberg, and *The World of Jimmy Connors* by Jim Burke.

Peter Rowley looks at *Ken Rosewall: Twenty Years at the Top* by describing his early years through his professional career including his peak, decline, and comeback. In *The Return of a Champion: Pancho Gonzales' Golden Year 1964* Dave Anderson describes one week at the United States Professional

Tennis Championships and focuses on its star, Pancho Gonzales. Andrew Drysdale tells about the tennis triumphs and tragedies of his South African brother in *Beyond Match Point: The Cliff Drysdale Story*. He describes his brother's role in the international tennis scene and his leadership in his country's Davis Cup play. *Crowded Galleries* by Mabel Brookes includes her life story as well as that of her husband, Norman Brookes, a tennis champion, Davis Cup captain, and longtime leader of Australian tennis. *Nasty: Ilie Nastase vs. Tennis* by Richard Evans candidly describes the vices of this volatile player as well as his lesser-known virtues. Evans describes Nastase as a clown, an entertainer, and a champion as well as an often times obscene, out-of-control player. Mariana Borg recalls her life with Bjorn Borg in *Love Match: My Life with Bjorn* while emphasizing his fifth Wimbledon victory. Bill Tilden and Stephen Merrihew in *Match Play and the Spin of the Ball* provide technique instruction and a biography of Tilden's career. Merrihew describes Tilden's early years, disappointing years, Davis Cup play, matches against Bill Johnston, and Wimbledon and United States victories. Based on his January 13, and January 20, 1975, articles in *Sports Illustrated*, Frank Deford graphically recounts a brilliant career and a sad truth in *Big Bill Tilden: The Triumphs and the Tragedy*. Half of the book describes Tilden's tennis career, while the remainder emphasizes his early life, his estrangement from his family, and his trials and conviction for homosexuality.

Roy Wilder in *Friend of Tennis* describes his lifelong involvement with tennis as an umpire. He also profiles tennis personalities and colors his description of this sport with numerous anecdotes. *Jean Hoxie: The Robin Hood of Tennis* is a portrayal of this outstanding teacher's commitment to tennis by Jean Pitrone. *"Teach Tennant": The Story of Eleanor Tennant the Greatest Tennis Coach in the World* also describes the star-studded career of the coach of Alice Marble, Pauline Betz, and Maureen Connolly. Nancy Spain describes Tennant's years at the Golden Gate Park and in Beverly Hills, her instruction of Hollywood stars, and the making of a champion's game. Teddy Tinling, a celebrated fashion designer and tennis umpire, recalls his love affair with the sport in *Tinling: Sixty Years in Tennis*.

There have also been a number of collective biographies of tennis players. Valentine Hall provides the first biographical sketches of prominent players in *Lawn Tennis in America* in 1888. Former champion Helen Jacobs in *Gallery of Champions* (1970), a revision of a 1949 work, describes the careers of outstanding women players Suzanne Lenglen, Helen Wills, Hilde Sperling, Alice Marble, Dorothy Round Little, Molla Bjurstedt, Pauline Betz, Simone Mathieu, Cilli Aussem, Sarah Palfrey, Anita Lizana, Louise Brough, Margaret duPont, Betty Nuthall, and Margaret Scriven. George Sullivan provides short biographies of Margaret Court, Billie Jean King, Chris Evert, Evonne Goolagong, Rosemary Casals, and Virginia Wade in *Queens of the Court* in addition to analyzing the importance of their contributions to the growth of women's tennis. Teddy Tinling recounts his personal insights about the careers of the players he outfitted in *White Ladies*. Owen Davidson and Clarence Jones picture and describe the early great players Bill Tilden, Jean Borotra, Henri Cochet, Rene Lacoste, Ellsworth Vines, Fred Perry, Don Budge, Jack Kramer, Pancho Gonzales, Frank Sedgman, Lew Hoad, Roy Emerson, Ken Rosewall, and Rod Laver in *Lawn Tennis: The Great Ones*. With an emphasis on their victories at Wimbledon, *Great Women Tennis Players* by Davidson and Jones sketches the careers of champions from Charlotte Cooper, Lottie Dod, and Dorothea Lambert-Chambers through Maria Bueno, Margaret Court, and Billie Jean King. Trent Frayne's *Famous Tennis Players* includes Bill Tilden, Jean Borotra, Henri Cochet, Rene Lacoste, Jacques Brugnon, Fred Perry, Don Budge, Bobby Riggs, Jack Kramer, Pancho Gonzales, Rod Laver, Arthur Ashe, Ilie Nastase, Bjorn Borg, and Jimmy Connors. He pictures and recounts the careers of Suzanne Lenglen, Helen Wills, Helen Jacobs, Alice Marble, Maureen Connolly, Margaret Court, Althea Gibson, Virginia Wade, Evonne Goolagong, Billie Jean King, Chris Evert, and Martina Navratilova in *Famous Women Tennis Players*.

Paul Metzler examines the *Great Players of Australian Tennis*, and renown Australian player and Davis Cup captain Harry

Hopman offers biographical sketches of male players and an account of the 1950–1956 Davis Cup tournaments in *Aces and Places*. It includes career highlights of Jack Crawford, Gottfried von Cramm, John Bromwich, Adrian Quist, Bobby Riggs, Yvon Petra, Jack Kramer, Pancho Gonzales, Ted Shroeder, Budge Patty, Pancho Segura, Dick Savitt, Frank Sedgman, Ken McGregor, Mervyn Rose, Lennart Bergelin, Sven Davidson, Vic Seixas, Jaroslav Drobny, Tony Trabert, Rex Hartwig, Lew Hoad, and Ken Rosewall. *Lawn Tennis: Analytical Studies of the World's Greatest Players* by Louis Stanley analyzes the strokes and styles of Louise Brough, Joy Mottram, Jean Borotra, and Ken McGregor. Edward Potter lists titles won and the three-year (1952–1954) performance records of eighty-three male and forty-three female players in *The World's Leading Tennis Players*. Gordon Forbes' *A Handful of Summers*, Melchior Di-Giacamo and Eugene Scott's *The Tennis Experience*, B. H. L. Hart's *The Lawn Tennis Masters Unveiled*, Arthur Myers' *Leaders of Lawn Tennis*, and Catherine Bell and Roy Peter's *Passing Shots* describe the lives and careers of several tennis champions. John McPhee in *Levels of the Game* provides a narrative of a match between Arthur Ashe and Clark Graebner in the semi-finals of the first United States Open Championship. He contrasts the lives and styles of play of these two stars. In *Short Circuit* the focus is on the players on the men's professional tennis circuit. Michael Mewshaw describes the use of drugs, financial controversies, gambling, throwing matches, and the unwillingness of the tennis establishment to acknowledge these problems. Peter Bodo takes a biographical-psychological look at professional tennis in *Inside Tennis: A Season on the Pro Tour*.

The history of the All-England Championships is told through biographies and significant matches in a 1934 publication, *Wimbledon Who's Who and Tennis Celebrities*, in Charles Landon's *Classic Moments of Wimbledon*, Virginia Wade and Jean Rafferty's *Ladies of the Court: A Century of Women at Wimbledon*, Terry Todd's *The Tennis Players from Pagan Rites to Strawberries and Cream*, and Gwen Robyns' *Wimbledon: The Hidden Drama*. Todd also traces the history of tennis. Bill Talbert and Pete Axthelm describe the 1881–1966 United States

Lawn Tennis Association men's singles champions in *Tennis Observed*. The history of tennis as influenced by players is the focus of several books such as *Love and Faults: Personalities Who Have Changed the History of Tennis in My Lifetime* by Teddy Tinling and Rod Humphries, *Game! Set! Match!* and *Tennis Revolution* by Murray Janoff, and *The Tennis Set* by Rex Bellamy. Outstanding players along with their styles of play and their records form the basis of Paul Metzler's *Tennis Styles and Stylists* and Will Grimsley's *Tennis: Its History, People and Events*. Eugene Scott in *Tennis: Game of Motion* includes biographies and descriptions about historic matches. Herbert Wind reprints articles from *The New Yorker* to sketch the history of tennis and its outstanding players in *Game, Set, and Match: The Tennis Boom of the 1960s and 70s*.

Four other books comprehensively describe the leading players and their tennis achievements. These include *Bud Collins' Modern Encyclopedia of Tennis* by Bud Collins and Zander Hollander, David Emery's *Who's Who in International Tennis*, *The Concise Dictionary of Tennis* by Martin Hedges, and Maurice Brady's *Lawn Tennis Encyclopedia*. In Brady's biographies he highlights their major victories, style of play, and personal facts.

BIBLIOGRAPHY

Addie, Pauline Betz. *Wings on My Tennis Shoes*. London: S. Low, Marston, 1949.

Anderson, Dave. *The Return of a Champion: Pancho Gonzales' Golden Year 1964*. Englewood Cliffs, New Jersey: Prentice-Hall, 1973.

Ashe, Arthur. *Advantage Ashe*. New York: Coward-McCann, 1967.

Ashe, Arthur, and Amdur, Neil. *Off the Court*. New York: New American Library, 1981.

Ashe, Arthur, and Deford, Frank. *Arthur Ashe: Portrait in Motion*. Boston: Houghton Mifflin, 1975.

Austin, Henry Wilfred, and Konstam, Phyllis. *A Mixed Double*. London: Chatto and Windus, 1969.

Barker, Sue. *Playing Tennis*. London: Batsford, 1979.

Bell, Catherine, and Peter, Roy. *Passing Shots*. New York: Beaufort Books, 1983.

Bellamy, Rex. *The Tennis Set*. London: Cassell, 1972.

Bodo, Peter. *Inside Tennis: A Season on the Pro Tour*. New York: Delta Books, 1979.

Borg Bjorn. *The Bjorn Borg Story*. Chicago: H. Regnery, 1975.

Borg, Bjorn, and Scott, Eugene L. *Bjorn Borg: My Life and Game*. New York: Simon and Schuster, 1980.

Borg, Mariana. *Love Match: My Life with Bjorn*. New York: Dial Press, 1981.

Brady, Maurice. *Lawn Tennis Encyclopedia*. South Brunswick, New Jersey: A. S. Barnes, 1969.

Brookes, Mabel. *Crowded Galleries*. London: William Heinemann, 1956.

Budge, John Donald. *Don Budge: A Tennis Memoir*. New York: Viking Press, 1969.

Burke, Jim. *The World of Jimmy Connors*. New York: Leisure Books, 1976.

Burrow, Francis Russell. *My Tournaments*. London: Hodder and Stoughton, 1922.

Cochet, Henri, and Feuillet, Jacques. *Tennis*. Paris: Stock, 1980.

Collins, Bud, and Hollander, Zander, eds. *Bud Collins' Modern Encyclopedia of Tennis*. Garden City, New York: Dolphin Books, 1980.

Connolly, Maureen Catherine, and Gwynne, Tom. *Forehand Drive*. London: MacGibbon and Kee, 1957.

Court, Margaret Smith, and Lawrence, Donald Hevingham. *The Margaret Smith Story*. London: S. Paul, 1965.

Court, Margaret Smith, and McGann, George. *Court on Court, a Life in Tennis*. New York: Dodd, Mead, 1975.

Davidson, Owen, and Jones, Clarence Medlycott. *Great Women Tennis Players*. London: Pelham Books, 1971.

————. *Lawn Tennis: The Great Ones*. London: Pelham Books, 1970.

Davies, Mike. *Tennis Rebel*. London: Stanley Paul, 1962.

Deford, Frank. *Big Bill Tilden: The Triumphs and the Tragedy*. New York: Simon and Schuster, 1976.

Delamarre, Gilles. *Nastase Superstar*. Paris: Solar, 1974.

DiGiacomo, Melchior, and Scott, Eugene L. *The Tennis Experience*. New York: Rutledge Books, 1979.

Drobny, Jaroslav. *Champion in Exile*. London: Hodder and Stoughton, 1955.

Drysdale, Andrew. *Beyond Match Point: The Cliff Drysdale Story*. Cape Town: Purnell, 1968.

Emery, David. *Who's Who in International Tennis*. New York: Facts on File Publications, 1983.

Evans, Richard. *Nasty: Ilie Nastase vs. Tennis*. New York: Stein and Day, 1978.

Evert-Lloyd, Chris, and Amdur, Neil. *Chrissie: My Own Story*. New York: Simon and Schuster, 1982.

Forbes, Gordon. *A Handful of Summers*. New York: Mayflower Books, 1978.

Fraser, Neale, and McDonald, Ian. *Power Tennis*. London: Stanley Paul, 1962.

Frayne, Trent. *Famous Tennis Players*. New York: Dodd, Mead, 1977.

———. *Famous Women Tennis Players*. New York: Dodd, Mead and Company, 1979.

Gibson, Althea. *I Always Wanted to Be Somebody*. New York: Harper and Row, 1958.

Gonzales, Pancho. *Man with a Racket*. New York: A. S. Barnes, 1959.

Goolagong, Evonne, and Collins, Bud. *Evonne! On the Move*. New York: E. P. Dutton, 1975.

Grimsley, Will. *Tennis: Its History, People and Events*. Englewood Cliffs, New Jersey: Prentice-Hall, 1971.

Hall, Valentine Gill. *Lawn Tennis in America*. New York: D. W. Granbery and Company, 1889.

Hart, B. H. L. *The Lawn Tennis Masters Unveiled*. Bristol, England: Arrowsmith, 1926.

Hart, Doris. *Tennis with Hart*. Philadelphia: Lippincott, 1955.

Hedges, Martin. *The Concise Dictionary of Tennis*. New York: Mayflower Book, 1978.

Hellberg, Bjorn. *Bjorn Borg*. Goteborg, Sweden: Zinderman, 1977.

Hoad, Lew, and Pollard, Jack. *The Lew Hoad Story*. Englewood Cliffs, New Jersey: Prentice-Hall, 1958.

———. *My Game*. London: Hodder and Stoughton, 1958.

Hopman, Harry. *Aces and Places*. London: Cassell and Company, 1957.

Jacobs, Helen Hull. *Beyond the Game: An Autobiography*. Philadelphia: J. B. Lippincott, 1936.

———. *Gallery of Champions*. New York: A. S. Barnes, 1970.

Janoff, Murray. *Game! Set! Match!* New York: Stadia Sports Publishers, 1973.

———. *Tennis Revolution*. New York: Stadia Sports Publishers, 1974.

Jones, Ann. *A Game to Love*. London: Stanley Paul, 1971.

King, Billie Jean, and Chapin, Kim. *Billie Jean*. New York: Harper and Row, 1974.

King, Billie Jean, and Deford, Frank. *Billie Jean*. New York: Viking Press, 1982.

Kramer, Jack, and Deford, Frank. *The Game: My 40 Years in Tennis*. New York: G. P. Putnam's Sons, 1979.

Lambert-Chambers, Dorothea Douglass. *Lawn Tennis for Ladies*. New York: Outing Publishing Company, 1912.

Landon, Charles. *Classic Moments of Wimbledon*. Ashbourne, Derbyshire, England: Moorland Publishers, 1982.

Laver, Rodney George, and Collins, Bud. *The Education of a Tennis Player*. New York: Simon and Schuster, 1973.

McPhee, John A. *Levels of the Game*. New York: Farrar, Straus, and Giroux, 1969.

Metzler, Paul. *Great Players of Australian Tennis*. New York: Harper and Row, 1979.

———. *Tennis Styles and Stylists*. New York: Macmillan, 1969.

Mewshaw, Michael. *Short Circuit*. New York: Atheneum, 1983.

Mortimer, Angela. *My Waiting Game*. London: F. Muller, 1962.

Mulloy, Gardnar. *Advantage Striker*. London: Allan Wingate, 1959.

———. *The Will to Win: An Inside View of the World of Tennis*. New York: A. S. Barnes, 1960.

Myers, Arthur Wallis. *Captain Anthony Wilding*. London: Hodder and Stoughton, 1916.

———. *Leaders of Lawn Tennis*. London: Amateur Sports Publishing Company, 1912.

Okker, Tom Samuel. *Tennis Met Tom*. Bussum: Teleboek, 1970.

Pails, Dinny. *Set Points: My Tennis Story*. London: Angus and Robertson, 1953.

Patty, John Edward. *Tennis My Way*. London: Hutchinson, 1951.

Perry, Frederick John. *Fred Perry: An Autobiography*. London: The Hutchinson Publishing Group, 1984.

———. *My Story*. London: Hutchinson and Company, 1934.

———. *Perry on Tennis: Expert Advice for All on Lawn Tennis*. London: John C. Winston Company, 1937.

Pitrone, Jean. *Jean Hoxie: The Robin Hood of Tennis*. Hamtramck, Michigan: Avenue Publishing Company, 1984.

Potter, Edward Clarkson. *The World's Leading Tennis Players*. New York: n.p., 1954.

Richards, Renee. *Second Serve*. New York: Stein and Day, 1983.

Riessen, Marty, and Evans, Richard. *Match Point: A Candid View of Life on the International Tennis Circuit*. Englewood Cliffs, New Jersey: Prentice-Hall, 1973.

Riggs, Robert Larimore. *Tennis Is My Racket*. New York: Simon and Schuster, 1950.

Riggs, Robert Larimore, and McGann, George. *Court Hustler*. Philadelphia: Lippincott, 1973.

Robyns, Gwen. *Wimbledon: The Hidden Drama*. New York: Drake Publishers, 1974.

Rosewall, Ken, and Barrett, John. *Play Tennis with Rosewall: The Little Master and His Method*. London: Queen Anne Press, 1975.

Rowley, Peter. *Ken Rosewall: Twenty Years at the Top*. London: Cassell, 1976.

Sangster, Mike, and Ballantine, John. *Cannonball Tennis*. London: A. Barker, 1965.

Scott, Eugene. *Tennis: Game of Motion*. New York: Crown Publishers, 1973.

Smyth, John George. *Jean Borotra, the Bounding Basque: His Life of Work and Play*. London: Stanley Paul, 1974.

Spain, Nancy. *"Teach Tennant": The Story of Eleanor Tennant the Greatest Tennis Coach in the World*. London: Werner Laurie, 1953.

Stanley, Louis T. *Lawn Tennis: Analytical Studies of the World's Greatest Players*. London: Hutchinson's Library of Sports and Pastimes, 1951.

Sullivan, George. *Queens of the Court*. New York: Dodd, Mead, 1974.

Talbert, Wiliam F., and Axthelm, Pete. *Tennis Observed*. Barre, Massachusetts: Barre Publishers, 1967.

Talbert, William F., and Sharnik, John. *Playing for Life: Bill Talbert's Story*. Boston: Little, Brown, 1958.

Tilden, William Tatem. *Aces, Places, and Faults*. London: R. Hale, 1938.

———. *Me—the Handicap*. London: Methuen and Company, 1929.

———. *My Story, A Champion's Memoirs*. New York: Hellman, Williams, 1948.

Tilden, William Tatem, and Merrihew, Stephen Wallis. *Match Play and the Spin of the Ball*. New York: American Sports Publishing Company, 1925.

Tinling, Teddy. *Tinling: Sixty Years in Tennis*. Topsfield, Massachusetts: Merrimack Publishers Circle, 1984.

———. *White Ladies*. London: Stanley Paul, 1963.

Tinling, Teddy, and Humphries, Rod. *Love and Faults: Personalities Who Have Changed the History of Tennis in My Lifetime*. New York: Crown Publsihers, 1979.

Todd, Terry. *The Tennis Players from Pagan Rites to Strawberries and Cream*. Guernsey, British Isles: Vallency Press, 1979.

Truman, Christine. *Tennis Today*. London: A. Barker, 1961.

Vines, Ellsworth, and Vier, Gene. *Tennis: Myth and Method*. New York: Viking Press, 1978.

Wade, Virginia, and Rafferty, Jean. *Ladies of the Court: A Century of Women at Wimbledon*. New York: Atheneum, 1984.

Wade, Virginia, and Wallace, Mary Lou. *Courting Triumph*. London: Hodder and Stoughton, 1978.

Wightman, Hazel. *Better Tennis*. New York: Houghton Mifflin Company, 1933.

Wilder, Roy. *Friend of Tennis*. Lynn, Massachusetts: H. O. Zimman, 1962.

Wills, Helen. *Fifteen-Thirty: The Story of a Tennis Player*. New York: Charles Scribner's Sons, 1937.

Wison, Bobby. *My Side of the Net*. London: Stanley Paul, 1964.

Wimbledon Who's Who and Tennis Celebrities. London: E. J. Burrow, 1934.

Wind, Herbert Warren. *Game, Set, and Match: The Tennis Boom of the 1960s and 70s*. New York: Dutton, 1979.

11

Children's Books

Unlike many sporting pastimes, the leisurely game of tennis originated with adults in the 1870s. When children began to play the sport, they used the same equipment, rules, and strokes, so no special books were written for them. With only a few exceptions, not until the 1970s, in conjunction with the boom in the popularity of tennis, were instructional books written specifically for children. Also in that decade came a proliferation in biographies about tennis players written for youthful readers. These books plus a few others about the history of tennis reflect and also encourage an increase in television exposure and a growth in interest in this lifetime sport. These motivate children, often in their early years, to play the game seriously. Going to a summer tennis camp, attending a residential tennis academy, receiving a college athletic grant-in-aid, and turning professional while still a teenager may occur as a result of this enthusiasm for tennis.

French champion Suzanne Lenglen and Eustace White provided one of the first children's instructional books, *Lawn Tennis for Girls*, in 1920. They discuss the strokes, tactics, tournament play, and common faults plus Lenglen tells about her own play and the evolution of the ladies' game of tennis. Three books, all entitled *Tennis for Girls*, by Miriam Hall (1914), Florence Ballin (1926), and English player Dorothy Round

(1938) exist, although no comparable books are available for boys. Ballin uses photographs of women players to complement her discussion of the basic strokes and tactics as does Hall. Helen Jacobs, another champion, offers pointers about tennis play through her ten lessons for juniors in both *Tennis* and *The Young Sportsman's Guide to Tennis*.

The basic, fundamental strokes for children's learning are the focus of *The Basic Strokes, Tennis: Text, Serving and Returning Service,* and *Volleying and Lobs* by Paul Deegan. Robert Antonacci and Barbara Lockart explain the game and its history, give step-by-step descriptions and diagrams of the strokes, and add strategies in *Tennis for Young Champions.* Former champion Arthur Ashe and Louie Robinson provide individual lessons about the forehand, backhand, serve, auxiliary strokes, and strategies in *Getting Started in Tennis.* Along with the rules, etiquette, tips on exercise, practice, and equipment, they provide some tennis quizzes to test knowledge about technique and tactics. Fred Stolle and M. Appel in *Let's Play Tennis* and Harry Hopman in *Better Tennis for Boys and Girls* also offers instructions to children about proper technique. Hopman explains sportsmanship, tactics, practice, fitness and match preparation, too.

Merritt Cutler stresses the essentials of stroke production and simple tactics using many diagrams and some explanations in *The Tennis Book.* Among the topics he discusses are spin shots and the effects of spin, using the angles, and doubles play. *Let's Play Tennis* by Robin Davison-Lungley includes the basic and advanced strokes, tactics and training, and a brief history. This book shows children learning the strokes plus stars executing the shots.

Charles Coombs focuses on the strokes and match play in *Be a Winner in Tennis.* Robert La Marche instructs in the fundamental shots, use of practice drills, learning the simplified rules, court conduct, and elementary strategies in *Tennis Basics.* Lud Duroska's *Tennis for Beginners* provides stroke instruction, practice suggestions, and hints for play. *Tennis Is for Me* by Lowell Dickmeyer and Annette Chappell is the story of twelve-year-old Sandy, who is starting to learn about tennis through reading about the sport's technique.

Harry Leighton in *Tennis* and *Junior Tennis* instructs in the basic strokes. *Junior Tennis* uses children in the photographs as they learn proper stroke execution. In *Tennis* he relies primarily on photographs and cartoon-like diagrams with a short explanation of each shot. Susan Noel explains how to help juniors learn the basic strokes and how to prepare for competitive matches in *Instructions to Young Tennis Players.* Youthful readers learn about tennis with Michael as their guide to stroke development in Joseph Pizzat's *Tennis for Children.* Bill McCormick in *Tennis* describes this as the game for a lifetime. Strokes, tactics, doubles, etiquette, and conditioning are among the items he discusses. *Tennis* by George Seewagen and George Sullivan includes the strokes (basic and advanced), strategies, and etiquette. An easy-to-read instructional book, *Your Book of Lawn Tennis*, explains that lawn tennis is a game to be won, not a battle to win at all costs. (Thus, it condemns the temper tantrums of some stars.) Gerald Walter, a tennis correspondent for the *News Chronicle*, uses photographs of the stars to demonstrate the strokes and tactics. Coach Clarence Jones and tennis star Angela Buxton in *Starting Tennis* explain the game to players who do not have a coach and who have only limited competitive opportunities. They discuss when to hit the ball, body position when stroking, quality practice plus mental rehearsal, and tactics, such as eight golden rules for match play, correct tactics to make the most of your strokes, avoiding mistakes, and varying pace and length of returns. Dorothy Phillips in *Winning Tennis* and H. E. Millen in *Lawn Tennis and Its Coaching in Schools for Girls* also focus on the basics. Clare Riessan and Mark Cox explain tennis terms, scoring, equipment, and stroke technique in *Tennis: A Basic Guide.* Former champion Ken Rosewall discusses the fundamentals and proper attitudes toward practice in *Ken Rosewall on Tennis.*

Two children learn to play tennis and participate in their first tournament in Eugene Baker's *I Want to Be a Tennis Player. Learning to Play Better Tennis* also stresses learning the basics. Gary Paulsen humorously looks at the different aspects of tennis using photographs of professional players in *Forehanding and Backhanding: If You're Lucky.* Cartoons by Charles Schulz help instruct children in the fundamentals in

Snoopy's Tennis Book: Featuring Snoopy at Wimbledon and Snoopy's Tournament Tips.

Competitive Tennis: A Guide for Parents and Young Players by David Benjamin explains the education of a young tennis player by discussing starting out, the tournament trail, and the college tennis scene including lessons, equipment, parents' roles, match pressure, college choices and tennis scholarships, coaches, and satellite events. Part II of his book illustrates this process by introducing the 1978 National Collegiate Athletic Association Championship and the making of its champion, John McEnroe. Nick Bollettieri and Barry McDermott describe the foremost training facility of junior champions, the Tennis Academy in Bradenton, Florida, in *Nick Bollettieri's Junior Tennis*. The Bollettieri way combines academic schooling at the year-round school with rigorous tennis coaching, which emphasizes motivation, concentration, and dedication. While stroke production is a key, he advocates that each player's aptitude and spirit dictates the use of which techniques work best. Court drills and practice form the backbone of the academy's program, but the independence of the coaching and proper relationships between the parents and young tennis aspirants are also essential.

Tennis Love: A Parents' Guide to the Sport by Billie Jean King and Greg Hoffman describes the various types of tennis parents, the fundamental strokes, lessons, camps, conditioning, practice, the mental game, (concentration and strategy), and the emotional game of motivation, temperament, and sportsmanship. Lessons including warm-up exercises, stroke instructions, practice drills, and tennis talk comprise Carol Kleinman's *You Can Teach Your Child Tennis: A 30-Day Guide to Tennis Readiness*. Bob Huang and Arthur Shay provide progressive lessons in *Teaching Your Child Tennis*. These lessons are as follows: 1) warm-up and grip; 2) palm tennis, throw and catch; 3) beginning bounce drills; 4) forehand and backhand drop and hit drills; 5) tennis touch with a ball on the racket; 6) hand-eye coordination drills; 7) backhand drills; 8) serve; 9) run and retrieve; 10) use of ping-pong to learn strategy. *Tennis and Kids: The Family Connection* focuses on parents' use of SCORE as the missing link in helping them serve as their child's best pro. Self-discipline, concentration, optimism, relaxation, and enjoyment are the components of Jim Fannin and John Mullin's recommendations to maximize the results of practice while keeping everything in perspective. *A Handbook for Junior Tennis Tournament Players* helps players and their parents know what to expect when they enter these competitive events.

By far the greatest number of children's tennis books are the fifty-one biographies. Interestingly thirty-six of these feature female players with ten of them focusing on Chris Evert-Lloyd. Linda Jacobs writes mostly about this young champion's professional career beginning at age eighteen and about her determination to be herself in *Chris Evert: Tennis Pro*. Jay Smith in *Chris Evert* highlights her career through her 1974 Wimbledon championship. Lynn Haney's *Chris Evert: The Young Champion* in covering her professional career also includes some information about her opponents—Julie Anthony, Evonne Goolagong, Martina Navratilova, and Billie Jean King. *Sports Star: Chris Evert* by S. H. Burchard portrays Evert's youthful rise to stardom including a brief personal sketch, learning the game, the United States Nationals in 1971, amateur successes, the Wimbledon Championships in 1972 and 1974, and her early professional career. Mary Jo O'Shea in *Winning Tennis Star: Chris Evert* focuses more on her life and personality than on her championships. Betty Phillips traces Evert's life from lessons from her father at age six to her number one ranking in *Chris Evert: First Lady of Tennis*. The importance of her family provides the foundation for her tennis achievements according to Francene Sabin in *Set Point: The Story of Chris Evert*. Other biographies of her championship career are *Chris! The Sports Career of Chris Evert Lloyd* by James Hahn and Lynn Hahn, *Chris Evert: Princess of Tennis* by Julian May, and *Chris Evert: Women's Tennis Champion* by Dorothy Schmitz.

Billie Jean King's life and tennis career are the focus of eight children's biographies. James Olsen in *Billie Jean King: The Lady of the Court* highlights her personal life, amateur career, championships, and her efforts to change tennis. Jim Baker focuses on her professional career including World Team Tennis and her promotion of equity for women in *Billie Jean King*. Besides discussing her introduction to and early years in tennis through the famous King-Riggs extravaganza, Julian May in *Billie Jean King: Tennis Champion* also stresses her opposition to tennis' outdated regulations. *Sports Hero: Billie Jean King* by Marshall Burchard and Sue Burchard discusses her introduction to tennis, decision to concentrate on tennis, first Wimbledon championship, attaining the number one ranking, and the King-Riggs match. The Burchards in their biography and Leila Gemme in *King on the Court: Billie Jean King* stress her promotion of the women's professional tennis circuit. Gemme also discusses her efforts to change the tennis establishment to make tennis a sport for all. Thomas Braun in *Billie Jean King*, James Hahn and Lynn Hahn in *King!: The Sports Career of Billie Jean King*, and Ann Morse in *Tennis Champion: Billie Jean King* also write about this outstanding player.

The teenage champion Tracy Austin was the subject of eight biographies published prior to her graduation from high school. Gloria Miklowitz in *Tracy Austin* describes the tennis successes of her brothers and sisters as well as her rapid ascent to stardom. James Hahn and Lynn Hahn in *Tracy Austin: Powerhouse in Pinafore* and *Tracy Austin: Teenage Superstar* by Nancy Robison trace her early years in tennis through her 1977 appearance in the Wimbledon Championships, the youngest at age fourteen ever to compete. Robison two years later updated Austin's career in *Tracy Austin: Teen Tennis Champion*. In 1977 Austin became *Tennis Magazine's* Rookie of the Year, while in 1979 she won the United States Open. S. H. Burchard in *Tracy Austin* highlights her brief career beginning at age eight with her first junior tournament victory. Anne Harler in *Tracy Austin: Teenage Champion* and Elizabeth Van Steenwyk in *Tracy Austin: Teenage Champion*, and Peter Talbert in *Tracy Austin: Tennis Wonder* also trace her early career.

Jimmy Connors leads the men with five children's biographies. Larry Batson in *Jimmy Connors* highlights his early years and the beginning of his career as does Marshall Burchard in *Sports Hero: Jimmy Connors*, Jay Smith in *Fiery Tennis Star: Jimmy Connors*, and Francene Sabin in *Jimmy Connors: King of the Courts*. Margaret Ogan and George Ogan emphasize his strong personality and will to win in *Smashing: Jimmy Connors*.

Bjorn Borg, Evonne Goolagong, Arthur Ashe, Rosemary Casals, Andrea Jaeger, and Martina Navratilova are subjects of four, three, four, two, two, and two children's biographies respectively. Generally, these focus on their early years and on tennis championships. Larry Audette in *Bjorn Borg*, James Hahn and Lynn Hahn in *Bjorn Borg: The Coolest Ace*, Gary Libman in *Bjorn Borg*, and Michel Sutter in *Borg Story* describe the early years and brief, yet outstanding, career of this baseliner. Charles Morse and Ann Morse in *Evonne Goolagong*, D.J. Herda in *Free Spirit, Evonne Goolagong*, and Linda Jacobs in *Evonne Goolagong: Smiles and Smashes* highlight her career with a focus on her 1971 Wimbledon Championship. *Raising a Racket: Rosie Casals* by Alida Thacher and *Rosemary Casals: The Rebel Rosebud* by Linda Jacobs emphasize her promotion of women's tennis and how she becomes a rebel to the tennis establishment. Problems with the Czechoslovakian government led Martina Navratilova to defect to the United States to pursue her professional career according to Edward Dolan and Richard Lyttle in *Martina Navratilova* and Linda Jacobs in *Martina Navratilova: Tennis Fury*. Charles Morse in *Arthur Ashe*, Julian May in *Arthur Ashe: Dark Star of Tennis*, Linda Jacobs in *Arthur Ashe: Alone in the Crowd*, and Louie Robinson in *Arthur Ashe: Portrait in Motion* describe the struggles of the first black male champion as he moved atop the elite sport of tennis. Julianna Fogel and Mary Watkins in *Andrea Jaeger, Tennis Champion* and Ray Sons' *Andrea Jaeger: Pro in Ponytails* describe the youngest tennis pro ever (in 1980) and her early tournament successes.

Single children's biographies describe the lives and careers of *Pancho Gonzales* by Charles Morse and *Stan Smith* by Sam Hasegawn. S. H. Burchard in *John McEnroe* describes his early years in tennis through his becoming at age eighteen the youngest semi-finalist at Wimbledon. Alice Marble in 1947 wrote the first tennis biography and the only tennis autobiography for children. In *The Road to Wimbledon* she describes in detail her early years in sports, her acceptance of tennis as a lady-like game, her early amateur successes, her illnesses, and her return to championship play and attainment of the number one ranking.

In addition to these books, a few children's works include biographical sketches about both past and present cham-

pions. Nathan Aaseng discusses the *Winning Men of Tennis*
and *Winning Women of Tennis*. The careers of Bill Tilden,
Pancho Gonzales, Rod Laver, Arthur Ashe, Jimmy Connors,
Bjorn Borg, Guillermo Vilas, and John McEnroe comprise the
first. The second includes the championship performances of
Helen Wills, Althea Gibson, Margaret Court, Billie Jean
King, Chris Evert-Lloyd, Evonne Goolagong, Martina Navratilova, and Tracy Austin. In *Women in Sports: Tennis*
Marion Meade describes the struggles of women's professional tennis to attain financial success by highlighting the
careers of the Old Lady Billie Jean King, Rosemary "Rosebud" Casals, Chris Evert, the Cinderella in sneakers, Evonne
Goolagong, the panther, and Margaret Court, the mighty
mouse. The careers of Chris Evert, Evonne Goolagong, Billie
Jean King, Jimmy Connors, Bjorn Borg, and Arthur Ashe
comprise *Winners on the Tennis Court* by William Glickman.
Andrew Lawrence in *Tennis: Great Stars, Great Moments*
gives brief biographical sketches and playing style analyses
of Bill Tilden, Don Budge, Pancho Gonzales, Ken Rosewall,
Rod Laver, Arthur Ashe, Jimmy Connors, Suzanne Lenglen,
Helen Wills, Billie Jean King, Chris Evert, and Evonne Goolagong. Some of the profiles focus around a single exciting
match, such as Lenglen versus Wills. In *Famous Modern
American Women Athletes*, Helen Jacobs describes one outstanding female athlete from eight sports. Billie Jean King's
career is the focus for tennis.

Joseph Cook in *Famous Firsts in Tennis* uses a brief description and a photograph of initial events and the first individuals
to accomplish certain feats in tennis' history. He includes the
first tennis court in the United States, men's and women's
national champions, United States' player to win at Wimbledon, stylist as a player, big game player, grand slam winner,
black to win a major championship, power volleyer, and player
to affect society. Maureen Reardon in *Match Point* discusses
the history of tennis, the championships at Wimbledon, outstanding players, and significant individuals and their contributions. Bryan Cutress uses the stars to describe and to illustrate
the game, and he also examines the various championships,

the men's, women's, and junior circuits, and the money side of the game in *Tennis*. Julian May provides biographies and photographs of the champions in *Forest Hills and the American Tennis Championship*. These include Bill Tilden, Helen Wills, Don Budge, Bobby Riggs, Alice Marble, Pancho Gonzales, Maureen Connolly, Althea Gibson, Arthur Ashe, Billie Jean King, Jimmy Connors, and Chris Evert. In addition to a brief history of the All-England Championships, May sketches biographies of the stars of the famous center court in *Wimbledon World Tennis Focus*. He focuses on Helen Wills, Helen Jacobs, Don Budge, Rod Laver, Margaret Court, and Billie Jean King. Hal Higdon in *Champions of the Tennis Court* focuses on Bill Tilden, Suzanne Lenglen, Helen Wills, Don Budge, Bill Talbert, Jack Kramer, Pancho Gonzales, Maureen Connolly, Lew Hoad, Billie Jean King, and Arthur Ashe. *Winning Men of Tennis* and *Winning Women of Tennis* by Nathan Aaseng picture and highlight the careers of Bill Tilden, Pancho Gonzales, Rod Laver, Arthur Ashe, Jimmy Connors, Bjorn Borg, Guillermo Vilas, John McEnroe, Helen Wills, Althea Gibson, Margaret Court, Billie Jean King, Chris Evert-Lloyd, Evonne Goolagong, Martina Navratilova, and Tracy Austin.

What Is Tennis? looks at the history of tennis as an international game. Anthony Ravielli also discusses the techniques and strategies of the game and how to improve both. Karen Sweeney gives a brief history, defines terms, and identifies outstanding players in *Illustrated Dictionary for Young People*. In *The Tennis Book* Lawrence Lorimer provides an A to Z encyclopedia about tennis including terms, players' sketches, championships, greatest star, famous matches, rules, and strategies.

BIBLIOGRAPHY

Aaseng, Nathan. *Winning Men of Tennis*. Minneapolis: Lerner Publications Company, 1981.
———. *Winning Women of Tennis*. Minneapolis: Lerner Publications Company, 1981.

Antonacci, Robert J., and Lockart, Barbara D. *Tennis for Young Champions*. New York: McGraw-Hill, 1982.

Ashe, Arthur, and Robinson, Louie. *Getting Started in Tennis*. New York: Atheneum/SMI, 1977.

Audette, Larry. *Bjorn Borg*. New York: Quick Fox, 1979.

Baker, Eugene H. *I Want to Be a Tennis Player*. Chicago: Childrens Press, 1973.

Baker, Jim. *Billie Jean King*. New York: Grosset and Dunlap, 1974.

Ballin, Florence A. *Tennis for Girls*. New York: American Sports Publishing Company, 1926.

Batson, Larry. *Jimmy Connors*. Mankato, Minnesota: Creative Education, 1975.

Benjamin, David A. *Competitive Tennis: A Guide for Parents and Young Players*. New York: Lippincott, 1979.

Bollettieri, Nick, and McDermott, Barry. *Nick Bollettieri's Junior Tennis*. New York: Simon and Schuster, 1984.

Braun, Thomas. *Billie Jean King*. Mankato, Minnesota: Creative Education, 1976.

Burchard, Marshall. *Sports Hero: Jimmy Connors*. New York: Putnam, 1976.

Burchard, Marshall, and Burchard, Sue. *Sports Hero: Billie Jean King*. New York: Putnam, 1975.

Burchard, S. H. *John McEnroe*. New York: Harcourt Brace Jovanovich, 1979.

———. *Sports Star: Chris Evert*. New York: Harcourt Brace Jovanovich, 1976.

———. *Tracy Austin*. New York: Harcourt Brace Jovanovich, 1982.

Cook, Joseph J. *Famous Firsts in Tennis*. New York: Putnam, 1978.

Coombs, Charles Ira. *Be a Winner in Tennis*. New York: Morrow, 1975.

Cutler, Merritt. *The Tennis Book*. New York: McGraw-Hill Book Company, 1967.

Cutress, Bryan. *Tennis*. Morristown, New Jersey: Silver Burdett, 1980.

Davison-Lungley, Robin. *Let's Play Tennis*. London: Octopus Books, 1979.

Deegan, Paul J. *The Basic Strokes*. Mankato, Minnesota: Creative Education, 1976.

———. *Serving and Returning Service*. Mankato, Minnesota: Creative Education, 1976.

———. *Tennis: Text*. Mankato, Minnesota: Creative Education, 1976.

———. *Volleying and Lobs*. Mankato, Minnesota: Creative Education, 1976.

Dickmeyer, Lowell A., and Chappell, Annette Jo. *Tennis Is for Me*. Minneapolis: Lerner Publications Company, 1978.

Dolan, Edward F., Jr., and Lyttle, Richard B. *Martina Navratilova.* Garden City, New York: Doubleday, 1977.

Duroska, Led. *Tennis for Beginners.* New York: Grosset and Dunlap, 1975.

Fannin, Jim, and Mullin, John. *Tennis and Kids: The Family Connection.* Garden City, New York: Doubleday, 1979.

Fogel, Julianna A., and Watkins, Mary. *Andrea Jaeger: Tennis Champion.* New York: Lippincott, 1980.

Gemme, Leila B. *King on the Court: Billie Jean King.* Milwaukee: Raintree Editions, 1976.

Glickman, William G. *Winners on the Tennis Court.* New York: Franklin Watts, 1978.

Hahn, James, and Hahn, Lynn. *Bjorn Borg: The Coolest Ace.* St. Paul: EMC Corporation, 1979.

———. *Chris! The Sports Career of Chris Evert Lloyd.* Mankato, Minnesota: Crestwood House, 1981.

———. *King! The Sports Career of Billie Jean King.* Mankato, Minnesota: Crestwood House, 1981.

———. *Tracy Austin: Powerhouse in Pinafore.* St. Paul: EMC Corporation, 1978.

Hall, Miriam. *Tennis for Girls.* San Francisco: A. M. Robertson, 1914.

A Handbook for Junior Tennis Tournament Players. New York: United States Tennis Association, 1976.

Haney, Lynn. *Chris Evert: The Young Champion.* New York: Putnam, 1976.

Harler, Anne. *Tracy Austin: Teenage Champion.* Chicago: Childrens Press, 1980.

Hasegawn, Sam. *Stan Smith.* Mankato, Minnesota: Creative Education, 1975.

Herda, D. J. *Free Spirit: Evonne Goolagong.* Milwaukee: Raintree Editions, 1976.

Higdon, Hal. *Champions of the Tennis Court.* Englewood Cliffs, New Jersey: Prentice-Hall, 1971.

Hopman, Harry. *Better Tennis for Boys and Girls.* New York: Dodd, Mead, 1972.

Huang, Bob, and Shay, Arthur. *Teaching Your Child Tennis.* Chicago: Contemporary Books, 1979.

Jacobs, Helen Hull. *Famous Modern American Women Athletes.* New York: Dodd, Mead, 1975.

———. *Tennis.* Mankato, Minnesota: Creative Education, 1961.

———. *The Young Sportsman's Guide to Tennis.* New York: T. Nelson, 1961.

Jacobs, Linda. *Arthur Ashe: Alone in the Crowd*. St. Paul: EMC Corporation, 1976.

———. *Chris Evert: Tennis Pro*. St. Paul: EMC Corporation, 1974.

———. *Evonne Goolagong: Smiles and Smashes*. St. Paul: EMC Corporation, 1975.

———. *Martina Navratilova: Tennis Fury*. St. Paul: EMC Corporation, 1976.

———. *Rosemary Casals: The Rebel Rosebud*. St. Paul: EMC Corporation, 1975.

Jones, Clarence M., and Buxton, Angela. *Starting Tennis*. New York: Barron's Woodbury, 1977.

King, Billie Jean, and Hoffman, Greg. *Tennis Love: A Parents' Guide to the Sport*. New York: Macmillan, 1978.

Kleinman, Carol. *You Can Teach Your Child Tennis: A 30-Day Guide to Tennis Readiness*. New York: Popular Library, 1979.

La Marche, Robert J. *Tennis Basics*. Englewood Cliffs, New Jersey: Prentice-Hall, 1983.

Lawrence, Andrew. *Tennis: Great Stars, Great Moments*. New York: Putnam, 1976.

Learning to Play Better Tennis. London: Collins, 1974.

Leighton, Harry. *Junior Tennis*. New York: Sterling Publishing Company, 1974.

———. *Tennis*. New York: Sterling Publishing Company, 1962.

Lenglen, Suzanne, and White, Eustace E. *Lawn Tennis for Girls*. New York: American Sports Publishing Company, 1920.

Libman, Gary. *Bjorn Borg*. Mankato, Minnesota. Creative Education, 1979.

Lorimer, Lawrence T. *The Tennis Book*. New York: Random House, 1980.

Marble, Alice. *The Road to Wimbledon*. New York: Charles Scribner's Sons, 1947.

May, Julian. *Arthur Ashe: Dark Star of Tennis*. Mankato, Minnesota: Crestwood House, 1975.

———. *Billie Jean King: Tennis Champion*. Mankato, Minnesota: Crestwood House, 1974.

———. *Chris Evert: Princess of Tennis*. Mankato, Minnesota: Crestwood House, 1975.

———. *Forest Hills and the American Tennis Championship*. Mankato, Minnesota: Creative Education, 1976.

———. *Wimbledon World Tennis Focus*. Mankato, Minnesota: Creative Education, 1975.

McCormick, Bill. *Tennis*. New York: Watts, 1973.

Meade, Marion. *Women in Sports: Tennis*. New York: Harvey House, 1975.

Miklowitz, Gloria D. *Tracy Austin*. New York: Grossett and Dunlap, 1978.

Millen, H. E. *Lawn Tennis and Its Coaching in Schools for Girls*. London: Macaire, Mould and Company, 1927.

Morse, Ann R. *Tennis Champion: Billie Jean King*. Mankato, Minnesota: Creative Education, 1976.

Morse, Charles. *Arthur Ashe*. Mankato, Minnesota: Childrens Press, 1974.

————. *Pancho Gonzales*. Mankato, Minnesota: Childrens Press, 1974.

Morse, Charles, and Morse, Ann. *Evonne Goolagong*. Mankato, Minnesota: Childrens Press, 1974.

Noel, Susan. *Instructions to Young Tennis Players*. London: Museum Press, 1961.

Ogan, Margaret Nettles, and Ogan, George. *Smashing: Jimmy Connors*. Milwaukee: Raintree Editions, 1976.

Olsen, James T. *Billie Jean King: The Lady of the Court*. Mankato, Minnesota: Creative Education, 1974.

O'Shea, Mary Jo. *Winning Tennis Star: Chris Evert*. Mankato, Minnesota: Creative Education, 1977.

Paulsen, Gary. *Forehanding and Backhanding: If You're Lucky*. Chicago: Childrens Press, 1978.

Phillips, Betty Lou. *Chris Evert: First Lady of Tennis*. New York: J. Messner, 1977.

Phillips, Dorothy. *Winning Tennis*. New York: Troll Associates, 1974.

Pizzat, Joseph. *Tennis for Children*. Danville, Illinois: School Aid Company, 1954.

Ravielli, Anthony. *What Is Tennis?* New York: Atheneum/SMI, 1977.

Reardon, Maureen. *Match Point*. Milwaukee: Advanced Learning Concepts, 1975.

Riessen, Clare, and Cox, Mark. *Tennis: A Basic Guide*. New York: Lothrop, Lee and Shepard, 1969.

Robinson, Louie. *Arthur Ashe: Portrait in Motion*. Garden City, New York: Doubleday, 1967.

Robison, Nancy. *Tracy Austin: Teen Tennis Champion*. New York: Harvey House, 1980.

————. *Tracy Austin: Teenage Superstar*. New York: Harvey House, 1978.

Rosewall, Ken R. *Ken Rosewall on Tennis*. New York: F. Fell Publishers, 1978.

Round, Dorothy. *Tennis for Girls*. London: Nisbet, 1938.

Sabin, Francene. *Jimmy Connors: King of the Courts.* New York: Putnam, 1978.

———. *Set Point: The Story of Chris Evert.* New York: Putnam, 1977.

Schmitz, Dorothy C. *Chris Evert: Women's Tennis Champion.* Mankato, Minnesota: Crestwood House, 1978.

Schulz, Charles M. *Snoopy's Tennis Book: Featuring Snoopy at Wimbledon and Snoopy's Tournament Tips.* New York: Holt, Rinehart and Winston, 1979.

Seewagen, George L., and Sullivan, George. *Tennis.* Chicago: Follett Publishing Company, 1968.

Smith, Jay H. *Chris Evert.* Mankato, Minnesota: Creative Education, 1975.

———. *Fiery Tennis Star: Jimmy Connors.* Mankato, Minnesota: Creative Education, 1977.

Sons, Ray. *Andrea Jaeger: Pro in Ponytails.* Chicago: Childrens Press, 1981.

Stolle, Fred, and Appel, M. *Let's Play Tennis.* St. Paul: Wanderer Books, 1980.

Sutter, Michel. *Borg Story.* Paris: O. Orban, 1978.

Sweeney, Karen O'Connor. *Illustrated Tennis Dictionary for Young People.* New York: Harvey House, 1979.

Talbert, Peter. *Tracy Austin: Tennis Wonder.* New York, Putnam, 1979.

Thacher, Alida M. *Raising a Racket: Rosie Casals.* Milwaukee: Raintree Editions, 1976.

Van Steenwyk, Elizabeth. *Tracy Austin: Teenage Champion.* Chicago: Childrens Press, 1980.

Walter, Gerard. *Your Book of Lawn Tennis.* London: Faber and Faber, 1958.

12

Humor

Julian Marshall first looked at tennis poetically in 1884 in *Tennis Cuts and Quips, in Prose and Verse with Rules and Wrinkles. The Tennis Court Oath: A Book of Poems* by John Ashbery in 1962 examines the sport from a similar perspective, while Ed Gellert's *You're Not Too Old—To Win at Tennis* is in psalm form.

Gary Paulsen uses anecdotes and humor to describe the game of tennis to children in *Forehanding and Backhanding—If You're Lucky. Snoopy's Tennis Book: Featuring Snoopy at Wimbledon and Snoopy's Tournament Tips* by Charles Schulz appeals to tennis enthusiasts of all ages. Bill Keane use cartoons and caricatures to explain the *Deuce and Don'ts of Tennis*. The key is swinging the racket freely with resultant power according to Sally Huss in *How to Play Power Tennis with Ease*. Using cartoons Huss shows the stance, swing, serve, and smash.

Mary Poppenberg and Marlene Parrish humorously approach cooking and astrology in *I'd Rather Play Tennis Than Cook: A Cookbook for Tennis Buffs* and in *The I'd Rather Play Tennis Horoscope*. In their first book among the menus they provide are kitchen quick service, winner's dinner, backhand buffet, dinner for deuce as well as instructions for preparing several items such as the cannonball (a drink), a cucumber court salad, double fault potatoes, volley chops, and lazy lob surprise. Poppenberg and Parrish apply the characteristics of players having each astrological sign to their tennis styles, explain how to play against each, and list leading players under their appropriate signs in their second book.

Rex Lardner takes a hilarious look at *The Underhanded Serve: How to Play Dirty Tennis* in his 1968 book. He discusses the scorer's advantage, doubles troubles, the seven toughest courts, preparation for a tournament match, bizarre aspects of courtesy, and how to exploit your opponent using sounds and countersounds. Lardner's sequel is the equally humorous *The Fine Art of Tennis Hustling* which tells how a canny competitor can win by using various psychological ploys. He uses case histories and anecdotes to demonstrate ways to upset, confuse, and exasperate opponents. The key according to Lardner is to have a thorough knowledge of the rules in order to bend them to one's nefarious purposes. *Bill Cosby's Personal Guide to Tennis Power: Or Don't Lower the Lob, Raise the Net* offers instructions and illustrations by Bill Cosby, a television celebrity and tennis noncelebrity. While providing secrets for the remedial player, such as watch the ball, hit the ball with the strings, and know your place, he also comically shows how not to hit serves, forehands, backhands, and lobs.

Philip Hawk in 1937 uses photographs and cartoons to illustrate *Off the Racket: Tennis Highlights and Lowdowns*. A partial history of tennis is evident in his discussion of the standouts of tennis between 1896–1936. Primarily Hawk looks at the unusual aspects of the game such as a likability rating of players based on charm, grace, and personality (Eileen Whittingstall and Jean Borotra), tennis Santa Claus, the throwing of points or games, a bedtime story for eight grandchildren by a former women's champion, champs for hire into the professional ranks, informal words of tennis champions, and nutty things which never could happen. Hawk asks eighty-six questions to test the reader's tennis I.Q., too. Axel Kaufman utilizes humor throughout *Pardon Me, Your Forehand Is Showing: A Collection of Inside and Outside Information about Tennis*. He discusses the trapping and care of doubles partners, tennis and murder, how to be a popular or a controversial player, losemanship, and numerous other essential aspects of the game.

James Sanderson reassures tennis hackers everywhere that they are not alone in *Tennis Hacker's Handbook: How to Survive the Game and Learn to Love It*. He confronts the moral dilemma of avoiding the obligation to become an all-around player and explains how virtue may be the ruination of players. Cartoons show bad serving, a few cute moves at the net, inexperienced volleys, low lobs, how to win even when ahead, mixed doubles troubles, and inner tennis. Kurt Wallach verifies that *Tennis Is a Funny Racquet*, while Jack Roberts instructs using a sundry of humorous strokes in *So You're Going to Take Tennis Seriously*. He explains how to pick up balls, games, and partners, how to poach, cheat, and lie, and doubles as group therapy. He labels the action of a second ball hit to your backhand as indecent. In *How to Succeed in Tennis without Really Trying: The Easy Tennismanship Way to Do All the Things No Tennis Pro Can Teach You* Shepherd Mead humorously explains that it is never too late to succeed. Rather than becoming one of the seven types of tennis club outcasts that nobody wants to play, Mead tells how to have more partners as well as describes the seven castes of club tennis. He recommends brain-boggling ways to beat better players and then tricks to use against the brain-bogglers. He provides twelve handy ways to tell others and yourself that you are really not so bad as a player, plus he adds helpful advice for capturing, taming, and training doubles partners, training, watching tennis, hosting tennis parties, and using tennis to succeed in business.

David Wiltse's *Best Tennis Humor: It Only Hurts When I Serve* is an anthology containing twenty-eight humorous articles. Samples from this book are "No. 1—For a Week" by Barry Tarshis, "Doubles Advice—Attack the Chipmunk" by Wiltse, "Net Loss," by Russell Baker, and "A Few Frissons at Forest Hills" by Laurence Sheehan. *From the Bottom of the Tennis Ladder: For Those Who Claim It Is Only a Game* speaks to mature players involved in the social aspects of the game. John Crockett includes in this humorous book descriptions of the various status levels within tennis ladders, such as clubbers, ego-squashers, handhold on the ladder types, and hackers. Donald Sonneman and Nicholas Ourusoff describe *The Compleat Pocket Tennis Strategist* using a cat as a player. After explaining the fundamental strokes, the authors explain how to beat baseliners and how to exploit the opponents' weaknesses. Responsibilities are shown in doubles for the server, net player, receiver, and receiver's partner.

BIBLIOGRAPHY

Ashbery, John. *The Tennis Court Oath: A Book of Poems*. Middletown, Connecticut: Wesleyan University Press, 1962.

Cosby, William H. *Bill Cosby's Personal Guide to Tennis Power: Or Don't Lower the Lob, Raise the Net*. New York: Random House, 1975.

Crockett, John C. *From the Bottom of the Tennis Ladder: For Those Who Claim It Is Only a Game*. New York: Vantage, 1982.

Gellert, Ed. *You're Not Too Old—To Win at Tennis*. Boise, Idaho: Mountain States Press, 1984.

Hawk, Philip Bovier. *Off the Racket: Tennis Highlights and Lowdowns*. New York: American Lawn Tennis, 1937.

Huss, Sally Moore. *How to Play Power Tennis with Ease*. New York: Harcourt Brace Jovanovich, 1979.

Kaufmann, Axel. *Pardon Me, Your Forehand Is Showing: A Collection of Inside and Outside Information about Tennis*. New York: World Tennis, 1956.

Keane, Bill. *Deuce and Don'ts of Tennis*. Phoenix: O'Sullivan Woodside and Company, 1975.

Lardner, Rex. *The Fine Art of Tennis Hustling*. New York: Hawthorn Books, 1975.

———. *The Underhanded Serve: How to Play Dirty Tennis*. New York: Hawthorn Books, 1968.

Marshall, Julian. *Tennis Cuts and Quips, in Prose and Verse with Rules and Wrinkles*. London: Field and Tuer, 1884.

Mead, Shepherd. *How to Succeed in Tennis without Really Trying: The Easy Tennismanship Way to Do All the Things No Tennis Pro Can Teach You*. New York: McKay, 1977.

Paulsen, Gary. *Forehanding and Backhanding—If You're Lucky*. Chicago: Childrens Press, 1978.

Poppenberg, Mary Kay, and Parrish, Marlene. *The I'd Rather Play Tennis Horoscope*. Pittsburgh: MPM Productions, 1975.

———. *I'd Rather Play Tennis Than Cook...A Cookbook for Tennis Buffs*. Pittsburgh: Hoechstetter Printing Company, 1970.

Roberts, Jack. *So You're Going to Take Tennis Seriously*. New York: Workman Publishing, 1974.

Sanderson, James Dean. *Tennis Hacker's Handbook: How to Survive the Game and Learn to Love It*. New York: A. and W. Publishers, 1977.

Schulz, Charles M. *Snoopy's Tennis Book: Featuring Snoopy at Wimbledon and Snoopy's Tournament Tips*. New York: Holt, Rinehart and Winston, 1979.

Sonneman, Donald, and Ourusoff, Nicholas. *The Compleat Pocket Tennis Strategist*. Boulder, Colorado: Sonneman, 1973.

Wallach, Kurt. *Tennis Is a Funny Racquet*. Miami: E. A. Seemann 1973.

Wiltse, David, ed. *Best Tennis Humor: It Only Hurts When I Serve*. Norwalk, Connecticut: Golf Digest/Tennis, 1980.

13

Films

Annually the United States Tennis Association publishes a list of over 150 tennis films and video cassettes available from its national film library, commercial distributors, free-loan film services, and other film libraries. The majority of these films are either instructional or depict match highlights, while a few provide biographical sketches, history, and other tennis-related information. The films in this chapter come from that exhaustive list.

Instructional films featuring leading players, teaching professionals, and various others comprise the most numerous category of films and video cassettes. Generally, players either teach the strokes or serve as models of proper technique. *Billie Jean King's Tennis for Everyone* provides instruction in the fundamentals and strategies for players of all skill levels and ages. These thirteen films feature the serve, forehand, backhand, volley, strategy in singles play, doubles as a partnership, special shots, some good practice drills, do's and don'ts, don't practice your mistakes, more on serves (three basic types, returning serve, and views about serving), Billie Jean: a study in motion, and getting in shape. Margaret Court demonstrates proper stroke execution in *Margaret Court Instructional Films*. These two films feature the fundamentals, conditioning exercises, and practice drills. Billie Jean King along with Erik Van

Dillen show ground strokes and the serve in *On Tennis*, a two-part film.

Dennis Ralston, Wendy Overton, Marty Riessen, and Rosemary Casals exhibit playing techniques for the serve, return of serve, forehand, backhand, lob, volley, overhead, and doubles strategy in *Playing Better Tennis*. Ilie Nastase in *Tennis: The Nasty Way* exhibits proper technique for the forehand, backhand, serve, volley, and strategy shots. Ken Rosewall demonstrates the forehand, backhand, serve, volley, half volley, overhead, and lob in *Tennis with Ken Rosewall*. Dennis Ralston, Dick Stockton, and Dennis Van der Meer along with seven other pros demonstrate the fundamentals, the strokes, the strategies, equipment, and fitness in *Play Your Best Tennis*.

The Laver-Emerson Method Tennis Tutor provides basic instruction in the forehand, backhand, volley, and serve by Rod Laver and Roy Emerson. These four super 8 mm cartridges come in a kit along with *Courtside Companion*, an instructional guide. *The Fundamentals of Tennis* shows the basic court stance, forehand, backhand, volley, overhead, serve, return of serve, and doubles play as demonstrated by Tracy Austin, Rosemary Casals, Andrea Jaeger, and Virginia Wade. Bjorn Borg explains and demonstrates his strokes, match strategies, and mental preparedness concepts in *Tennis Lessons from Bjorn Borg*. Arthur Ashe, Stan Smith, Roscoe Tanner, and Brian Gottfried instruct in *Complete Tennis from the Pros*. This four-part program on video cassettes for beginners to advanced players includes the forehand, backhand, overhead, serve, return of serve, lob, volley, singles and doubles strategy, practice techniques, fitness, conditioning, and equipment. In *Tut Bartzen Tennis* this former Clay Court Champion demonstrates forehands, backhands, and net play.

Leading players frequently serve as demonstrators for proper techniques such as in *Approach to Tennis*, which shows singles play in the national championships. *Tennis Grips and Strokes* features several champions demonstrating grips, ground strokes, serve, volley, chop, overhead using slow motion, stop-action, and concept pointers. Seven top players demonstrate all the strokes while Vic Braden describes the action in *Practice with the Pros*. Julie Heldman and John Alexander offer instructional lessons in *Tennis Aces*. The first cassette includes the serve, return of serve, forehand, backhand, conditioning, equipment, and doubles, while the second offers hints about serve variations, correcting faults in serving, volley, smash, lob, drop shot, and conditioning. *Love, Tennis* in ten cassettes features six male players demonstrating the forehand, backhand, serve, return of serve, volley, lob, smash, singles and doubles strategy plus tennis jargon and scoring. While observing the playing styles of leading players, Jack Kramer explains their similarities and differences as well as offers some insights into the mental aspect of the game in *You're Playing at Wimbledon*.

Bjorn Borg: The Player, Chris Evert-Lloyd, Jimmy Connors, Hana Mandlikova, Vitas Gerulaitis, and *Yannick Noah* include analysis of the strokes of these outstanding players as well as brief personality sketches about the last three. *SyberVision Tennis* uses Stan Smith as a model for its stroke analysis. The instructional technique in this video cassette provides both visual and sensory imagery to enhance retention.

Several of the best instructional films feature teaching professionals explaining their methods. Bill Luffer shows that tennis is a popular lifetime sport in *Introduction to Tennis*. Dennis Van der Meer in *Elementary Tennis Instruction* explains his techniques for teaching young players through progressions. Van der Meer offers coaching aids and instruction in *Tennis* (D) which presents tactics for practice, the serve, return of serve, ground strokes, specialty shots, and singles and doubles play. *Tennis, Anyone?* features Van der Meer in a six-part video cassette series of an introduction, the serve, the forehand, the backhand, specialty strokes, and strategy and tactics. Allie Ritzenberg's *Let's Start with the Forehand* progressively demonstrates and analyzes all aspects of the forehand, backhand, serve, and net game strokes. In *The Winning Serve* Ritzenberg explains and shows the grips, stances, swing, and rhythm of the basic, slice, and twist serves. The *Vic Braden Tennis Training Films* feature this outstanding teacher in its fourteen films. The fundamentals he discusses are the forehand drive, backhand drive, half volley, approach shot, forehand volley, backhand volley, basic serve, overhead, advanced serve, lob, ball rotation, footwork, singles strategy, and doubles strategy. In *Quick Cures for Common Tennis Problems* Braden provides twenty-eight lessons to isolate and to cure faults.

Coach Dick Gould explains proper execution of forehands, backhands, lobs, moving the ball, serves, and volleys in *Tennis Instruction*. Gould's suggestions for group tennis instruction in forehand and backhand stroke fundamentals, applying these strokes, the serve, and net play are available in loop films and video cassette in Tennis (C). Paul Xanthos shows how to instruct large groups in *Tennis Class Organization*. Coach Gundars Tilmanis explains how to more effectively communicate fundamentals to players for their maximum retention in *Tennis Teaching Skills: The Sensual Approach*.

Welby Van Horn and Axel Kaufmann in *Tennis Fundamentals* provide detailed explanations of the forehand, backhand, and serve using Van Horn's balance system. The Athletic Institute's Sports Techniques series of eight super 8 mm film loops comprise *Tennis* (F). These include forehand strokes and variations, backhand strokes and variations, volley, basic serve, flat serve, American twist serve, and overhead. They are available with either male or female demonstrators. Another set of Athletic Institute instructional films Tennis (D) describes tactics for the 1980s (about practicing), serve, return of serve, ground strokes, specialty shots, singles play, and doubles play. *Tennis* (B) features the forehand, backhand, volley, and serve by Christopher Busa. In *The Groundstrokes* and *The Serve and Volley* Ken Stuart teaches these shots. Marty Shaw explains the why and the how in *Forehand and Backhand*. Coach Gary Thorne introduces beginners to the *Serve!* in six progressive steps and explains the slice and twist serves to advanced players. In *Strokes* Myron McNamara discusses the basic grip, footwork, and weight shift necessary for all ground strokes. *Tennis*(A) features Chet Murphy explaining the backhand, forehand, serve, volley, lob, smash, and footwork in two films. *Tennis Basics with Dennis Ralston* provides his analysis of the game as well as player demonstrations of the forehand, backhand, serve, and volley. *Tennis: Basic Tactics for Singles* describes and demonstrates the strategy for singles including where to serve, when to go to the net, when to volley, and basic offensive and defensive play. Similarly, movement on the court in relation to the ball and a partner, and situational offensive and defensive strategies comprise *Tennis: Basic Tactics for Doubles.*

A *Guide to Tennis* shows the fundamental techniques for ground strokes, volleys, drop shots, serves and returns, lobs, smashes, singles and doubles strategy as well as footwork, grips, and ball control. Diagrams and player demonstrations illustrate drills and ways to improve performance in *Practice for Tennis.* Ground strokes, serves, and volleys are taught in *Introskill Tennis*, while the ground strokes, net play, and the serve comprise *Tips for Tennis.* Elaine Mason demonstrates seven aspects of the game in *Tennis* (E). These loop films include the forehand, backhand, volley, serve, and footwork. *Tennis: How to Play the Game* sequentially teaches the fundamentals, ground strokes, serve and overhead, supplementary strokes, and strategies and tactics through five 35 mm (cassette) filmstrips. Players demonstrate especially for women the forehand strokes, one- and two-handed backhands, serves, volleys, half volleys, lobs, and footwork in *Women's Tennis.*

The history of women's tennis featuring costumes and styles of play is the subject of *You've Come a Long Way, Baby.* This film also shows the play of Billie Jean King, Chris Evert, Margaret Court, and Evonne Goolagong. *Great Moments in the History of Tennis* depicts the evolution of tennis by featuring Bill Tilden, Jack Kramer, Althea Gibson, and Billie Jean King. Peter Ustinov narrates *The Great English Garden Party* in celebration of Wimbledon's one hundred years of championships in this fifty-two-minute award-winning film. *First Game, First Set* highlights the origins and developments of tennis from its ancestor real tennis through today's popular professional sport.

A look at the past and the present comprises part of *Tennis Everybody's Game*, while Butch Buchholz also provides some instructions about how to play tennis. *The USTA: The First Hundred Years* on the occasion of its one hundredth anniversary describes the many contributions made by and leadership of this organization. Juniors, aspiring tournament players, and seniors are shown as tennis enthusiasts in this film. Players of all ages taking lessons along with some action of the leading players of the 1970s comprise *Tennis Everyone.*

Six players are the subjects of biographical films or video cassettes. The focus of the earliest film is the life and career of champion *Helen Wills Moody* who reigned as queen of tennis during the late 1920s and the 1930s. The film entitled *John Newcombe* is a portrayal of the World Championship of Tennis competition, plus it provides glimpses of his personal life. *Marty Riessen* is shown on tour as a professional player who experiences and overcomes the pressures of this elite competition. *The John McEnroe Story* tells about his successful career through highlights of him at Wimbledon, the U.S. Open, and in Davis Cup play. A personal look at *Billie Jean King* plus match sequences against Chris Evert are the focus of this film. *Advantage Borg!* tells about Bjorn Borg the individual and shows his championship techniques.

For children, two films describe in an entertaining way the processes for making *Tennis Balls* and *Tennis Shoes. Tennis Racquet*, a seven-minute cartoon, features Disney character Goofy playing tennis. Parental pressure is shown via *Tennis Mothers*, in which a young girl constantly faces her mother's philosophies about tennis competition.

The Tennis Match shows a doubles match with four men who seemingly argue about everything and the repercussions of their behaviors. Contrastingly, Vic Braden in *Play It Straight* humorously describes tennis etiquette, sportsmanship, and behavior. Vic Braden provides strategic advice for doubles in *Go for a Winner*, an entertaining film. *Vic Braden's Tennis for the Future* describes various aspects of the game by dispelling myths and by giving hints for improved technique. *The Van der Meer Clinic at Forest Hills* features Dennis Van der Meer explaining and showing problems that players experience and their correction. Vic Braden explains pointers for improved serves, strategies, net play, singles, and doubles in *Tone Up for Tennis*, another entertaining film. Braden continues to look at stroking techniques in *Winning Tennis Strokes* by advocating "laugh and win" through its thirty-three lessons.

How to Warm Up informs players about the body's need for

a proper warm-up as well as illustrates exercises to accomplish this goal. Improper and harmful activities and the rationale for warming up comprise *Why Warm Up?* Medical experts explain the problems and injuries that middle-aged sport participants encounter due to their infrequent activity in *The Weekend Athletes.* A portion of Rod Laver's advice in *What You Should Know about Tennis* focuses on warm-ups and conditioning. He also explains tennis terms, surfaces, game analyses, and equipment. Jeffrey Stapleton provides a repetitious workout for tennis, racquetball, squash, and badminton players in *Sportvision: Workout for Racquet Sports.*

Match highlights comprise the second largest category of films. Portions of the 1971–1972 and 1975–1982 U.S. Open Championships are on film. In 1971, the *Tournament* shows Chris Evert, Pancho Gonzales, Billie Jean King, and Stan Smith in action at Forest Hills. *The Pros* features Ilie Nastase's triumph over Arthur Ashe in the 1972 men's final. Semi-final action for the men and the women's and men's finals in 1975 comprises the *U.S. Open 1975.* Matches in the *U.S. Open 1976* include the men's semi-finals and the finals between Bjorn Borg and Jimmy Connors and Evonne Goolagong and Chris Evert. Guillermo Vilas and Chris Evert capture the *U.S. Open 1977,* the last one held at the West Side Tennis Club in Forest Hills, New York. From a field of youthful and veteran players, Jimmy Connors and Chris Evert emerge as the champions of the *U.S. Open 1978* at the new USTA National Tennis Center. In the *U.S. Open 1979* Tracy Austin becomes the youngest woman champion ever as she outlasts Chris Evert-Lloyd while John McEnroe defeats Vitas Gerulaitis for the men's title. McEnroe repeats his victory in the *U.S. Open 1980* beating Bjorn Borg while Evert-Lloyd regains her title by defeating Hana Mandlikova. In celebration of the United States Tennis Association's centennial, *U.S. Open 1981* includes action of past champions in addition to the quarter-finals, semi-finals, and finals as John McEnroe and Tracy Austin win the championships. The *U.S. Open 1982* shows Jimmy Connors and Chris Evert-Lloyd emerge victorious.

United States Open Clay Court Tennis Championships 1979, 1980, 1981, and 1982 spotlight these events and the victors.

Other tournament films in the United States focus on the 1976 and 1977 American Airlines events in *Duel in the Desert* and *Killer Instinct* respectively, the 1977 National Indoor Pro Championships in *In Pursuit of Number One*, and the 1977 *Volvo International Tennis Tournament. Aetna Wheelchair Tennis* features Brad Parks and Jim Worth at the 1980 Aetna World Cup.

The men's finals in the World Championship of Tennis are the focus in the following films: *Shoot Out at High Noon* (1971), *The Greatest Tennis Match of All Time* (1972), *The New Era* (1973), *65,000 Miles to Dallas* (1974), *Arthur Claims the Gold* (1975), *The Youngest Champion* (1976), *And Then There Was One* (1977), *Dallas '78* (1978), *Seven Days in May* (1979), and *The End of a Decade ... The Dawn of a New Era* (1980). Films of the 1969, 1973, and 1977–1979 Davis Cup finals are also available. Stan Smith, Bob Lutz, and Arthur Ashe battle Rumania's Ilie Nastase and Ion Tiriac in *Challenge*. Stan Smith, Tom Gorman, and Erik Van Dillen compete against Rod Laver and John Newcombe from Australia in *Davis Cup Impressions. We Shall Return* shows a defeat of the South African team, but Argentina emerges as the 1977 victor. Teams from South Africa, Chile, Sweden, and finally Great Britain lose in *Advantage, United States*. The United States retains the Davis Cup in *Tennis, American Style* following victories over Colombia, Argentina, Australia, and Italy in 1979.

The All-England Championships at Wimbledon are the feature of films every year since 1971 except 1973. *At 2 P.M. Precisely* includes match play of John Newcombe, Stan Smith, Rod Laver, Arthur Ashe, Pancho Gonzales, Margaret Court, Chris Evert, and Evonne Goolagong. *You're Playing at Wimbledon* emphasizes instruction rather than match results. Youthful stars Chris Evert and Jimmy Connors lead the *Revolution in Church Road* at the 1974 championships. The Evonne Goolagong-Billie Jean King and Arthur Ashe-Jimmy Connors finals along with a perspective about Wimbledon comprises *Ustinov at Wimbledon* with Peter Ustinov narrating. Chris Evert, Evonne Goolagong, Virginia Wade, Martina Navratilova, Sue Barker, Ilie Nastase, Bjorn Borg, Jimmy Connors, Arthur Ashe, and others are in action in *Mason at Wimbledon*. Virginia

Wade and Bjorn Borg capture the 100th year anniversary championship as special ceremonies add to the splendor of *Wimbledon 1977*. Borg wins his third title while Martina Navratilova captures her first in the *Wimbledon 1978* film which includes other match highlights. In *Wimbledon 1979* both champions repeat their victories. Borg wins a record-setting fifth consecutive championship in *Wimbledon 1980* while Navratilova loses in the semi-finals to Chris Evert-Lloyd who in turn falls to Evonne Goolagong-Cawley. John McEnroe dethrones Borg in *Wimbledon 1981* while Evert-Lloyd defeats Hana Mandlikova. In *Wimbledon 1982* Jimmy Connors and Martina Navratilova in their victories over McEnroe and Evert-Lloyd provide some spectacular match play.

Finally, *The National Tennis Rating Program* provides an explanation of the United States Tennis Association's player rating categories.

BIBLIOGRAPHY

Advantage Borg! [26–minute color 16 mm film ($6.50 rental) from Pennsylvania State University]

Advantage, United States. [24–minute color 16 mm film (free loan) from USTA National Film Library)

Aetna Wheelchair Tennis. [9 –minute color video cassette (free loan) and ($150) from Aetna Life and Casualty]

Approach to Tennis. [14–minute color 16 mm film ($7.35 rental) from Oklahoma State University or ($235) from Association Films]

Arthur Claims the Gold. [27–minute color 16 mm film ($35 rental) and ($295) from Sportlite and 53–minute color video cassette ($62, " and $120, ") from Sports World Cinema]

At 2 P.M. Precisely. [52–minute color 16 mm film (free loan) from USTA National Film Library]

Basic Tennis Skills in Action. [6–minute color 35 mm filmstrip ($25) from Eye Gate Media]

Billie Jean King. [22–minute color 16 mm film ($13.80 rental) from Oklahoma State University and ($380) from AIMS Media]

Billie Jean King's Tennis for Everyone. [10–minute color segments of each of 13 parts on 16 mm film ($13/segment rental) and ($145/segment) from Association Films and 60–minute color video-cassette ($64.95) from Sportlite]

Bjorn Borg: The Player. [20–minute color 16 mm film ($12 rental) from USTA National Film Library]

Challenge. [26–minute color 16 mm film ($50 rental) and ($225) from Sports Investors]

Chris Evert-Lloyd. [26–minute color 16 mm film ($12 rental) or video cassette ($80) from USTA National Film Library]

Complete Tennis from the Pros. [60–minute color video cassettes ($59.95, " and $120, ") from Sportlite]

Dallas '78. [27–minute color 16 mm film ($35 rental) and ($295) from Sportlite and 53 –minute color video cassette ($62, " and $120, ") from Sports World Cinema]

Davis Cup Impressions. [13–minute and 28–minute color 16 mm films (free loan) from Bell System Films]

Duel in the Desert. [27–minute color 16 mm film (free loan) from USTA National Film Library]

Elementary Tennis Instruction. [15–minute color 16 mm film (free loan) from USTA National Film Library]

The End of a Decade ... The Dawn of a New Era. [26–minute color 16 mm film ($35 rental) and ($295) from Sportlite]

First Game, First Set. [20–minute color 16 mm film ($12 rental) from USTA National Film Library]

Forehand and Backhand. [15–minute color 16 mm film ($14 rental) and ($240) from Association Films

The Fundamentals of Tennis. [video cassettes ($54.95 each) from Sportlite]

Go for a Winner. [37–minute color 16 mm film from Vic Braden Tennis College]

The Great English Garden Party. [52–minute color 16 mm film ($730) from Trans World International]

Great Moments in the History of Tennis. [40–minute B/W 16 mm film (free loan) from USTA National Film Library]

The Greatest Tennis Match of All Time. [26–minute color 16 mm film ($35 rental) and ($295) from Sportlite and 52–minute color video cassette ($62, " and $120, ") from Sports World Cinema]

The Groundstrokes. [22–minute color 16 mm film (free loan) from USTA National Film Library]

Guide to Tennis. [22–minute color 16 mm film ($30/day rental) and ($350) from Brentwood]

Hana Mandlikova. [20–minute color 16 mm film ($12 rental) from USTA National Film Library]

Helen Wills Moody. [15–minute B/W video cassette from Two Star Films]

How to Warm Up. [35 mm filmstrip ($10 rental) and ($20) and slides ($30) from Association Films]

In Pursuit of Number One. [25–minute color 16 mm film ($35 rental) and ($200) and 53–minute color video cassette ($62, " and $120, ") from Sports World Cinema]

Introduction to Tennis. [14–minute color 16 mm film ($8.65) from Oklahoma State University]

Introskill Tennis. [3 –minute color super 8 mm cartridges ($24.95 each) from Champions on Film and Video]

Jimmy Connors. [26–minute color 16 mm film ($12 rental) and video cassette ($80) from USTA National Film Library]

The John McEnroe Story. [60–minute color video cassette ($54.95) from Sportlite]

John Newcombe. [22–minute color 16 mm film ($50 rental) from Sportlite]

Killer Instinct. [30–minute color 16 mm film ($35 rental) and ($200) and 53–minute color video cassette ($62, " and $120, ") from Sports World Cinema]

The Laver-Emerson Method Tennis Tutor. [2 –minute color super 8 mm cartridges ($49.95/kit) from Sportlite]

Let's Start with the Forehand. [23–minute color 16 mm film ($14.50) from Pennsylvania State University]

Love, Tennis. [30–minute color video cassette ($30/week each rental) and ($120 each) from Maryland Center for Public Broadcasting]

Margaret Court Instructional Films. [25–minute color 16 mm films ($12/unit rental) from USTA National Film Library and ($75/unit) from Scholastic Coach]

Marty Riessen. [22–minute color 16 mm film ($50 rental) from Sportlite]

Mason at Wimbledon. [52–minute color 16 mm film (free loan) from Rolex Watch U.S.A. and ($730) from Trans World International]

The National Tennis Rating Program. [30–minute color 16 mm film ($12 rental) and ($175) and video cassette ($8 rental) and ($60) from USTA National Film Library]

The New Era. [26 –minute color 16 mm film ($35 rental) and ($295) from Sportlite and 51 –minute color video cassette ($62, " and $120, ") from Sports World Cinema]

On Tennis. [15–minute color 16 mm films ($9.25/unit) from Indiana University]

Play It Straight. [30–minute color 16 mm film ($41 rental) and ($400) and video cassette ($41 rental) and ($400) from Johnson-Nyquist Productions]

Play Your Best Tennis. [80–minute color video cassettes ($49.95 each) from Caravatt Communications]

Playing Better Tennis. [25–minute color 16 mm film ($100 rental) and ($300) from Sports Films and Talents and super 8 mm film ($275) from Sports Films and Talents]

Practice for Tennis. [20–minute color 16 mm film ($12 rental) from USTA National Film Library]

Practice with the Pros. [28–minute color 16 mm film from Vic Braden Tennis College]

The Pros. [25–minute color 16 mm film ($50 rental) and ($225) and super 8 mm cartridges ($150) from Sports Investors]

Quick Cures for Common Tennis Problems. [57–minute video cassette ($69.96) from Johnson-Nyquist Productions]

Revolution in Church Road. [52–minute color 16 mm film ($45 rental) and ($394) and video cassette ($62, " and $120, ") from Sports World Cinema]

Serve! [14–minute B/W or color 16 mm film ($40 rental and $200 B/W and $295 color) from Sportlite]

The Serve and Volley. [16–minute color 16 mm film (free loan) from USTA National Film Library]

Seven Days in May. [26–minute color 16 mm film ($35 rental) and ($295) from Sportlite]

Shoot Out at High Noon. [26–minute color 16 mm film ($35 rental) and ($295) from Sportlite and video cassette ($62, " and $120, ") from Sports World Cinema]

65,000 Miles to Dallas. [25–minute color 16 mm film ($35 rental) and ($295) from Sportlite and 51 –minute color video cassette ($62, " and $120, ") from Sports World Cinema]

Sportvision: Workout for Racquet Sports. [60–minute video cassette ($39) from SPORTection, Inc.]

Strokes. [12 –minute color 16 mm film ($15/day rental) and ($185) from Brentwood]

SyberVision Tennis. [60–minute color video cassette ($89.95) from SyberVision Systems, Inc.]

Tennis. (A) [6–7–minute color 16 mm films ($79 each), super 8 mm cartridges ($24.95 each), and video cassette ($82, " and $107, ") from Champions on Film and Video]

Tennis. (B) [20–minute color 16 mm film ($285) and video cassette ($44.50, " and $149.50, ") from Forest Hills Productions]

Tennis. (C) [20–minute color 16 mm films ($40/segment rental) from Karol Media and ($305 each) from Athletic Institute, super 8 mm cassettes and film loops ($225 each) from Athletic Institute, and video cassettes ($815, " and $883, ") from Athletic Institute]

Tennis. (D) [9–minute color 16 mm films ($30/segment rental) from
    Karol Media and ($140 each) from Athletic Institute, super 8
    mm films and 35 mm filmstrips ($125) from Athletic Institute,
    and video cassette ($685) from Athletic Institute]

Tennis. (E) [1 –minute color, silent loop films ($50) and video cassettes
    ($55–$60) from Scope Productions]

Tennis. (F) [3 –minute color silent 8 mm film loops ($24.95/loop) from
    Athletic Institute]

Tennis Aces. [30–minute color video cassette ($125 each rental) and
    ($39.95 each, " and $250 each, ") from Video Tape Network]

Tennis, American Style. [24–minute color 16 mm film (free loan) from
    USTA National Film Library]

Tennis, Anyone? [30–minute color video cassette ($125 rental) and
    ($200, " and $300, ") from Time-Life Video]

Tennis Balls. [4–minute color 16 mm film ($35 rental) and ($125) and
    video cassette ($65) from Films, Inc.]

Tennis: Basic Tactics for Doubles. [13–minute color 16 mm film ($10.50
    rental) from Kent State University and ($240) from BFA Ed-
    ucational Media and video cassette ($36 rental) and ($150) from
    BFA Educational Media]

Tennis: Basic Tactics for Singles. [13–minute color 16 mm film ($11.50
    rental) from Pennsylvania State University and ($240) from
    BFA Educational Media and video cassette ($36 rental) and
    ($150) from BFA Educational Media]

Tennis Basics with Dennis Ralston. [8– and 10–minute color 16 mm
    films ($8.50/each rental) from Kent State University and ($160
    each) from Churchill Films and video cassettes ($160 each) from
    Churchill Films]

Tennis Class Organization. [15–minute color 16 mm film (free loan)
    from USTA National Film Library]

Tennis Everybody's Game. [28–minute color 16 mm film (free loan)
    from Association Films]

Tennis Everyone. [26–minute color 16 mm film (free loan) from West
    Glen Films and ($300) from Sportlite]

Tennis Fundamentals. [30–minute color 16 mm film ($425) from Ten-
    nis Films International]

Tennis Grips and Strokes. [11–minute color 16 mm film ($6 rental)
    from Indiana University and ($185) from BFA Educational Me-
    dia and video cassette ($28 rental) and ($125) from BFA Edu-
    cational Media]

Tennis: How to Play the Game. [14–minute color 35 mm filmstrips
    ($30 each) from Encyclopedia Britannica Educational
    Corporation]

Tennis Instruction. [18–minute color super 8 mm reels ($39.95 each)
and cartridges ($53.45 each) from Sportlite]

Tennis Lessons from Bjorn Borg. [60–minute color video cassette ($69.95
each) from Sportlite]

The Tennis Match. [16–minute color 16 mm film ($25 rental) and
($265) and video cassettes ($25 rental) and ($185) from Phoenix
Films]

Tennis Mothers. [14–minute color 16 mm film ($265) from Carousel
Films]

Tennis: The Nasty Way. [13– and 14–minute color 16 mm films ($8.50/
segment rental) from Kent State University and ($265/unit)
from AIMS Media and video cassettes ($265 each) from AIMS
Media]

Tennis Racquet. [7–minute color 16 mm film ($35 rental) and ($180
license) from Walt Disney]

Tennis Shoes. [4–minute color 16 mm film ($35 rental) and ($125) and
video cassette ($65) from Films, Inc.]

Tennis Teaching Skills: The Sensual Approach. [25–minute color video
cassette ($49.95, " and $59.95, ") from Advantage Video]

Tennis with Ken Rosewall. [25–minute color 16 mm film ($12 rental)
from USTA National Film Library]

And Then There Was One. [26 –minute color 16 mm film ($35 rental)
and ($295) from Sportlite and 53 –minute color video cassette
($62, " and $120, ") from Sports World Cinema]

Tips for Tennis. [11–minute color 16 mm films (free loan) from the
Coca Cola Company]

Tone Up for Tennis. [24–minute color 16 mm film from Vic Braden
Tennis College]

Tournament. [25–minute color 16 mm film ($50 rental) and ($255)
and super 8 mm cartridges ($150) from Sports Investors]

Tut Bartzen Tennis. [15–minute B/W 16 mm film ($40) from Sportlite]

U.S. Open 1975. [24–minute color 16 mm film ($35 rental) and ($192)
and 51–minute color video cassette ($62, " and $120, ") from
Sports World Cinema]

U.S. Open 1976. [30–minute color 16 mm film ($35 rental) and ($200)
and video cassette ($62, " and $120, ") from Sports World Cinema]

U.S. Open 1977. [25–minute color 16 mm film ($35 rental) and ($216)
from Sports World Cinema]

U.S. Open 1978. [24–minute color 16 mm film ($35 rental) and ($192)
from Sports World Cinema]

U.S. Open 1979. [20–minute color 16 mm film (free loan) from USTA
National Film Library and ($350) from WW Films]

U.S. Open 1980. [27–minute color 16 mm film (free loan) from USTA and ($350) from WW Films]

U.S. Open 1981. [27–minute color 16 mm film ($12 rental) and ($300) from USTA National Film Library]

U.S. Open 1982. [27–minute color 16 mm film ($12 rental) from USTA National Film Library and video cassette ($75) from WW Films]

United States Open Clay Court Tennis Championships. (1979) [25–minute color 16 mm film (free loan) from USTA National Film Library]

United States Open Clay Court Tennis Championships. (1980) [27–minute color 16 mm film (free loan) from USTA National Film Library]

United States Open Clay Court Championships. (1981) [28–minute color 16 mm film ($12 rental) from USTA National Film Library]

U.S. Open Clay Court Championships. (1982) [28–minute color 16 mm film ($12 rental) from USTA National Film Library]

USTA: The First Hundred Years. [28–minute color 16 mm film (free loan) USTA National Film Library and ($350) from Bay State Productions]

Ustinov at Wimbledon. (1975) [52–minute color 16 mm film (free loan) from Rolex Watch U.S.A. and ($730) from Trans World International and video cassette ($62, " and $120, ") from Sports World Cinema]

The Van der Meer Clinic at Forest Hills. [14–minute color 16 mm film (free loan) from USTA National Film Library]

Vic Braden's Tennis for the Future. [20–minute color 16 mm film (free loan) from USTA National Film Library]

Vic Braden Tennis Training Films. [3– and 5–minute color 16 mm films ($1043), super 8 mm films or cassettes, ($60—$90), and video cassettes ($320 each) from Johnson-Nyquist Productions]

Vitas Gerulaitis. [20–minute color 16 mm film ($12 rental) from USTA National Film Library]

Volvo International Tennis Tournament. [20–minute color 16 mm film (free loan) from USTA National Film Library]

We Shall Return. [24–minute color 16 mm film (free loan) from USTA National Film Library]

The Weekend Athletes. [48–minute color 16 mm film ($65/week rental) and ($695) and video cassette ($695) from Best Films]

What You Should Know about Tennis. [30–minute color 16 mm film (free loan) from USTA National Film Library]

Why Warm Up? [35 mm filmstrip ($10 rental) and ($20) and slides ($130) from Association Films]

Wimbledon 1977. [52–minute color 16 mm film (free loan) from Rolex Watch U.S.A. and ($730) from Trans World International]

Wimbledon 1978. [52–minute color 16 mm film (free loan) from Rolex Watch U.S.A. and ($730) from Trans World International]

Wimbledon 1979. [52–minute color 16 mm film (free loan) from Rolex Watch U.S.A. and ($730) from Trans World International]

Wimbledon 1980. [52–minute color 16 mm film (free loan) from Rolex Watch U.S.A. and ($730) from Trans World International]

Wimbledon 1981. [52–minute color 16 mm film (free loan) from Rolex Watch U.S.A. and ($730) from Trans World International]

Wimbledon 1982. [52–minute color 16 mm film (free loan) from Rolex Watch U.S.A. and ($730) from Trans World International]

The Winning Serve. [15–minute color 16 mm film ($260) from Golden Door]

Winning Tennis Strokes. [60–minute video cassette ($69.95) from Johnson-Nyquist Productions]

Women's Tennis. [3 –minute color super 8 mm loop films ($24.95 each) from Champions on Film and Video]

Yannick Noah. [37–minute color 16 mm film ($12 rental) from USTA National Film Library]

The Youngest Champion. [26–minute color 16 mm film ($35 rental) and ($295) from Sportlite and video cassette ($62, " and $120, ") from Sports World Cinema]

You're Playing at Wimbledon. [27–minute color 16 mm film ($12 rental) from USTA National Film Library and 51–minute color video cassette ($62, " and $120, ") from Sports World Cinema]

You've Come a Long Way, Baby. [25–minute color 16 mm film ($50 rental) and ($225) and video cassette ($150) from Sports Investors]

DISTRIBUTOR ADDRESS LIST

Advantage Video
16325 S.W. Boones Ferry Road
Lake Oswego, OR 97034

Aetna Life and Casualty
Audio-Visual Resources, DA02
Hartford, CT 06516
203–273–0123

AIMS Media
626 Justin Avenue
Glendale, CA 91201
213–240–9300

Association Films
866 Third Avenue
New York, NY 10022
212–935–4210

Athletic Institute
200 Castle Wood Drive
North Palm Beach, FL 33408
305–842–3600

Bay State Productions
35 Springfield Street
Agawam, MA 01001
413–786–4454

Bell and Howell Video Systems Division
720 Landwehr Road
Northbrook, IL 60062

Best Films
Box 725
Delmar, CA 92014
714–755–9327

BFA Educational Media
A Division of Phoenix Films
468 Park Avenue South
New York, NY 10016
212–684–5910

Brentwood Productions
P.O. Box 49956
Los Angeles, CA 90049
213–472–0868

Caravatt Communications and Home Entertainment
551 Fifth Avenue
New York, NY 10176

Carousel Films
241 East 34th Street, Room 304
New York, NY 10016
212–683–1660

Champions on Film and Video
P.O. Box 1941
Ann Arbor, MI 48106
313–761–5175

Churchill Films
662 North Robertson Boulevard
Los Angeles, CA 90069
213–657–5110

The Coca Cola Company
Media Center/NAT-2
P.O. Drawer 1734
Atlanta, GA 30301
404–898–2606

Encyclopedia Britannica Educational Corporation
425 North Michigan Avenue
Chicago, IL 60611
312–321–6800
800–621–3900

Eye Gate Media
146–1 Archer Avenue
Jamaica, NY 11435
212–291–9100

Films, Inc.
733 Green Bay Road
Wilmette, IL 60091
800–323–4222

Forest Hills Productions
Box A619, Madison Square Station
New York, NY 10010
212–473–4413

Golden Door Productions
Tenth and Parker
Berkeley, CA 94710
415–849–3571

Indiana University
Audio Visual Center
Bloomington, IN 47405
812–355–2103

Johnson-Nyquist Productions, Inc.
23854 Via Fabricante, D-1
Mission Viejo, CA 92691
714–770–5777

Karol Media
625 From Road
Paramus, NJ 07652
201–262–4170

Kent State University
Audio Visual Services
Kent, OH 44242
216–672–3456

Maryland Center for Public Broadcasting
Program Circulation Manager
Owings Mills, MD 21117
301–356–5600

Oklahoma State University
Audio Visual Center
Stillwater, OK 74078
405–624–7216

Pennsylvania State University
Audio Visual Services
Special Services Building
University Park, PA 16801
814–865–6314

Phoenix Films
468 Park Avenue South
New York, NY 10016
212–684–5910

Rolex Watch U.S.A.
665 5th Avenue
New York, NY 10022
212–758–7700

Scholastic Coach Athletic Services
50 West 44th Street
New York, NY 10036
212–944–7700, ext. 746

Scope Productions
P.O. Box 206
Ahwahnee, CA 93601
209–683–6003

SPORTection
Toronto, Canada

Sportlite Films
230 North Michigan Avenue
Chicago, IL 60601
312–236–8955

Sports Films and Talents
12755 State Highway 55
Minneapolis, MN 55441
612–540–5970

Sports Investors, Inc.
1107 Broadway, 7th Floor
New York, NY 10010
212–741–2323

Sports World Cinema
P.O. Box 17022
Salt Lake City, UT 84117
801–486–3925

SyberVision Systems, Inc.
2450 Washington Avenue, Dept. 270
San Leandro, CA 94577

Tennis Films International
44 Puritan Road
Newton Highlands, MA 02161
617–244–3883

Time-Life Video
100 Eisenhower Drive
P.O. Box 644
Paramus, NJ 07652
201–843–4545

Trans World International
2–4 Wendell Road
London W12 9RT
England
01–743–7501

Two Star Films
P.O. Box 495
Saint James, NY 11780
516–584–7285

USTA National Film Library
729 Alexander Road
Princeton, NJ 08540
609–452–2580

Vic Braden Tennis College
22000 Plano Trabuco Canyon Road
Trabuco Canyon, CA 92678

Video Tape Network
33 East 68th Street
New York, NY 10021
212–570–1200

W W Films
1650 Broadway, 4th Floor
New York, NY 10019
212–541–9441

Walt Disney Education Media Company
500 South Buena Vista Street
Burbank, CA 91521
213–840–1726

West Glen Films
1430 Broadway
New York, NY 10018
212–921–0966

14

Tennis in General Works, General and Specific Periodicals, and Promotional Organizations

Tennis is a part of numerous comprehensive sports books, the focus of several specific periodicals, and a feature in other sports publications. In addition to the written word, some tennis organizations promote participation, the development of junior players, and the training of instructors.

Of the numerous general works that discuss all sports, most briefly recount the history of tennis and describe its growth while another group briefly explains how to play each sport. Illustrative of this later group are books such as *Rules of the Game*, a complete illustrated encyclopedia of all the sports of the world, *Sports Skills: A Conceptual Approach to Meaningful Movement* by Beverly Seidel, Fay Biles, Grace Figley, and Bonnie Neuman, *Physical Education Handbook* by Don Seaton, Neil Schmottlach, Irene Clayton, Howard Leibee, and Lloyd Messersmith, and *Sports and Recreational Activities of Men and Women* by Dale Mood, Frank Musker, and David Armbruster. These and other similar books briefly describe the rules, the techniques, the terminology, and the strategies of many sports.

The general sport history works describe the evolution of all sports as they relate to developments in society as a whole. John Betts' *America's Sporting Heritage, 1850–1950* and Wells Twombly's *200 Years of Sport in America: A Pageant of a Nation at Play* are good examples since neither focuses on tennis as much as describing its development within a larger context. John Arlott's *The Oxford Companion to World Sports and Games* devotes eighteen pages to the game, its championships, and international play. Frederick Cozens and Florence Stumpf provide a brief history of the game plus information about junior programs, the Olympics, vacation spots, school programs, and tennis as a recreational sport in *Sports in American Life*. The history of tennis and its stars is the focus of *The Official Encyclopedia of Sports* by John Pratt and Jim Benagh. *Sport: Mirror of American Life* by Robert Boyle includes a cursory overview of tennis. Descriptions of early champions and a history of the game comprise *Annals of American Sport* by John Krout. In *The Encyclopedia of Sports* Frank Menke explains the history of tennis and provides listings of the champions in Davis Cup, Wightman Cup, Federation Cup, Wimbledon, United States, intercollegiate, French, early professional tours, World Championship of Tennis, Virginia Slims, and World Team Tennis events. Menke's *The All-Sports Record Book* chronicles the players who won the United States' nationals, clay, hard, indoor, public parks, intercollegiate, and veterans' events, Wimbledon, Australian, Canadian, French, and Australasia championships, Davis Cup and Wightman Cup matches, United States rankings, professional events, and records of outstanding players. Ralph Hickok's *New Encyclopedia of Sports* decribes tennis' development and some of its stars in addition to listing champions. Herbert Wind's *The Gilded Age of Sport* includes three articles about tennis—one about the game in Australia, another about Gussie Moran, and the third about Hazel Wightman. Wind's *The Realm of Sport* is an anthology of classic works about the world's great sporting events and personalities. Among the topics of its ten tennis articles are Suzanne Lenglen, the Davis Cup, Bill Tilden, and Wimbledon.

Paula Welch and Harold Lerch in *History of American Physical Education and Sport* and Betty Spears and Richard Swanson in *History of Sport and Physical Activity in the United States* examine the development of sports in this country. Both also include a look at the Olympic Games, including tennis between 1896 and 1924. In *Saga of American Sport* John Lucas and Ronald Smith focus on early American sport, sport in transition, and twentieth century sport. Their discussion of women in sport, blacks in sport, and intercollegiate sport is especially timely and analytical. After a brief look at early games, Benjamin Rader describes in depth the age of the player (the elite, the outsiders, and sporting ideology), the age of the spectator (heroes, team sports, individual sports, professional and college sports), and equal opportunity for blacks and women in *American Sports: From the Age of Folk Games to the Age of Spectators*. *Sports in the Western World* by William Baker begins its tracing of sport history in early societies, especially in Greece, highlights the English popularization of modern games, and explains the positive and negative aspects of sports in the United States today. The athletes and their sports, the patrons who organize, govern, and promote contests, the spectators, and the commentators are the constants in this historical narrative.

While popular magazines from *Playboy* to *Mademoiselle* and *Newsweek* to *Times* occasionally have feature articles about tennis stars or events, none of these has a column devoted just to tennis. Enthusiasts would be more likely to find instructional advice in the *Athletic Journal, The Coaching Clinic,* or *Scholastic Coach*. In each of these monthly publications high school and college coaches describe playing techniques, strategies, drills, and philosophies. *Athletic Business* is a monthly magazine for the planning, financing, and operating of athletic, recreational, and fitness programs and facilities. *Women's Sports and Fitness* (monthly) and *Sports Illustrated* (weekly) include coverage of all sports including but not emphasizing tennis.

Numerous tennis periodicals appeared through its over a century of development as a popular pastime and a competitive sport. In some cases the exact dates of the first and last issues are impossible to determine. The United States National Lawn Tennis Association published the *Official Lawn Tennis Bulletin* monthly from 1894–1898, except weekly July 4 through September 12. Like most of these periodicals it included tournament results, player profiles, and general information about tennis. Between 1929–1932 the United States Lawn Tennis Association issued *Tennis* on a monthly basis which replaced the *Bulletin*. *American Lawn Tennis* (also known as *The Racquet*) from April 15, 1907–October 1953 was another monthly publication of this group. Replacing the United States Lawn Tennis Association's *Official News, Tennis U.S.A.* (monthly) offered features and instructional advice until May 1979. Jahial Paret issued *Lawn Tennis* (monthly) between May 1901–April 1903. He included tennis results, articles, and notices. *Lawn Tennis* from April 1907, is the English Lawn Tennis Association's official bulletin. On an irregular basis the Eastern Lawn Tennis Association published the *William M. Fischer Lawn Tennis Library Record* between March 1949–August 1960.

Currently at least ten countries other than the United States, including Australia, Denmark, England, France, Italy, Japan, the Netherlands, South Africa, Sweden, and Switzerland, have tennis magazines. In the United States *Tennis, Magazine of the Racquet Sports* has the largest circulation of any tennis publication according to its advertising. Since May 1965 this monthly has provided instructional tips from current champions and teaching professionals, feature articles about players, tournament previews and results, equipment, travel, and related tennis miscellany. *World Tennis*, the monthly magazine of the membership of the United States Tennis Association since June 1953, offers similar instruction, results, and features. It has regular articles about equipment, travel, kids and tennis, and tennis around the world.

Tennis...Buyers Guide, semi-annually since 1984, *Tennis Industry Magazine*, eleven issues a year since September 1972, and *Tennis/Racquet Trade*, monthly since 1972, provide extensive listings of tennis equipment, clothing, and supplies. *Inside Women's Tennis*, a bimonthly international newspaper devoted to women's professional tennis, includes tournament results and stories, international rankings, upcoming events, and features. Similarly, the Association of Tennis Professionals, a men's group, issues its *International Tennis Weekly*. The Professional Tennis Registry publishes its *Tennis Pro Magazine* bimonthly as does the United States Professional Tennis Association in *Advantage Magazine*—both containing instructional advice from their memberships of teaching professionals. The Tennis Foundation of North America issues *Net Friends News*, a bimonthly news bulletin. The American Tennis Association helps promote tennis for blacks of all ages through its quarterly *Black Tennis*

Magazine. The National Foundation of Wheelchair Tennis publishes *Two Bounce News* (bimonthly) informing individuals with physical disabilities about clinics, camps, and tournaments available to them. *Tennis Week* (1974) is a thirty-issue per year, tabloid format periodical that lists current happenings in tennis.

Tennis organizations (see Appendix A) exist to promote tennis for all ages, skill levels, and specific groups. This may include the sponsorship of competitive events, publication of periodicals, improvement in quality of play, or recognition of outstanding players.

The American Medical Tennis Association (1967) organizes tennis tournaments for physicians and their families. The American Tennis Association began in 1916 to conduct tennis tournaments and to promote training programs for blacks. Children receive encouragement to play tennis in schools, playgrounds, and parks through the National Junior Tennis League (1969). In 1923 the National Public Parks Tennis Association joined together interested tennis groups at the public park level to encourage tennis programs for all. The United States Recreational Tennis Association (1976) promotes recreational tennis through the use of the United States Handicap/Rating Tennis System and sponsors tennis events. The Tennis Foundation of North America (1975) represents manufacturers of tennis equipment, apparel, accessories, builders, and trade publications in the promotion of competitive and recreational tennis.

The Women's Tennis Association (1973) helps organize professional women's tennis tournaments and represents its membership in tennis matters. World rankings and various promotional efforts have been among the responsibilities of the Association of Tennis Professionals since 1972 as they seek to improve male players' and spectators' tennis. Instructors and college coaches beginning in 1927 sought to improve tennis instruction through the activities of the United States Professional Tennis Association. The Professional Tennis Registry (1976) certifies and registers tennis teaching professionals, conducts clinics and workshops, and sponsors competition.

The National Foundation of Wheelchair Tennis (1980) and the Wheelchair Tennis Players Association (1980) share in the development of tennis programs for individuals with physical disabilities. The players' group promotes fairness and uniformity in the tournaments which the first association sponsors. The National Foundation also provides camps, clinics, junior programs, and on court demonstrations.

Newspaper and magazine writers, broadcast journalists, and photographers from several countries publicize tennis through their United States Tennis Writers Association. The United States Tennis Association (1881) represents over 210,000 members. In addition to its sponsorship of numerous national tournaments, it seeks to develop tennis as a recreational and fitness sport and to maintain high standards of amateurism, fair play, and sportsmanship. It promotes developmental programs for junior players, as well as sponsors this country's Davis Cup, Wightman Cup, and Federation Cup teams for juniors and adults. Since 1913 the International Tennis Federation has encouraged and developed the sport and has sought to ensure application of the international tennis code by the members of the national associations in seventy-seven countries.

The National Tennis Hall of Fame opened in 1954 at the Newport Casino Tennis Club, the original home of the men's national singles championship, through the leadership of James Van Alen and the approval of the United States Tennis Association. In 1976 it recognized the first international honorees. Selection is based on character and sportsmanship in addition to championship play or significant contributions to tennis. The honorees are listed in Appendix B. The renamed International Tennis Hall of Fame contains an outstanding reference library, many out-of-print books, early rackets, the Sears Bowl (the first national championship trophy), and two acres of tennis courts. The Citizens Savings Tennis Hall of Fame (1949) also recognizes outstanding players and tennis contributors (See Appendix C). This is one of its thirty-one halls of fame that honor athletes from all sports.

General sports books and journals along with specialized periodicals and organizations explain the history of tennis as well as inform people about the latest champions, playing styles, tournaments, and equipment. Each plays a valuable role in popularizing and promoting the sport of tennis.

BIBLIOGRAPHY: GENERAL WORKS

Arlott, John, ed. *The Oxford Companion to World Sports and Games.* London: Oxford University Press, 1975.

Baker, William J. *Sports in the Western World.* Totowa, New Jersey: Rowman and Littlefield, 1982.

Betts, John R. *America's Sporting Heritage, 1850–1950.* Reading, Massachusetts: Addison: Wesley Publishing Company, 1974.

Boyle, Robert H. *Sport: Mirror of American Life.* Boston: Little, Brown, and Company, 1963.

Cozens, Frederick W., and Stumpf, Florence S. *Sports in American Life.* New York: Arno Press, 1976.

Hickok, Ralph. *New Encyclopedia of Sports.* New York: McGraw-Hill Book Company, 1977.

Krout, John Allen. *Annals of American Sport.* Pageant of America Series, vol. 15. New Haven: Yale University Press, 1929.

Lucas, John A., and Smith, Ronald A. *Saga of American Sport.* Philadelphia: Lea and Febiger, 1978.

Menke, Frank G. *The All-Sports Record Book.* New York: A. S. Barnes and Company, 1950.

———. *The Encyclopedia of Sports.* 6th ed. New York: A. S. Barnes and Company, 1977.

Mood, Dale, Musker, Frank F., and Armbruster, David. *Sports and Recreational Activities for Men and Women.* St. Louis: C. V. Mosby Company, 1983.

Pratt, John Lowell, and Benagh, Jim. *The Official Encyclopedia of Sports.* New York: Franklin Watts, 1964.

Rader, Benjamin G. *American Sports: From the Age of Folk Games to the Age of Spectators.* Englewood Cliffs, New Jersey: Prentice-Hall, 1983.

Rules of the Game. New York: Paddington Press, 1974.

Seaton, Don C., et al. *Physical Education Handbook.* 7th ed. Englewood Cliffs, New Jersey: Prentice-Hall, 1983.

Seidel, Beverly L., et al. *Sports Skills: A Conceptual Approach to Meaningful Movement.* Dubuque, Iowa: William C. Brown Company Publishers, 1980.

Spears, Betty, and Swanson, Richard A., 2nd ed. *History of Sport and Physical Activity in the United States.* Dubuque, Iowa: William C. Brown Publishers, 1983.

Twombly, Wells. *200 Years of Sport in America: A Pageant of a Nation at Play.* New York: McGraw-Hill, 1976.

Welch, Paula D., and Lerch, Harold A. *History of American Physical Education and Sport.* Springfield, Illinois: Charles C. Thomas, 1981.
Wind, Herbert Warren. *The Gilded Age of Sport.* New York: Simon and Schuster, 1961.
————. *The Realm of Sport.* New York: Simon and Schuster, 1966.

BIBLIOGRAPHY: GENERAL SPORT JOURNALS

Athletic Business. 1842 Hoffman Street, Suite 201, Madison, Wisconsin 53704
Athletic Journal. 1719 Howard Street, Evanston, Illinois 60202
The Coaching Clinic. Princeton Educational Publishers, CN 5245, Princeton, New Jersey 08540
Scholastic Coach. 50 West 44th Street, New York, New York 10036
Sports Illustrated. Time, Inc., Time and Life Building, New York, New York 10020
Women's Sports and Fitness. 310 Town and Country Village, Palo Alto, California 94301

BIBLIOGRAPHY: TENNIS PERIODICALS

Advantage Magazine. United States Professional Tennis Association, 1621 Gulf of Mexico Drive, Longboat Key, Florida 33548.
American Lawn Tennis (The Racquet). United States Lawn Tennis Association.
Black Tennis Magazine. American Tennis Association, 475 Riverside Drive, Suite 439, New York, New York 10115.
Inside Women's Tennis. Women's Tennis Association, 1604 Union Street, San Francisco, California 94123.
International Tennis Weekly. Association of Tennis Professionals, 319 Country Club Road, Garland, Texas 75040.
Lawn Tennis. London: Lawn Tennis Association.
Net Friends News. Tennis Foundation of North America, 200 Castlewood Court, North Palm Beach, Florida 33408.
Official Lawn Tennis Bulletin. United States National Lawn Tennis Association.
Paret, Jahiel Parmly. *Lawn Tennis.* New York: Lawn Tennis Publishing Company.
Tennis. United States Lawn Tennis Association.

Tennis... Buyers Guide. Ziff Davis Publishing Company, One Park
    Avenue, New York, New York, 10016.
Tennis Industry Magazine. Industry Publishers, Inc., 1545 N.E. 123rd
    Street, North Miami, Florida 33161.
Tennis, Magazine of the Racquet Sports. Golf Digest/Tennis, Inc., 495
    Westport Avenue, P.O. Box 5350, Norwalk, Connecticut 06856.
Tennis Pro Magazine. Professional Tennis Registry, P.O. Box 5902,
    Hilton Head Island, South Carolina 29938.
Tennis/Racquet Trade. Charnin Building, Room 1749, 122 East 42nd
    Street, New York, New York 10017.
Tennis Week. Tennis News, Inc., 1007 Broadway, New York, New
    York 10010.
Tennis U.S.A. United States Lawn Tennis Association.
Two Bounce News. National Foundation of Wheelchair Tennis. 3857
    Birch Street, Newport Beach, California 92660.
William M. Fischer Lawn Tennis Library Record. Eastern Lawn Ten-
    nis Association.
World Tennis. 1515 Broadway, New York, New York 10036.

Appendix A

Tennis Organizations

American Medical Tennis Association
P.O. Box 183
Alton, Illinois 62002
(618) 462–6841

American Tennis Association
475 Riverside Drive
Suite 439
New York, New York 10115
(212) 870–2660

Association of Tennis Professionals
319 Country Club Road
Garland, Texas 75040
(214) 494–5991

Citizens Savings
Hall of Fame Athletic Museum
9800 S. Sepulveda Boulevard
Los Angeles, California 90045
(213) 670–7550

International Tennis Federation
2 Avenue George Bennett
F-75016
Paris, France
651 21 09

International Tennis Hall of Fame
194 Bellevue Avenue
Newport, Rhode Island 02840
(401) 846–4567

National Foundation of Wheelchair Tennis
3857 Birch Street
Newport Beach, California 92660
(714) 851–1707

National Junior Tennis League
25 West 39th Street
Suite 1105
New York, New York 10018
(212) 869–3322

National Public Parks Tennis Association
P.O. Box 60076
Los Angeles, California 90060
(213) 622–6123

Professional Tennis Registry
P.O. Box 5902
Hilton Head Island, South Carolina 29938
(800) 845–6138

Tennis Foundation of North America
200 Castlewood Court
North Palm Beach, Florida 33408
(305) 848–1026

United States Professional Tennis Association
1621 Gulf of Mexico Drive
Longboat Key, Florida 33548
(813) 383–5555

United States Recreational Tennis Association
3112 Adderly Court
Silver Spring, Maryland 20906
(301) 598–4819

United States Tennis Association
51 E. 42nd Street
New York, New York 10017
(212) 949–9112

United States Tennis Association Education and Research Center
729 Alexander Road
Princeton, New Jersey 08540
(609) 452–2580

United States Tennis Writers Association
c/o H.O. Zimman, Inc.
156 Broad Street
Lynn, Massachusetts 01901
(617) 598–9230

Wheelchair Tennis Players Association
3857 Birch Street
Newport Beach, California 92660
(714) 669–1453

Appendix B

International Tennis Hall of Fame

Pauline Betz Addie
George T. Adee
Fred B. Alexander
Wilmer L. Allison
Manuel Alonso
Juliette Atkinson
Lawrence A. Baker
Maud Barger-Wallach
Karl Behr
Jean Borotra
Maureen Connolly Brinker
John Bromwich
Norman Everard Brookes
Mary K. Browne
Jacques Brugnon
J. Donald Budge
Maria Bueno
May Sutton Bundy
Mabel Cahill
Oliver S. Campbell
Malcolm Chace
Dorothea Lambert-Chambers
Louise Brough Clapp
Clarence Clark
Joseph S. Clark

William J. Clothier
Henri Cochet
Margaret Smith Court
Gofttfried von Cramm
John H. Crawford
Allison Danzig
Sarah Palfrey Danzig
Dwight F. Davis
Lottie Dod
John H. Doeg
H. Laurence Doherty
Reginald Doherty
Jaroslav Drobny
Margaret Osborne duPont
Dr. James Dwight
Roy Emerson
Pierre Etchebaster
Robert Falkenburg
Neale Fraser
Charles S. Garland
Althea Gibson
Kathleen McKane Godfree
Richard A. Gonzales
Bryan M. Grant, Jr.
Clarence Griffin

Gustaf V, King of Sweden
Harold H. Hackett
Ellen Forde Hansell
Darlene R. Hard
Doris Hart
Gladys Heldman
William E. Hester
Lewis Hoad
Harry Hopman
Fred Hovey
Joseph R. Hunt
Francis T. Hunter
Shirley Fry Irvin
Helen Hull Jacobs
William Johnston
Perry Jones
John A. Kramer
Rene Lacoste
Al Laney
William A. Larned
Arthur D. Larsen
Rod Laver
Suzanne Lenglen
George M. Lott, Jr.
Maurice McLoughlin
W. Donald McNeill
C. Gene Mako
Molla Bjurstedt Mallory
Alice Marble
Alastair B. Martin
William McChesney Martin
Elizabeth H. Moore
Gardnar Mulloy
R. Lindley Murray
Julian S. Myrick
Arthur C. Nielsen, Sr.
Rafael Osuna
Mary Ewing Outerbridge
Frank A. Parker
Budge Patty
Theodore R. Pell

Frederick J. Perry
Tom Pettitt
Adrian Quist
Ernest Renshaw
William Renshaw
Vincent Richards
Robert L. Riggs
Helen Wills Roark
Ellen C. Roosevelt
Kenneth Rosewall
Elizabeth Ryan
Manuel Santana
Richard Savitt
Frederick R. Schroeder
Eleonora Sears
Richard D. Sears
Frank Sedgman
Pancho Segura
E. Victor Seixas, Jr.
Francis X. Shields
Betty Nuthall Shoemaker
Henry W. Slocum, Jr.
William F. Talbert
William T. Tilden, II
Lance Tingay
Bertha Townsend Toulmin
Tony Trabert
James H. Van Alen
John Van Ryn
H. Ellsworth Vines
Marie Wagner
Holcombe Ward
Watson Washburn
Malcolm D. Whitman
Hazel Hotchkiss Wightman
Anthony Wilding
Richard Norris Williams, II
Sidney B. Wood
Robert D. Wrenn
Beals C. Wright

Appendix C

Citizens Savings Tennis Hall of Fame

Addie, Pauline Betz
Allison, Wilmer Lawson, Jr.
Atkinson, Juliette
Brinker, Maureen Connolly
Browne, Mary K.
Budge, J. Donald
Bundy, May Sutton
Campbell, Oliver Samuel
Clapp, Louise Brough
Danzig, Sarah Palfrey Cooke
Darben, Althea Gibson
Davis, Dwight Filley
Denny, Victor (c)
duPont, Margaret Osborne
Gonzales, Richard A.
Gunter, Nancy Richey
Hard, Darlene R.
Hart, Doris
Irvin, Shirley Fry
Jacobs, Helen Hull
Johnston, William
Jones, Perry T. (c)
King, Billie Jean Moffitt
Kramer, John Albert

Larned, William A.
Lott, George M., Jr.
McKinley, Charles R.
McLoughlin, Maurice Evans
Mako, Gene
Mallory, Molla Bjurstedt
Marble, Alice
Moore, Elizabeth H.
Murray, R. Lindley
Myrick, Julian S. (c)
Parker, Frank A.
Richards, Vincent
Riggs, Robert Lorimer
Roark, Helen Wills Moody
Ryan, Elizabeth
Schroeder, Frederick R., Jr.
Sears, Richard Dudley
Seixas, Elias Victor, Jr.
Tilden, William Tatem, III
Trabert, Marion
Vines, H. Ellsworth
Ward, Holcombe
Whitman, Malcolm D.
Wightman, Hazel Hotchkiss
Williams, Richard Norris, II
Wrenn, Robert D.

(c) = contributors, all other players

Appendix D

Champions of Team Competitions

DAVIS CUP FINALS

1900 U.S. d. Britain, 3–0
1901 No match
1902 U.S. d. Britain, 3–2
1903 Britain d. U.S., 4–1
1904 Britain d. Belgium, 5–0
1905 Britain d. U.S., 5–0
1906 Britain d. U.S., 5–0
1907 Australasia d. Britain, 3–2
1908 Australasia d. U.S., 3–2
1909 Australasia d. U.S., 5–0
1910 No match
1911 Australasia d. U.S., 5–0
1912 Britain d. Australasia, 3–2
1913 U.S. d. Britain, 3–2
1914 Australasia d. U.S., 3–2
1915–18 No matches
1919 Australasia d. Britain, 4–1
1920 U.S. d. Australasia, 5–0
1921 U.S. d. Japan, 5–0
1922 U.S. d. Australasia, 4–1
1923 U.S. d. Australasia, 4–1
1924 U.S. d. Australasia, 5–0
1925 U.S. d. France, 4–1
1926 U.S. d. France, 4–1
1927 France d. U.S., 3–2
1928 France d. U.S., 4–1
1929 France d. U.S., 3–2
1930 France d. U.S., 4–1
1931 France d. Britain, 3–2
1932 France d. U.S., 3–2
1933 Britain d. France, 3–2
1934 Britain d. U.S., 4–1
1935 Britain d. U.S., 5–0
1936 Britain d. Australia, 3–2
1937 U.S. d. Britain, 4–1
1938 U.S. d. Australia, 3–2
1939 U.S. d. Australia, 3–2
1940–45 No matches
1946 U.S. d. Australia, 5–0
1947 U.S. d. Australia, 4–1
1948 U.S. d. Australia, 5–0
1949 U.S. d. Australia, 4–1
1950 Australia d. U.S., 4–1
1951 Australia d. U.S., 3–2
1952 Australia d. U.S., 4–1
1953 Australia d. U.S., 3–2
1954 U.S. d. Australia, 3–2
1955 Australia d. U.S., 5–0

1956 Australia d. U.S., 5–0
1957 Australia d. U.S., 3–2
1958 U.S. d. Australia, 3–2
1959 Australia d. U.S., 3–2
1960 Australia d. Italy, 4–1
1961 Australia d. Italy, 5–0
1962 Australia d. Mexico, 5–0
1963 U.S. d. Australia, 3–2
1964 Australia d. U.S., 3–2
1965 Australia d. Spain, 4–1
1966 Australia d. India, 4–1
1967 Australia d. Spain, 4–1
1968 U.S. d. Australia, 4–1
1969 U.S. d. Rumania, 5–0
1970 U.S. d. West Germany, 5–0
1971 U.S. d. Rumania, 3–2
1972 U.S. d. Rumania, 3–2
1973 Australia d. U.S., 5–0
1974 South Africa d. India
    (default)
1975 Sweden d. Czechoslovakia,
    3–2
1976 Italy d. Chile, 3–2
1977 Australia d. Italy, 3–1
1978 U.S. d. Britain, 4–1
1979 U.S. d. Italy, 5–0
1980 Czechoslovakia d. Italy,
    4–1
1981 U.S. d. Argentina, 3–1
1982 U.S. d. France, 4–1
1983 Australia d. Sweden, 3–2
1984 Sweden d. U.S., 4–1

THE WIGHTMAN CUP

1923 U.S. d. Britain, 7–0
1924 Britain d. U.S., 6–1
1925 Britain d. U.S., 4–3
1926 U.S. d. Britain, 4–3
1927 U.S. d. Britain, 4–3
1928 Britain d. U.S., 4–3
1929 U.S. d. Britain, 4–3
1930 Britain d. U.S., 4–3

1931 U.S. d. Britain, 5–2
1932 U.S. d. Britain, 4–3
1933 U.S. d. Britain, 4–3
1934 U.S. d. Britain, 5–2
1935 U.S. d. Britain, 4–3
1936 U.S. d. Britain, 4–3
1937 U.S. d. Britain, 6–1
1938 U.S. d. Britain, 5–2
1939 U.S. d. Britain, 5–2
1940–45 No matches
1946 U.S. d. Britain, 7–0
1947 U.S. d. Britain, 7–0
1948 U.S. d. Britain, 6–1
1949 U.S. d. Britain, 7–0
1950 U.S. d. Britain, 7–0
1951 U.S. d. Britain, 6–1
1952 U.S. d. Britain, 5–2
1953 U.S. d. Britain, 7–0
1954 U.S. d. Britain, 6–0
1955 U.S. d. Britain, 6–1
1956 U.S. d. Britain, 5–2
1957 U.S. d. Britain, 6–1
1958 Britain d. U.S., 4–3
1959 U.S. d. Britain, 4–3
1960 Britain d. U.S., 4–3
1961 U.S. d. Britain, 6–1
1962 U.S. d. Britain, 4–3
1963 U.S. d. Britain, 6–1
1964 U.S. d. Britain, 5–2
1965 U.S. d. Britain, 5–2
1966 U.S. d. Britain, 4–3
1967 U.S. d. Britain, 6–1
1968 Britain d. U.S., 4–3
1969 U.S. d. Britain, 5–2
1970 U.S. d. Britain, 4–3
1971 U.S. d. Britain, 4–3
1972 U.S. d. Britain, 5–2
1973 U.S. d. Britain, 5–2
1974 Britain d. U.S., 6–1
1975 Britain d. U.S., 5–2
1976 U.S. d. Britain, 5–2
1977 U.S. d. Britain, 7–0
1978 Britain d. U.S., 4–3

1979 U.S. d. Britain, 7–0
1980 U.S. d. Britain, 5–2
1981 U.S. d. Britain, 7–0
1982 U.S. d. Britain, 6–1
1983 U.S. d. Britain, 6–1
1984 U.S. d. Britain, 5–2

FEDERATION CUP FINALS

1963 U.S. d. Australia, 2–1
1964 Australia d. U.S., 2–1
1965 Australia d. U.S., 2–1
1966 U.S. d. West Germany, 3–0
1967 U.S. d. Britain, 2–0
1968 Australia d. Netherlands, 3–0
1969 U.S. d. Australia, 2–1
1970 Australia d. West Germany, 3–0
1971 Australia d. Britain, 3–0
1972 South Africa d. Britain, 2–1
1973 Australia d. South Africa, 3–0
1974 Australia d. U.S., 2–1
1975 Czechoslovakia d. Australia, 3–0
1976 U.S. d. Australia, 2–1
1977 U.S. d. Australia, 2–1
1978 U.S. d. Australia, 2–1
1979 U.S. d. Australia, 3–0
1980 U.S. d. Australia, 3–0
1981 U.S. d. Britain, 3–0
1982 U.S. d. West Germany, 3–0
1983 Czechoslovakia d. West Germany, 2–1
1984 Czechoslovakia d. Australia, 2–1

Appendix E

United States Champions

Years in which there were two champions are marked with asterisks. The first name listed was champion of the amateur event, and the second was champion of the open event.

MEN'S SINGLES

1881 Richard Sears
1882 Richard Sears
1883 Richard Sears
1884 Richard Sears
1885 Richard Sears
1886 Richard Sears
1887 Richard Sears
1888 Henry Slocum
1889 Henry Slocum
1890 Oliver Campbell
1891 Oliver Campbell
1892 Oliver Campbell
1893 Robert Wrenn
1894 Robert Wrenn
1895 Frederick Hovey
1896 Robert Wrenn
1897 Robert Wrenn
1898 Malcolm Whitman
1899 Malcolm Whitman
1900 Malcolm Whitman
1901 William Larned
1902 William Larned
1903 Laurence Doherty
1904 Holcombe Ward
1905 Beals Wright
1906 William Clothier
1907 William Larned
1908 William Larned
1909 William Larned
1910 William Larned
1911 William Larned
1912 Maurice McLoughlin
1913 Maurice McLoughlin
1914 Richard Williams
1915 Bill Johnston
1916 Richard Williams
1917 Lindley Murray
1918 Lindley Murray
1919 Bill Johnston
1920 Bill Tilden

1921 Bill Tilden
1922 Bill Tilden
1923 Bill Tilden
1924 Bill Tilden
1925 Bill Tilden
1926 Rene Lacoste
1927 Rene Lacoste
1928 Henri Cochet
1929 Bill Tilden
1930 John Doeg
1931 Ellsworth Vines
1932 Ellsworth Vines
1933 Fred Perry
1934 Fred Perry
1935 Wilmer Allison
1936 Fred Perry
1937 Don Budge
1938 Don Budge
1939 Bobby Riggs
1940 Don McNeill
1941 Bobby Riggs
1942 Ted Schroeder
1943 Joseph Hunt
1944 Frank Parker
1945 Frank Parker
1946 Jack Kramer
1947 Jack Kramer
1948 Pancho Gonzales
1949 Pancho Gonzales
1950 Art Larsen
1951 Frank Sedgman
1952 Frank Sedgman
1953 Tony Trabert
1954 Vic Seixas
1955 Tony Trabert
1956 Ken Rosewall
1957 Mal Anderson
1958 Ashley Cooper
1959 Neale Fraser
1960 Neale Fraser
1961 Roy Emerson
1962 Rod Laver
1963 Rafael Osuna

1964 Roy Emerson
1965 Manuel Santana
1966 Fred Stolle
1967 John Newcombe
*1968 Arthur Ashe
1968 Arthur Ashe
*1969 Stan Smith
*1969 Rod Laver
1970 Ken Rosewall
1971 Stan Smith
1972 Ilie Nastase
1973 John Newcombe
1974 Jimmy Connors
1975 Manuel Orantes
1976 Jimmy Connors
1977 Guillermo Vilas
1978 Jimmy Connors
1979 John McEnroe
1980 John McEnroe
1981 John McEnroe
1982 Jimmy Connors
1983 Jimmy Connors
1984 John McEnroe

WOMEN'S SINGLES

1887 Ellen Hansell
1888 Bertha Townsend
1889 Bertha Townsend
1890 Ellen Roosevelt
1891 Mabel Cahill
1892 Mabel Cahill
1893 Aline Terry
1894 Helen Helwig
1895 Juliette Atkinson
1896 Elizabeth Moore
1897 Juliette Atkinson
1898 Juliette Atkinson
1899 Marion Jones
1900 Myrtle McAteer
1901 Elizabeth Moore
1902 Marion Jones
1903 Elizabeth Moore
1904 May Sutton

1905 Elizabeth Moore
1906 Helen Homans
1907 Evelyn Sears
1908 Maud Barger-Wallach
1909 Hazel Hotchkiss
1910 Hazel Hotchkiss
1911 Hazel Hotchkiss
1912 Mary Browne
1913 Mary Browne
1914 Mary Browne
1915 Molla Bjurstedt
1916 Molla Bjurstedt
1917 Molla Bjurstedt
1918 Molla Bjurstedt
1919 Hazel Wightman
1920 Molla Mallory
1921 Molla Mallory
1922 Molla Mallory
1923 Helen Wills
1924 Helen Wills
1925 Helen Wills
1926 Molla Mallory
1927 Helen Wills
1928 Helen Wills
1929 Helen Wills
1930 Betty Nuthall
1931 Helen Moody
1932 Helen Jacobs
1933 Helen Jacobs
1934 Helen Jacobs
1935 Helen Jacobs
1936 Alice Marble
1937 Anita Lizana
1938 Alice Marble
1939 Alice Marble
1940 Alice Marble
1941 Sarah Cooke
1942 Pauline Betz
1943 Pauline Betz
1944 Pauline Betz
1945 Sarah Cooke
1946 Pauline Betz
1947 Louise Brough

1948 Margaret duPont
1949 Margaret duPont
1950 Margaret duPont
1951 Maureen Connolly
1952 Maureen Connolly
1953 Maureen Connolly
1954 Doris Hart
1955 Doris Hart
1956 Shirley Fry
1957 Althea Gibson
1958 Althea Gibson
1959 Maria Bueno
1960 Darlene Hard
1961 Darlene Hard
1962 Margaret Smith
1963 Maria Bueno
1964 Maria Bueno
1965 Margaret Smith
1966 Maria Bueno
1967 Billie Jean King
*1968 Margaret Court
*1968 Virginia Wade
*1969 Margaret Court
*1969 Margaret Court
1970 Margaret Court
1971 Billie Jean King
1972 Billie Jean King
1973 Margaret Court
1974 Billie Jean King
1975 Chris Evert
1976 Chris Evert
1977 Chris Evert
1978 Chris Evert
1979 Tracy Austin
1980 Chris Evert-Lloyd
1981 Tracy Austin
1982 Chris Evert-Lloyd
1983 Martina Navratilova
1984 Martina Navratilova

MEN'S DOUBLES

1881 Clarence Clark–F. W.
      Taylor

1882 Richard Sears–James
     Dwight
1883 Richard Sears–James
     Dwight
1884 Richard Sears–James
     Dwight
1885 Richard Sears–Joseph
     Clark
1886 Richard Sears–James
     Dwight
1887 Richard Sears–James
     Dwight
1888 Oliver Campbell–V. G.
     Hall
1889 Henry Slocum–H. Taylor
1890 V. G. Hall–Clarence
     Hobart
1891 Oliver Campbell–Robert
     Huntington
1892 Oliver Campbell–Robert
     Huntington
1893 Clarence Hobart–Fred
     Hovey
1894 Clarence Hobart–Fred
     Hovey
1895 Malcolm Chace–Robert
     Wrenn
1896 Carr Neel–Samuel Neel
1897 Leo Ware–George Sheldon
1898 Leo Ware–George Sheldon
1899 Holcombe Ward–Dwight
     Davis
1900 Holcombe Ward–Dwight
     Davis
1901 Holcombe Ward–Dwight
     Davis
1902 Reginald Doherty–
     Laurence Doherty
1903 Reginald Doherty–
     Laurence Doherty
1904 Holcombe Ward–Beals
     Wright
1905 Holcombe Ward–Beals
     Wright

1906 Holcombe Ward–Beals
     Wright
1907 Fred Alexander–Harold
     Hackett
1908 Fred Alexander–Harold
     Hackett
1909 Fred Alexander–Harold
     Hackett
1910 Fred Alexander–Harold
     Hackett
1911 Raymond Little–Gustave
     Touchard
1912 Maurice McLoughlin–
     Thomas Bundy
1913 Maurice McLoughlin–
     Thomas Bundy
1914 Maurice McLoughlin–
     Thomas Bundy
1915 Bill Johnston–Clarence
     Griffin
1916 Bill Johnston–Clarence
     Griffin
1917 Fred Alexander–Harold
     Throckmorton
1918 Bill Tilden–Vincent
     Richards
1919 Norman Brookes–Gerald
     Patterson
1920 Bill Johnston–Clarence
     Griffin
1921 Bill Tilden–Vincent
     Richards
1922 Bill Tilden–Vincent
     Richards
1923 Bill Tilden–Brian Norton
1924 Howard Kinsey–Robert
     Kinsey
1925 Richard Williams–Vincent
     Richards
1926 Richard Williams–Vincent
     Richards
1927 Bill Tilden–Francis
     Hunter

1928 George Lott–John Hennessey
1929 George Lott–John Doeg
1930 George Lott–John Doeg
1931 Wilmer Allison–John Van Ryn
1932 Ellsworth Vines–Keith Gledhill
1933 George Lott–Les Stoefen
1934 George Lott–Les Stoefen
1935 Wilmer Allison–John Van Ryn
1936 Don Budge–Gene Mako
1937 Gottfried von Cramm–Henner Henkel
1938 Don Budge–Gene Mako
1939 Adrian Quist–John Bromwich
1940 Jack Kramer–Ted Schroeder
1941 Jack Kramer–Ted Schroeder
1942 Gardnar Mulloy–Bill Talbert
1943 Jack Kramer–Frank Parker
1944 Don McNeill–Robert Falkenburg
1945 Gardnar Mulloy–Bill Talbert
1946 Gardnar Mulloy–Bill Talbert
1947 Jack Kramer–Ted Schroeder
1948 Gardnar Mulloy–Bill Talbert
1949 John Bromwich–Bill Sidwell
1950 John Bromwich–Frank Sedgman
1951 Ken McGregor–Frank Sedgman
1952 Mervyn Rose–Vic Seixas

1953 Rex Hartwig–Mervyn Rose
1954 Vic Seixas–Tony Trabert
1955 Kosel Kamo–Atsushi Miyagi
1956 Lew Hoad–Ken Rosewall
1957 Ashley Cooper–Neale Fraser
1958 Alex Olmedo–Hamilton Richardson
1959 Neale Fraser–Roy Emerson
1960 Neale Fraser–Roy Emerson
1961 Charles McKinley–Dennis Ralston
1962 Rafael Osuna–Antonio Palafox
1963 Charles McKinley–Dennis Ralston
1964 Charles McKinley-Dennis Ralston
1965 Roy Emerson–Fred Stolle
1966 Roy Emerson–Fred Stolle
1967 John Newcombe–Tony Roche
*1968 Bob Lutz–Stan Smith
*1968 Bob Lutz–Stan Smith
*1969 Dick Crealy–Allan Stone
*1969 Ken Rosewall–Fred Stolle
1970 Pierre Barthes–Nikki Pilic
1971 John Newcombe–Roger Taylor
1972 Cliff Drysdale–Roger Taylor
1973 John Newcombe–Owen Davidson
1974 Bob Lutz–Stan Smith
1975 Jimmy Connors–Ilie Nastase
1976 Marty Riessen–Tom Okker
1977 Bob Hewitt–Frew McMillan
1978 Bob Lutz–Stan Smith

1979 Peter Fleming–John
McEnroe
1980 Bob Lutz–Stan Smith
1981 Peter Fleming–John
McEnroe
1982 Kevin Curren–Steve
Denton
1983 Peter Fleming–John
McEnroe
1984 John Fitzgerald–Thomas
Smid

WOMEN'S DOUBLES

1890 Ellen Roosevelt–Grace
Roosevelt
1891 Mable Cahill–Fellowes
Morgan
1892 Mabel Cahill–A. M.
McKinley
1893 Aline Terry–Hattie Butler
1894 Helen Helwig–Juliette
Atkinson
1895 Helen Helwig–Juliette
Atkinson
1896 Elizabeth Moore–Juliette
Atkinson
1897 Juliette Atkinson–
Kathleen Atkinson
1898 Juliette Atkinson–
Kathleen Atkinson
1899 Jane Craven–Myrtle
McAteer
1900 Edith Parker–Hallie
Champlin
1901 Juliette Atkinson–Myrtle
McAteer
1902 Juliette Atkinson-Marion
Jones
1903 Elizabeth Moore–Carrie
Neely
1904 May Sutton–Miriam Hall

1905 Helen Homans–Carrie
Neely
1906 L. S. Coe–D. S. Platt
1907 Marie Weimer–Carrie
Neely
1908 Evelyn Sears–Margaret
Curtis
1909 Hazel Hotchkiss–Edith
Rotch
1910 Hazel Hotchkiss–Edith
Rotch
1911 Hazel Hotchkiss–Eleanor
Sears
1912 Dorothy Green–Mary
Browne
1913 Mary Browne–Mrs. R. H.
Williams
1914 Mary Browne–Mrs. R. H.
Williams
1915 Hazel Wightman–Eleanor
Sears
1916 Molla Bjurstedt–Eleanor
Sears
1917 Molla Bjurstedt–Eleanor
Sears
1918 Marion Zinderstein–
Eleanor Goss
1919 Marion Zinderstein–
Eleanor Goss
1920 Marion Zinderstein–
Eleanor Goss
1921 Mary Browne–Mrs. R. H.
Williams
1922 Marion Zinderstein-
Jessup–Helen Wills
1923 Kathleen McKane–Phyllis
Covell
1924 Hazel Wightman–Helen
Wills
1925 Mary Browne–Helen Wills
1926 Elizabeth Ryan–Eleanor
Goss
1927 Kathleen Godfree–
Ermyntrude Harvey

1928 Hazel Wightman–Helen
Wills
1929 Phoebe Watson–Peggy
Michell
1930 Betty Nuthall–Sarah
Palfrey
1931 Betty Nuthall–Eileen
Whittingstall
1932 Helen Jacobs–Sarah
Palfrey
1933 Betty Nuthall–Freda
James
1934 Helen Jacobs–Sarah
Palfrey
1935 Helen Jacobs–Sarah
Fabyan
1936 Marjorie Van Ryn–Carolin
Babcock
1937 Sarah Fabyan–Alice
Marble
1938 Sarah Fabyan–Alice
Marble
1939 Sarah Fabyan–Alice
Marble
1940 Sarah Fabyan–Alice
Marble
1941 Sarah Cooke–Margaret
Osborne
1942 Louise Brough–Margaret
Osborne
1943 Louise Brough–Margaret
Osborne
1944 Louise Brough–Margaret
Osborne
1945 Louise Brough–Margaret
Osborne
1946 Louise Brough–Margaret
Osborne
1947 Louise Brough–Margaret
Osborne
1948 Louise Brough–Margaret
duPont
1949 Louise Brough–Margaret
duPont

1950 Louise Brough–Margaret
duPont
1951 Shirley Fry–Doris Hart
1952 Shirley Fry–Doris Hart
1953 Shirley Fry–Doris Hart
1954 Shirley Fry–Doris Hart
1955 Louise Brough–Margaret
duPont
1956 Louise Brough–Margaret
duPont
1957 Louise Brough–Margaret
duPont
1958 Jeanne Arth–Darlene
Hard
1959 Jeanne Arth–Darlene
Hard
1960 Maria Bueno–Darlene
Hard
1961 Darlene Hard–Lesley
Turner
1962 Maria Bueno–Darlene
Hard
1963 Robyn Ebbern–Margaret
Smith
1964 Billie Jean Moffitt–Karen
Susman
1965 Carole Graebner–Nancy
Richey
1966 Maria Bueno–Nancy
Richey
1967 Rosemary Casals–Billie
Jean King
*1968 Maria Bueno–Margaret
Court
*1968 Maria Bueno–Margaret
Court
*1969 Margaret Court–Virginia
Wade
*1969 Francoise Durr–Darlene
Hard
1970 Margaret Court–Judy
Dalton
1971 Rosemary Casals–Judy
Dalton

1972 Francoise Durr–Betty Stove

1973 Margaret Court–Virginia Wade

1974 Billie Jean King–Rosemary Casals

1975 Margaret Court–Virginia Wade

1976 Linky Boshoff–Ilana Kloss

1977 Martina Navratilova–Betty Stove

1978 Billie Jean King–Martina Navratilova

1979 Betty Stove–Wendy Turnbull

1980 Billie Jean King–Martina Navratilova

1981 Kathy Jordan–Anne Smith

1982 Rosemary Casals–Wendy Turnbull

1983 Martina Navratilova–Pam Shriver

1984 Martina Navratilova–Pam Shriver

MIXED DOUBLES

1892 Mabel Cahill–Clarence Hobart

1893 Ellen Roosevelt–Clarence Hobart

1894 Juliette Atkinson–Edwin Fischer

1895 Juliette Atkinson–Edwin Fischer

1896 Juliette Atkinson–Edwin Fischer

1897 Laura Henson–D. L. Magruder

1898 Carrie Neely–Edwin Fischer

1899 Elizabeth Rastall–Albert Hoskins

1900 Margaret Hunnewell–Alfred Codman

1901 Marion Jones–Raymond Little

1902 Elizabeth Moore–Wylie Grant

1903 Helen Chapman–Harry Allen

1904 Elizabeth Moore–Wylie Grant

1905 Mr. & Mrs. Clarence Hobart

1906 Sarah Coffin–Edward Dewhurst

1907 May Sayres–Wallace Johnson

1908 Edith Rotch–Nathaniel Niles

1909 Hazel Hotchkiss–Wallace Johnson

1910 Hazel Hotchkiss–Joseph Carpenter

1911 Hazel Hotchkiss–Wallace Johnson

1912 Mary Browne–Richard Williams

1913 Mary Browne–Bill Tilden

1914 Mary Browne–Bill Tilden

1915 Hazel Wightman–Harry Johnson

1916 Eleonora Sears–Willie Davis

1917 Molla Bjurstedt–Irving Wright

1918 Hazel Wightman–Irving Wright

1919 Marion Zinderstein–Vincent Richards

1920 Hazel Wightman–Wallace Johnson

1921 Mary Browne–William Johnston

1922 Molla Mallory–Bill Tilden

1923 Molla Mallory–Bill Tilden
1924 Helen Wills–Vincent Richards
1925 Kathleen McKane–John Hawkes
1926 Elizabeth Ryan–Jean Borotra
1927 Eileen Bennett–Henri Cochet
1928 Helen Wills–John Hawkes
1929 Betty Nuthall–George Lott
1930 Edith Cross–Wilmer Allison
1931 Betty Nuthall–George Lott
1932 Sarah Palfrey–Fred Perry
1933 Elizabeth Ryan–Ellsworth Vines
1934 Helen Jacobs–George Lott
1935 Sarah Fabyan–Enrique Maier
1936 Alice Marble–Gene Mako
1937 Sarah Fabyan–Don Budge
1938 Alice Marble-Don Budge
1939 Alice Marble–Harry Hopman
1940 Alice Marble–Bobby Riggs
1941 Sarah Cooke–Jack Kramer
1942 Louise Brough–Ted Schroeder
1943 Margaret Osborne–Bill Talbert
1944 Margaret Osborne–Bill Talbert
1945 Margaret Osborne–Bill Talbert
1946 Margaret Osborne–Bill Talbert
1947 Louise Brough–John Bromwich
1948 Louise Brough–Tom Brown
1949 Louise Brough–Eric Sturgess

1950 Margaret duPont–Kenneth McGregor
1951 Doris Hart–Frank Sedgman
1952 Doris Hart–Frank Sedgman
1953 Doris Hart–Vic Seixas
1954 Doris Hart–Vic Seixas
1955 Doris Hart–Vic Seixas
1956 Margaret duPont–Ken Rosewall
1957 Althea Gibson–Kurt Nielsen
1958 Margaret duPont–Neale Fraser
1959 Margaret duPont–Neale Fraser
1960 Margaret duPont–Neale Fraser
1961 Margaret Smith–Robert Mark
1962 Margaret Smith–Fred Stolle
1963 Margaret Smith–Ken Fletcher
1964 Margaret Smith–John Newcombe
1965 Margaret Smith–Fred Stolle
1966 Donna Fales–Owen Davidson
1967 Billie Jean King–Owen Davidson
1968 Mary Ann Eisel–Peter Curtis
*1969 Patti Hogan–Paul Sullivan
*1969 Margaret Court–Marty Riessen
1970 Margaret Court–Marty Riessen
1971 Billie Jean King–Owen Davidson

1972 Margaret Court–Marty
    Riessen
1973 Billie Jean King–Owen
    Davidson
1974 Pam Teeguarden–Geoff
    Masters
1975 Rosemary Casals–Dick
    Stockton
1976 Billie Jean King–Phil
    Dent
1977 Betty Stove–Frew
    McMillan

1978 Betty Stove–Frew
    McMillan
1979 Greer Stevens–Bob Hewitt
1980 Wendy Turnbull–Marty
    Riessen
1981 Anne Smith–Kevin Curren
1982 Anne Smith–Kevin Curren
1983 Elizabeth Sayers–John
    Fitzgerald
1984 Manuela Maleeva–Tom
    Gullikson

Appendix F

Wimbledon Champions

MEN'S SINGLES

1877 Spencer Gore
1878 Frank Hadow
1879 John Hartley
1880 John Hartley
1881 William Renshaw
1882 William Renshaw
1883 William Renshaw
1884 William Renshaw
1885 William Renshaw
1886 William Renshaw
1887 Herbert Lawford
1888 Ernest Renshaw
1889 William Renshaw
1890 William Hamilton
1891 Wilfred Baddeley
1892 Wilfred Baddeley
1893 Joshua Pim
1894 Joshua Pim
1895 Wilfred Baddeley
1896 Harold Mahoney
1897 Reggie Doherty
1898 Reggie Doherty
1899 Reggie Doherty

1900 Reggie Doherty
1901 Arthur Gore
1902 Laurie Doherty
1903 Laurie Doherty
1904 Laurie Doherty
1905 Laurie Doherty
1906 Laurie Doherty
1907 Norman Brookes
1908 Arthur Gore
1909 Arthur Gore
1910 Anthony Wilding
1911 Anthony Wilding
1912 Anthony Wilding
1913 Anthony Wilding
1914 Norman Brookes
1915–18 Not held
1919 Gerald Patterson
1920 Bill Tilden
1921 Bill Tilden
1922 Gerald Patterson
1923 William Johnston
1924 Jean Borotra
1925 Rene Lacoste
1926 Jean Borotra
1927 Henri Cochet

1928 Rene Lacoste
1929 Henri Cochet
1930 Bill Tilden
1931 Sidney Wood
1932 Ellsworth Vines
1933 Jack Crawford
1934 Fred Perry
1935 Fred Perry
1936 Fred Perry
1937 Don Budge
1938 Don Budge
1939 Bobby Riggs
1940–45 Not held
1946 Yvon Petra
1947 Jack Kramer
1948 Bob Falkenburg
1949 Ted Schroeder
1950 Budge Patty
1951 Dick Savitt
1952 Frank Sedgman
1953 Vic Seixas
1954 Jaroslav Drobny
1955 Tony Trabert
1956 Lew Hoad
1957 Lew Hoad
1958 Ashley Cooper
1959 Alex Olmedo
1960 Neale Fraser
1961 Rod Laver
1962 Rod Laver
1963 Chuck McKinley
1964 Roy Emerson
1965 Roy Emerson
1966 Manuel Santana
1967 John Newcombe
1968 Rod Laver
1969 Rod Laver
1970 John Newcombe
1971 John Newcombe
1972 Stan Smith
1973 Jan Kodes
1974 Jimmy Connors
1975 Arthur Ashe

1976 Bjorn Borg
1977 Bjorn Borg
1978 Bjorn Borg
1979 Bjorn Borg
1980 Bjorn Borg
1981 John McEnroe
1982 Jimmy Connors
1983 John McEnroe
1984 John McEnroe

WOMEN'S SINGLES

1884 Maud Watson
1885 Maud Watson
1886 Blanche Bingley
1887 Lottie Dod
1888 Lottie Dod
1889 Blanche Bingley-Hillyard
1890 L. Rice
1891 Lottie Dod
1892 Lottie Dod
1893 Lottie Dod
1894 Blanche Bingley-Hillyard
1895 Charlotte Cooper
1896 Charlotte Cooper
1897 Blanche Bingley-Hillyard
1898 Charlotte Cooper
1899 Blanche Bingley-Hillyard
1900 Blanche Bingley-Hillyard
1901 Charlotte Cooper-Sterry
1902 Muriel Robb
1903 Dorothea Douglas
1904 Dorothea Douglas
1905 May Sutton
1906 Dorothea Douglas
1907 May Sutton
1908 Charlotte Sterry
1909 Dora Boothby
1910 Dorothea Lambert-
       Chambers
1911 Dorothea Lambert-
       Chambers
1912 Ethel Thomson-Larcombe

1913 Dorothea Lambert-
    Chambers
1914 Dorothea Lambert-
    Chambers
1915–18 Not held
1919 Suzanne Lenglen
1920 Suzanne Lenglen
1921 Suzanne Lenglen
1922 Suzanne Lenglen
1923 Suzanne Lenglen
1924 Kitty McKane
1925 Suzanne Lenglen
1926 Kitty Godfree
1927 Helen Wills
1928 Helen Wills
1929 Helen Wills
1930 Helen Moody
1931 Cilly Aussem
1932 Helen Moody
1933 Helen Moody
1934 Dorothy Round
1935 Helen Moody
1936 Helen Jacobs
1937 Dorothy Round
1938 Helen Moody
1939 Alice Marble
1940–45 Not held
1946 Pauline Betz
1947 Margaret Osborne
1948 Louise Brough
1949 Louise Brough
1950 Louise Brough
1951 Doris Hart
1952 Maureen Connolly
1953 Maureen Connolly
1954 Maureen Connolly
1955 Louise Brough
1956 Shirley Fry
1957 Althea Gibson
1958 Althea Gibson
1959 Maria Bueno
1960 Maria Bueno
1961 Angela Mortimer

1962 Karen Susman
1963 Margaret Smith
1964 Maria Bueno
1965 Margaret Smith
1966 Billie Jean King
1967 Billie Jean King
1968 Billie Jean King
1969 Ann Jones
1970 Margaret Court
1971 Evonne Goolagong
1972 Billie Jean King
1973 Billie Jean King
1974 Chris Evert
1975 Billie Jean King
1976 Chris Evert
1977 Virginia Wade
1978 Martina Navratilova
1979 Martina Navratilova
1980 Evonne Goolagong
1981 Chris Evert-Lloyd
1982 Martina Navratilova
1983 Martina Navratilova
1984 Martina Navratilova

MEN'S DOUBLES

1879 L. R. Erskine–Herbert
    Lawford
1880 William Renshaw–Ernest
    Renshaw
1881 William Renshaw–Ernest
    Renshaw
1882 John Hartley–R. T.
    Richardson
1883 C. W. Grinstead–C. E.
    Welldon
1884 William Renshaw–Ernest
    Renshaw
1885 William Renshaw–Ernest
    Renshaw
1886 William Renshaw–Ernest
    Renshaw

1887 Herbert Wilberforce–P. B. Lyon

1888 William Renshaw–Ernest Renshaw

1889 William Renshaw–Ernest Renshaw

1890 Joshua Pim–F. O. Stoker

1891 Wilfred Baddeley–Herbert Baddeley

1892 E. W. Lewis–H. S. Barlow

1893 Joshua Pim–F. O. Stoker

1894 Wilfred Baddeley–Herbert Baddeley

1895 Wilfred Baddeley–Herbert Baddeley

1896 Wilfred Baddeley–Herbert Baddeley

1897 Reggie Doherty–Laurie Doherty

1898 Reggie Doherty–Laurie Doherty

1899 Reggie Doherty–Laurie Doherty

1900 Reggie Doherty–Laurie Doherty

1901 Reggie Doherty–Laurie Doherty

1902 Sidney Smith–Frank Riseley

1903 Reggie Doherty–Laurie Doherty

1904 Reggie Doherty–Laurie Doherty

1905 Reggie Doherty–Laurie Doherty

1906 Sidney Smith–Frank Riseley

1907 Norman Brookes–Anthony Wilding

1908 Anthony Wilding–M. J. G. Ritchie

1909 Arthur Gore–Roper Barrett

1910 Anthony Wilding–M. J. G. Ritchie

1911 Andre Gobert–Max Decugis

1912 Roper Barrett–Charles Dixon

1913 Roper Barrett–Charles Dixon

1914 Norman Brookes–Anthony Wilding

1915–18 Not held

1919 R. V. Thomas–Pat Wood

1920 Richard Williams–Chuck Garland

1921 Randolph Lycett–Max Woosnam

1922 John Anderson–Randolph Lycett

1923 Leslie Godfree–Randolph Lycett

1924 Frank Hunter–Vincent Richards

1925 Jean Borotra–Rene Lacoste

1926 Jacques Brugnon–Henri Cochet

1927 Frank Hunter–Bill Tilden

1928 Jacques Brugnon–Henri Cochet

1929 Wilmer Allison–John Van Ryn

1930 Wilmer Allison–John Van Ryn

1931 George Lott–John Van Ryn

1932 Jean Borotra–Jacques Brugnon

1933 Jean Borotra–Jacques Brugnon

1934 George Lott–Lester Stoefen

1935 Jack Crawford–Adrian Quist

1936 Pat Hughes–Raymond
     Tuckey
1937 Don Budge–Gene Mako
1938 Don Budge–Gene Mako
1939 Ellwood Cooke–Bobby
     Riggs
1940–45 Not held
1946 Tom Brown–Jack Kramer
1947 Bob Falkenburg–Jack
     Kramer
1948 John Bromwich–Frank
     Sedgman
1949 Pancho Gonzales–Frank
     Parker
1950 John Bromwich–Adrian
     Quist
1951 Ken McGregor–Frank
     Sedgman
1952 Ken McGregor–Frank
     Sedgman
1953 Lew Hoad–Ken Rosewall
1954 Rex Hartwig–Mervyn Rose
1955 Rex Hartwig–Lew Hoad
1956 Lew Hoad–Ken Rosewall
1957 Budge Patty–Gardnar
     Mulloy
1958 Sven Davidson–Ulf
     Schmidt
1959 Roy Emerson–Neale
     Fraser
1960 Rafael Osuna–Dennis
     Ralston
1961 Roy Emerson–Neale
     Fraser
1962 Bob Hewitt–Fred Stolle
1963 Rafael Osuna–Antonio
     Palafox
1964 Bob Hewitt–Fred Stolle
1965 John Newcombe–Tony
     Roche
1966 Ken Fletcher–John
     Newcombe
1967 Bob Hewitt–Frew
     McMillan

1968 John Newcombe–Tony
     Roche
1969 John Newcombe–Tony
     Roche
1970 John Newcombe–Tony
     Roche
1971 Roy Emerson–Rod Laver
1972 Bob Hewitt–Frew
     McMillan
1973 Ilie Nastase–Jimmy
     Connors
1974 John Newcombe–Tony
     Roche
1975 Vitas Gerulaitis–Sandy
     Mayer
1976 Brian Gottfried–Raul
     Ramirez
1977 Ross Case–Geoff Masters
1978 Bob Hewitt–Frew
     McMillan
1979 Peter Fleming–John
     McEnroe
1980 Peter McNamara–Paul
     McNamee
1981 Peter Fleming–John
     McEnroe
1982 Peter McNamara–Paul
     McNamee
1983 Peter Fleming–John
     McEnroe
1984 Peter Fleming–John
     McEnroe

WOMEN'S DOUBLES

1913 R. J. McNair–Dora
     Boothby
1914 A. M. Morton–Elizabeth
     Ryan
1915–18 Not held
1919 Suzanne Lenglen–
     Elizabeth Ryan

1920 Suzanne Lenglen–
     Elizabeth Ryan
1921 Suzanne Lenglen–
     Elizabeth Ryan
1922 Suzanne Lenglen–
     Elizabeth Ryan
1923 Suzanne Lenglen–
     Elizabeth Ryan
1924 Hazel Wightman–Helen
     Wills
1925 Suzanne Lenglen–
     Elizabeth Ryan
1926 Mary Browne–Elizabeth
     Ryan
1927 Helen Wills–Elizabeth
     Ryan
1928 Peggy Saunders–Phoebe
     Watson
1929 Peggy Michell–Phoebe
     Watson
1930 Helen Moody–Elizabeth
     Ryan
1931 Phyllis Mudford–Dorothy
     Barron
1932 Doris Metaxa–Josane
     Sigart
1933 Simone Mathieu–Elizabeth
     Ryan
1934 Simone Mathieu–Elizabeth
     Ryan
1935 Freda James–Kay
     Stammers
1936 Freda James–Kay
     Stammers
1937 Simone Mathieu–Adeline
     Yorke
1938 Sarah Fabyan–Alice
     Marble
1939 Sarah Fabyan–Alice
     Marble
1940–45 Not held
1946 Louise Brough–Margaret
     Osborne

1947 Pat Todd–Doris Hart
1948 Louise Brough–Margaret
     duPont
1949 Louise Brough–Margaret
     duPont
1950 Louise Brough–Margaret
     duPont
1951 Doris Hart–Shirley Fry
1952 Doris Hart–Shirley Fry
1953 Doris Hart–Shirley Fry
1954 Louise Brough–Margaret
     duPont
1955 Angela Mortimer–Anne
     Shilcock
1956 Angela Buxton–Althea
     Gibson
1957 Althea Gibson–Darlene
     Hard
1958 Maria Bueno–Althea
     Gibson
1959 Jeanne Arth–Darlene
     Hard
1960 Maria Bueno–Darlene
     Hard
1961 Karen Hantze–Billie Jean
     Moffitt
1962 Billie Jean Moffitt–Karen
     Susman
1963 Maria Bueno–Darlene
     Hard
1964 Margaret Smith–Lesley
     Turner
1965 Maria Bueno–Billie Jean
     Moffitt
1966 Maria Bueno–Nancy
     Richey
1967 Rosemary Casals–Billie
     Jean King
1968 Rosemary Casals–Billie
     Jean King
1969 Margaret Court–Judy
     Tegart
1970 Rosemary Casals–Billie
     Jean King

1971 Rosemary Casals–Billie
Jean King
1972 Billie Jean King–Betty
Stove
1973 Rosemary Casals–Billie
Jean King
1974 Peggy Michel–Evonne
Goolagong
1975 Ann Kiyomura–Kazuko
Sawamatsu
1976 Chris Evert–Martina
Navratilova
1977 Helen Cawley–Joanne
Russell
1978 Kerry Reid–Wendy
Turnbull
1979 Billie Jean King–Martina
Navratilova
1980 Kathy Jordan–Anne Smith
1981 Martina Navratilova–Pam
Shriver
1982 Martina Navratilova–Pam
Shriver
1983 Martina Navratilova–Pam
Shriver
1984 Martina Navratilova–Pam
Shriver

MIXED DOUBLES

1913 Hope Crisp–C. O. Tuckey
1914 James Parke–Ethel
Larcombe
1915–18 Not held
1919 Randolph Lycett–Elizabeth
Ryan
1920 Gerald Patterson–Suzanne
Lenglen
1921 Randolph Lycett–Elizabeth
Ryan
1922 Pat Wood–Suzanne
Lenglen

1923 Randolph Lycett–Elizabeth
Ryan
1924 Brian Gilbert–Kitty
McKane
1925 Jean Borotra–Suzanne
Lenglen
1926 Leslie Godfree–Kitty
Godfree
1927 Francis Hunter–Elizabeth
Ryan
1928 Pat Spence–Elizabeth
Ryan
1929 Francis Hunter–Helen
Wills
1930 Jack Crawford–Elizabeth
Ryan
1931 George Lott–Anna Harper
1932 Enrique Maier–Elizabeth
Ryan
1933 Gottfried von Cramm–
Hilda Krahwinkel
1934 Miko Ryuki–Dorothy
Round
1935 Fred Perry–Dorothy Round
1936 Fred Perry–Dorothy Round
1937 Don Budge–Alice Marble
1938 Don Budge–Alice Marble
1939 Bobby Riggs–Alice Marble
1940–45 Not held
1946 Tom Brown–Louise
Brough
1947 John Bromwich–Louise
Brough
1948 John Bromwich–Louise
Brough
1949 Eric Sturgess–Sheila
Summers
1950 Eric Sturgess–Louise
Brough
1951 Frank Sedgman–Doris
Hart
1952 Frank Sedgman–Doris
Hart

1953 Vic Seixas–Doris Hart
1954 Vic Seixas–Doris Hart
1955 Vic Seixas–Doris Hart
1956 Vic Seixas–Shirley Fry
1957 Mervyn Rose–Darlene Hard
1958 Bob Howe-Loraine Coghlan
1959 Rod Laver–Darlene Hard
1960 Rod Laver–Darlene Hard
1961 Fred Stolle–Lesley Turner
1962 Neale Fraser–Margaret duPont
1963 Ken Fletcher–Margaret Smith
1964 Fred Stolle–Lesley Turner
1965 Ken Fletcher–Margaret Smith
1966 Ken Fletcher–Margaret Smith
1967 Owen Davidson–Billie Jean King
1968 Ken Fletcher–Margaret Court
1969 Fred Stolle–Ann Jones
1970 Ilie Nastase–Rosemary Casals

1971 Owen Davidson–Billie Jean King
1972 Ilie Nastase–Rosemary Casals
1973 Owen Davidson–Billie Jean King
1974 Owen Davidson–Billie Jean King
1975 Martin Riessen–Margaret Court
1976 Tony Roche–Francoise Durr
1977 Bob Hewitt–Greer Stevens
1978 Frew McMillan–Betty Stove
1979 Bob Hewitt–Greer Stevens
1980 John Austin–Tracy Austin
1981 Frew McMillan–Betty Stove
1982 Kevin Curren–Anne Smith
1983 John Lloyd–Wendy Turnbull
1984 John Lloyd–Wendy Turnbull

Appendix G

Women's Intercollegiate Champions

SINGLES

1958 Darlene Hard, Pomona
1959 Donna Floyd, William & Mary
1960 Linda Vail, Oakland City
1961 Tory Ann Fretz, Occidental
1962 Roberta Alison, Alabama
1963 Roberta Alison, Alabama
1964 Jane Albert, Stanford
1965 Mimi Henreid, UCLA
1966 Cecelia Martinez, San Francisco State
1967 Patsy Rippy, Odessa Junior
1968 Emilie Burrer, Trinity
1969 Emilie Burrer, Trinity
1970 Laura DuPont, North Carolina
1971 Pam Richmond, Arizona State
1972 Janice Metcalf, Redlands
1973 Janice Metcalf, Redlands
1974 Carrie Meyer, Marymount
1975 Stephanie Tolleson, Trinity
1976 Barbara Hallquist, USC
1977 Barbara Hallquist, USC
1978 Stacy Margolin, USC
1979 Kathy Jordan, Stanford
1980 Anne White, Rollins
1981 Anna Maria Fernandez, USC
*1982 Heather Crowe, Indiana (AIAW)
*1982 Alycia Moulton, Stanford (NCAA)
1983 Beth Herr, USC
1984 Lisa Spain, Georgia

DOUBLES

1958 Sue Metzger–Erika Puetz
1959 Joyce Pniewski–Phyllis Saganski
1960 Susan Butt–Linda Vail

*Two national championships were held in 1982.

1961 Tory Ann Fretz–Mary Sherar
1962 Linda Yeomans–Carol Hanks
1963 Roberta Alison–Justina Bricka
1964 Connie Jaster–Carol Loop
1965 Nancy Falkenberg–Cynthia Goeltz
1966 Yale Stockwell–Libby Weiss
1967 Jane Albert–Julie Anthony
1968 Emilie Burrer–Becky Vest
1969 Emilie Burrer–Becky Vest
1970 Pam Farmer–Connie Capozzi
1971 Peggy Michel–Pam Richmond
1972 Peggy Michel–Pam Richmond
1973 Linda Rupert–Cathy Beene
1974 Anne Lebedeff–Karen Reinke
1975 Donna Stockton–Joanne Russell
1976 Susie Hagey–Diane Morrison
1977 Jodi Applebaum–Tery Saiganik
1978 Sherry Acker–Judy Acker
1979 Kathy Jordan–Alycia Moulton
1980 Trey Lewis–Anne White
1981 Caryn Copeland–Alycia Moulton
1982 T. Blumentritt–S. Rudd (AIAW)
     Lynn Lewis–Heather Ludloff (NCAA)
1983 Louise Allen–Gretchen Rush
1984 Linda Gates–Elise Burgin

Appendix H

Men's Intercollegiate Champions

SINGLES

1882 H. A. Taylor, Harvard
1883 Joseph Clark, Harvard
1884 W. P. Knapp, Yale
1885 W. P. Knapp, Yale
1886 G. M. Brinley, Trinity
1887 P. S. Sears, Harvard
1888 P. S. Sears, Harvard
1889 R. P. Huntington, Jr., Yale
1890 Fred Hovey, Harvard
1891 Fred Hovey, Harvard
1892 William Larned, Cornell
1893 M. G. Chase, Brown
1894 M. G. Chase, Yale
1895 M. G. Chase, Yale
1896 Malcolm Whitman,
    Harvard
1897 S. G. Thompson, Princeton
1989 Leo Ware, Harvard
1899 Dwight Davis, Harvard
1900 Raymond Little, Princeton
1901 Fred Alexander, Princeton
1902 William Clothier, Harvard

1903 E. B. Dewhurst, Penn
1904 Robert LeRoy, Columbia
1905 E. B. Dewhurst, Penn
1906 Robert LeRoy, Columbia
1907 Peabody Gardner, Jr.,
    Harvard
1908 Nat Niles, Harvard
1909 Wallace Johnson, Penn
1910 R. A. Holden, Jr., Yale
1911 E. H. Whitney, Harvard
1912 George Church, Princeton
1913 Richard Williams, II,
    Harvard
1914 George Church, Princeton
1915 Richard Williams, II,
    Harvard
1916 Colket Caner, Harvard
1917–18 Not held
1919 Charles Garland, Yale
1920 L. M. Banks, Yale
1921 Philip Neer, Stanford
1922 Lucien Williams, Yale
1923 Carl Fischer, Philadelphia
    Osteopathic

1924 Wallace Scott, Washington
1925 Edward Chandler, California
1926 Edward Chandler, California
1927 Wilmer Allison, Texas
1928 Julius Seligson, Lehigh
1929 Berkeley Bell, Texas
1930 Clifford Sutter, Tulane
1931 Keith Gledhill, Stanford
1932 Clifford Sutter, Tulane
1933 Jack Tidball, UCLA
1934 Gene Mako, USC
1935 Wilbur Hess, Rice
1936 Ernest Sutter, Tulane
1937 Ernest Sutter, Tulane
1938 Frank Guernsey, Rice
1939 Frank Guernsey, Rice
1940 Donald McNeill, Kenyon
1941 Jospeh Hunt, Navy
1942 Frederick Schroeder, Jr., Stanford
1943 Pancho Segura, Miami
1944 Pancho Segura, Miami
1945 Pancho Segura, Miami
1946 Robert Falkenburg, USC
1947 Gardner Larned, William & Mary
1948 Harry Likas, San Francisco
1949 Jack Tuero, Tulane
1950 Herbert Flam, UCLA
1951 Tony Trabert, Cincinnati
1952 Hugh Stewart, USC
1953 Hamilton Richardson, Tulane
1954 Hamilton Richardson, Tulane
1955 Jose Aguero, Tulane
1956 Alejandro Olmedo, USC
1957 Barry MacKay, Michigan
1958 Alejandro Olmedo, USC
1959 Whitney Reed, San Jose State

1960 Larry Nagler, UCLA
1961 Allen Fox, UCLA
1962 Rafael Osuna, USC
1963 Dennis Ralston, USC
1964 Dennis Ralston, USC
1965 Arthur Ashe, Jr., UCLA
1966 Charles Pasarell, UCLA
1967 Bob Lutz, USC
1968 Stan Smith, USC
1969 Joaquin Loyo-Mayo, USC
1970 Jeff Borowiak, UCLA
1971 Jimmy Connors, UCLA
1972 Dick Stockton, Trinity
1973 Sandy Mayer, Jr., Stanford
1974 John Whitinger, Stanford
1975 Billy Martin, UCLA
1976 Bill Scanlon, Trinity
1977 Matt Mitchell, Stanford
1978 John McEnroe, Stanford
1979 Kevin Curren, Texas
1980 Robert Van't Hof, USC
1981 Tim Mayotte, Stanford
1982 Mike Leach, Michigan
1983 Greg Holmes, Utah
1984 Michael Pernfors, Georgia

DOUBLES

1882 Joseph Clark–Howard Taylor
1883 Howard Taylor–R. E. Presbrey
1884 W. P. Knapp–W. V. S. Thorne
1885 W. P. Knapp–A. L. Shipman
1886 W. P. Knapp–W. L. Thacher
1887 P. S. Sears–Quincy Shaw, Jr.
1888 V. G. Hall–Oliver Campbell
1889 Oliver Campbell–A. E. Wright

1890 Quincy Shaw, Jr.–S. T. Chase

1891 Fred Hovey–Robert Wrenn

1892 Robert Wrenn–F. B. Winslow

1893 M. G. Chace–C. R. Budlong

1894 M. G. Chace–A. E. Foote

1895 M. G. Chace–A. E. Foote

1896 Leo Ware–W. M. Scudder

1897 Leo Ware–Malcolm Whitman

1898 Leo Ware–Malcolm Whitman

1899 Holcombe Ward–Dwight Davis

1900 Fred Alexander–Raymond Little

1901 H. A. Plummer–S. L. Russell

1902 William Clothier–E. W. Leonard

1903 B. Colston–E. Clapp

1904 Karl Behr–G. Bodman

1905 E. B. Dewhurst–H. B. Register

1906 E. B. Wells–A. Spaulding

1907 Nat Niles–A. S. Dabney

1908 H. M. Tilden–A. Thayer

1909 Wallace Johnson–A. Thayer

1910 Dean Mathey–Burnham Dell

1911 Dean Mathey–C. T. Butler

1912 George Church–W. H. Mace

1913 Watson Washburn–J. J. Armstrong

1914 Richard Williams, II– Richard Harte

1915 Richard Williams, II– Richard Harte

1916 Colket Caner–Richard Harte

1917–18 Not held

1919 Colket Garland–K. N. Hawkes

1920 A. Wilder–L. Wiley

1921 Brooks Fenno, Jr.–William Feibleman

1922 James Davies–Philip Neer

1923 Lew White–Louis Thalheimer

1924 Lew White–Louis Thalheimer

1925 Gervais Hills–Gerald Stratford

1926 Edward Chandler–Tom Stow

1927 John Van Ryn–Kenneth Appel

1928 Ralph McElevenny–Alan Herrington

1929 Benjamin Gorchakoff– Arthur Kussman

1930 Dolf Muehleisen–Robert Muench

1931 Bruce Barnes–Karl Kamrath

1932 Keith Gledhill–Joseph Coughlin

1933 Joseph Coughlin–Sam Lee

1934 Gene Mako–Philip Castlen

1935 Paul Newton–Richard Bennett

1936 Bennett Dey–William Seward

1937 Richard Bennett–Paul Newton

1938 Joseph Hunt–Lewis Wetherell

1939 Douglas Imhoff–Robert Peacock

1940 Lawrence Dee–James Wade

1941 Charles Olewine–Charles Mattmann

1942 Frederick Schroeder, Jr.–
Lawrence Dee
1943 John Hickman–Walter
Driver
1944 John Hickman–Felix
Kelley
1945 Pancho Segura–Tom
Burke
1946 Robert Falkenburg–Tom
Falkenburg
1947 Sam Match–Bobby Curtis
1948 Fred Kovaleski–Bernard
Bartzen
1949 Jim Brink–Fred Fisher
1950 Herbert Flam–Gene
Garrett
1951 Earl Cochell–Hugh
Stewart
1952 Hugh Ditzler–Clifton
Mayne
1953 Lawrence Huebner–Robert
Perry
1954 Ronald Livingston–Robert
Perry
1955 Francisco Contreras–
Joaquin Reyes
1956 Francisco Contreras–
Alejandro Olmedo
1957 Crawford Henry–Ronald
Holmberg
1958 Edward Atkinson–
Alejandro Olmedo
1959 Crawford Henry–Ronald
Holmberg
1960 Larry Nagler–Allen Fox
1961 Rafael Osuna–Ramsey
Earnhart
1962 Rafael Osuna–Ramsey
Earnhart

1963 Rafael Osuna–Dennis
Ralston
1964 William Bond–Dennis
Ralston
1965 Arthur Ashe–Ian
Crookenden
1966 Ian Crookenden–Charles
Pasarell
1967 Bob Lutz–Stan Smith
1968 Bob Lutz–Stan Smith
1969 Joaquin Loyo-Mayo–
Marcelo Lara
1970 Pat Cramer–Luis Garcia
1971 Jeff Borowiak–Haroon
Rahim
1972 Sandy Mayer, Jr.–Roscoe
Tanner
1973 Sandy Mayer, Jr.–Jim
Delaney
1974 Jim Delaney–John
Whitlinger
1975 Bruce Manson–Butch
Walts
1976 Peter Fleming–Ferdi
Taygan
1977 Chris Lewis–Bruce
Manson
1978 John Austin–Bruce
Nichols
1979 Erick Iskersky–Ben
McKown
1980 Rodney Harmon–Mel
Purcell
1981 David Pate–Karl Richter
1982 Peter Doohan–Pat Serrett
1983 Ola Malmquist–Allen
Miller
1984 Kelly Jones–Jerome Jones

Appendix I

USTA Junior Champions

GIRLS' 18 SINGLES

1918 Katherine Porter
1919 Katherine Gardner
1920 Louise Dixon
1921 Helen Wills
1922 Helen Wills
1923 Helen Hooker
1924 Helen Jacobs
1925 Helen Jacobs
1926 Louise McFarland
1927 Marjorie Gladman
1928 Sarah Palfrey
1929 Sarah Palfrey
1930 Sarah Palfrey
1931 Ruby Bishop
1932 Helen Fulton
1933 Bonnie Miller
1934 Helen Pedersen
1935 Patricia Henry
1936 Margaret Osborne
1937 Barbara Winslow
1938 Helen Bernhard
1939 Helen Bernhard
1940 Louise Brough

1941 Louise Brough
1942 Doris Hart
1943 Doris Hart
1944 Shirley Fry
1945 Shirley Fry
1946 Helen Pastall
1947 Nancy Chaffee
1948 Beverly Baker
1949 Maureen Connolly
1950 Maureen Connolly
1951 Anita Kanter
1952 Julia Ann Sampson
1953 Mary Ann Ellenberger
1954 Barbara Breit
1955 Barbara Breit
1956 Miriam Arnold
1957 Karen Hantze
1958 Sally Moore
1959 Karen Hantze
1960 Karen Hantze
1961 Victoria Palmer
1962 Victoria Palmer
1963 Julie Heldman
1964 Mary Ann Eisel
1965 Jane Bartkowicz

1966 Jane Bartkowicz
1967 Jane Bartkowicz
1968 Kristy Pigeon
1969 Sharon Walsh
1970 Sharon Walsh
1971 Chris Evert
1972 Ann Kiyomura
1973 Carrie Fleming
1974 Rayni Fox
1975 Beth Norton
1976 Lynn Epstein
1977 Tracy Austin
1978 Tracy Austin
1979 Andrea Jaeger
1980 Kate Gompert
1981 Lisa Bonder
1982 Leigh Ann Eldredge
1983 Caroline Kuhlman
1984 Melissa Gurney

GIRLS' 18 DOUBLES

1919 Elizabeth Warren–
Penelope Anderson
1920 Virginia Carpenter–Helen
Sewell
1921 Virginia Carpenter–Ceres
Baker
1922 Helen Wills–Helen Hooker
1923 Helen Hooker–Elizabeth
Hilleary
1924 Francis Curtis–Margaret
Palfrey
1925 Marjorie Morrill–Louise
Slocum
1926 Mianne Palfrey–Sarah
Palfrey
1927 Marjorie Gladman–Jo
Cruickshank
1928 Mianne Palfrey–Sarah
Palfrey
1929 Mianne Palfrey–Sarah
Palfrey

1930 Helen Marlow–Mercedes
Marlow
1931 Alice Marble–Bonnie
Miller
1932 Gracyn Wheeler–
Katherine Winthrop
1933 Bonnie Miller–Frances
Herron
1934 May Hope Doeg–Priscilla
Merwin
1935 Hope Knowles–Patricia
Cumming
1936 Margaret Osborne–Elinor
Dawson
1937 Helen Bernhard–Patricia
Cumming
1938 Margaret Jessee–Joan
Bigler
1939 Patricia Canning–
Marguerita Madden
1940 Doris Hart–Neillie Sheer
1941 Louise Brough–Gertrude
Moran
1942 M. R. Donnelly–Barbara
Brooke
1943 Doris Hart–Shirley Fry
1944 Margaret Varner–Jean
Doyle
1945 Margaret Varner–Jean
Doyle
1946 Barbara Wilkins–Mary
Cunningham
1947 Nancy Chaffee–Beverly
Baker
1948 Beverly Baker–Marjorie
McCord
1949 Maureen Connolly–Lee
Van Keuren
1950 Maureen Connolly–
Patricia Zellmer
1951 Elaine Lewicki–Bonnie
MacKay
1952 Mary Ann Ellenberger–
Linda Mitchell

1953 Nancy Dwyer–Mary Ann
     Ellenberger
1954 Barbara Breit–Darlene
     Hard
1955 Barbara Breit–Diane
     Wootton
1956 Mary Ann Mitchell–Rosa
     Maria Reyes
1957 Sally Moore–Helene Weill
1958 Karen Hantze–Helene
     Weill
1959 Karen Hantze–Kathy
     Chabot
1960 Karen Hantze–Kathy
     Chabot
1961 Victoria Palmer–Judy
     Alvarez
1962 Jane Albert–Mary Arfaras
1963 Jane Albert–Stephanie
     DeFina
1964 Mary Ann Eisel–Wendy
     Overton
1965 Jane Bartkowicz–Valerie
     Ziegenfuss
1966 Jane Bartkowicz–Valerie
     Ziegenfuss
1967 Jane Bartkowicz–Valerie
     Ziegenfuss
1968 Kristy Pigeon–Denise
     Carter
1969 Gail Hansen–Patty Ann
     Reese
1970 Nancy Ornstein–Kristien
     Kemmer
1971 Janet Newberry–Eliza
     Pande
1972 Marita Redondo–Laurie
     Tenney
1973 Susan Boyle–Janet May
1974 Barbara Hallquist–Ann
     Bruning
1975 Roberta McCallum–Lea
     Antonoplis

1976 Sherry Acker–Anne Smith
1977 Lea Antonoplis–Kathy
     Jordan
1978 Tracy Austin–Anna Maria
     Fernandez
1979 Andrea Jaeger–Susy
     Jaeger
1980 Louise Allen–Marian
     Kremer
1981 Linda Gates–Gretchen
     Rush
1982 Amy Holton–Kathy Holton
1983 Mary Norwood–Susan
     Russo
1984 Stephanie London–Cammy
     MacGregor

GIRLS' 16 SINGLES

1962 Kathy Blake
1963 Jane Bartkowicz
1964 Jane Bartkowicz
1965 Jane Bartkowicz
1966 Linda Tuero
1967 Kristien Kemmer
1968 Janet Newberry
1969 Eliza Pande
1970 Chris Evert
1971 Laurie Fleming
1972 Marita Redondo
1973 Betsy Nagelsen
1974 Zenda Liess
1975 Lea Antonoplis
1976 Mareen Louie
1977 Linda Siegel
1978 Tracy Austin
1979 Kathleen Horvath
1980 Zina Garrison
1981 Carolina Kuhlman
1982 Terry Phelps
1983 Grace Kim
1984 M. J. Fernandez

GIRLS' 16 DOUBLES

1962 Stepanie DeFina–Jean
   Danilovich
1963 Rosemary Casals–Pixie
   Lamm
1964 Paulette Verzin–Patsy
   Rippy
1965 Jane Bartkowicz–Valerie
   Ziegenfuss
1966 Connie Capozzi–Linda
   Tuero
1967 Gail Hansen–Patty Ann
   Reese
1968 Kristien Kemmer–Janet
   Newberry
1969 Susan Epstein–Chris Evert
1970 Barbara Downs–Ann
   Kiyomura
1971 Ann Kiyomura–Marita
   Redondo
1972 Jeanne Evert–Kathy
   Kuykendall
1973 Robin Tenny–Susan
   Mehmedbasich
1974 Sherry Acker–Anne Smith
1975 Lea Antonoplis–Berta
   McCallum
1976 Lucia Fernandez–Trey
   Lewis
1977 Tracy Austin–Maria
   Fernandez
1978 Pam Shriver–Barbara
   Potter
1979 Kathleen Horvath–Pilar
   Vasquez
1980 Andrea Leand–Susan
   Mascarin
1981 Beverly Bowes–Stephanie
   Savides
1982 Sonia Hahn–Terry Phelps
1983 Shawn Foltz–Niurka
   Sodupe

1984 Nicole Arendt–Jennifer
   Young

GIRLS' 14 SINGLES

1962 Jane Bartkowicz
1963 Jane Bartkowicz
1964 Linda Tuero
1965 Connie Capozzi
1966 Patty Ann Reese
1967 Karin Benson
1968 Chris Evert
1969 Laurie Fleming
1970 Marita Redondo
1971 Jeanne Evert
1972 Robin Tenney
1973 Zenda Liess
1974 Jennifer Balent
1975 Tracy Austin
1976 Tracy Austin
1977 Shelly Solomon
1978 Andrea Jaeger
1979 Beverly Bowes
1980 Lisa Bonder
1981 Marianne Werdel
1982 Grace Kim
1983 Stephanie Rehe
1984 Lucinda Gurney

GIRLS' 14 DOUBLES

1962 Paulette Verzin–Patsy
   Rippy
1963 Jane Bartkowicz–Ginger
   Pfeiffer
1964 Patricia Montano–Kristy
   Pigeon
1965 Marjorie Gengler–Alice
   deRochemont
1966 Karin Benson–Marcelyn
   Louie
1967 Whitney Grant–Janet
   Newberry

1968 Chris Evert–Susan Epstein
1969 Ann Kiyomura–Susan
     Kraft
1970 Marita Redondo–Gretchen
     Gait
1971 Jeanne Evert–Judy
     Gfroerer
1972 Beth Bondurant–Lynn
     Epstein
1973 Jamie Balsden–Roberta
     McCallum
1974 Jennifer Balent–Mareen
     Louie
1975 Betty Newfield–Caroline
     Stoll
1976 Ellen March–Joanie
     Holzschich
1977 Susan Mascarin–Anna
     Van Walleghem
1978 Andrea Jaeger–Beverly
     Bowes
1979 Not completed
1980 Lisa Bonder–Joni Urban
1981 Jennifer Fuchs–Nicole
     Stafford
1982 Katrina Adams–Gail
     Gibson
1983 Trisha Laux–Kathleen
     Monczka
1984 Deborah Graham–Julie
     Willett

GIRLS' 12 SINGLES

1962 Connie Capozzi
1963 Connie Capozzi
1964 Patty Ann Reese
1965 Marcelyn Louie
1966 Christine Bartkowicz
1967 Ann Kiyomura
1968 Marna Louie
1969 Jeanne Evert
1970 Lynn Epstein

1971 Sherry Acker
1972 Mareen Louie
1973 Linda Siegel
1974 Tracy Austin
1975 Shelly Solomon
1976 Susan Mascarin
1977 Andrea Jaeger
1978 Margaret Hopkins
1979 Kathy Rinaldi
1980 Marianne Werdel
1981 Stephanie Rehe
1982 Mary Joe Fernandez
1983 Holly Lloyd
1984 Luanne Spadea

GIRLS' 12 DOUBLES

1962 Jane Lawson–Connie
     Capozzi
1963 Connie Capozzi–Gene
     Shapiro
1964 Marcelyn Louie–Karin
     Benson
1965 Karin Benson–Marcelyn
     Louie
1966 Susan Epstein–Chris Evert
1967 Lisa Barry–Laurie
     Fleming
1968 Kathy May–Gretchen Galt
1969 Judy Gfroerer–Jeanne
     Evert
1970 Susan Wright–Susan
     Hagey
1971 Lea Antonoplis–Sherry
     Acker
1972 Mareen Louie–Sue
     Rasmussen
1973 Betty Newfield–Caroline
     Stoll
1974 Tracy Austin–Kelly Henry
1975 Susan Mascarin–Anna
     Van Walleghem

1976 Andrea Jaeger–Beverly Bowes
1977 Andrea Jaeger–Beverly Bowes
1978 Kathy Rinaldi–Nicole Stafford
1979 Lynn Nabors–Ginny Purdy
1980 Clare Evert–Raka Raychaudhuri
1981 Stephanie London–Cammy MacGregor
1982 Nicole Ashare–Amy Frazier
1983 Lucinda Gurney–Kristen Phebus
1984 Kimberly Po–Veena Prabhaker

BOYS' 18 SINGLES

1916 Harold Throckmorton
1917 Charles Garland
1918 Harold Taylor
1919 Vincent Richards
1920 Vincent Richards
1921 Vincent Richards
1922 Arnold Jones
1923 George Lott, Jr.
1924 George Lott, Jr.
1925 Cranston Holman
1926 John Doeg
1927 Francis Shields
1928 Francis Shields
1929 Keith Gledhill
1930 Wilmer Hines
1931 Jack Lynch
1932 Frank Parker
1933 Donald Budge
1934 Gene Mako
1935 Bobby Riggs
1936 Julius Heldman
1937 Joseph Hunt
1938 David Freeman

1939 Frederick Schroeder, Jr.
1940 Robert Carrothers, Jr.
1941 Budge Patty
1942 Budge Patty
1943 Robert Falkenburg
1944 Robert Falkenburg
1945 Herbert Flam
1946 Herbert Flam
1947 Herbert Behrens
1948 Gilbert Bogley
1949 Gilbert Bogley
1950 Hamilton Richardson
1951 Ted Rogers
1952 Jack Frost
1953 John Lesch
1954 Gerald Moss
1955 Esteban Reyes
1956 Rod Laver
1957 Alan Roberts
1958 Butch Buchholz, Jr.
1959 Dennis Ralston
1960 William Lenoir
1961 Charles Pasarell
1962 Mike Belkin
1963 Cliff Richey
1964 Stan Smith
1965 Bob Lutz
1966 Stephen Avoyer
1967 Jeff Borowiak
1968 Robert McKinley
1969 Erik van Dillen
1970 Brian Gottfried
1971 Raul Ramirez
1972 Pat DuPre
1973 Billy Martin
1974 Ferdi Taygan
1975 Howard Schoenfield
1976 Larry Gottfried
1977 Van Winitsky
1978 David Dowlen
1979 Scott Davis
1980 Sammy Giammalva
1981 Jimmy Brown

1982 John Letts
1983 Aaron Krickstein
1984 Ricky Brown

BOYS' 18 DOUBLES

1918 Vincent Richards–Harold
     Taylor
1919 Frank Anderson–Cecil
     Donaldson
1920 Harold Godshall–Robert
     Hinckley
1921 Arnold Jones–William
     Ingraham
1922 Arnold Jones–William
     Ingraham
1923 George Lott, Jr.–Julius
     Sagalowsky
1924 George Lott, Jr.–Thomas
     McGlinn
1925 Malcolm Hill–Henry
     Johnson, Jr.
1926 Berkeley Bell–James
     Quick
1927 Alphonso Smith–Edward
     Jacobs
1928 Francis Shields–Barry
     Wood
1929 Ellsworth Vines–Keith
     Gledhill
1930 Wilmer Hines–Judge
     Beaver
1931 Kendall Cram–Judge
     Beaver
1932 Jack Lynch–Gene Mako
1933 Gene Mako–Ben Day
1934 Gene Mako–Lawrence
     Nelson
1935 Bobby Riggs–Joseph Hunt
1936 Joseph Hunt–Julius
     Heldman
1937 Joseph Hunt–John
     Moreno, Jr.

1938 David Freeman–Welby
     Van Horn
1939 John Kramer–C. E.
     Olewine
1940 R. D. Carrothers, Jr.–D. C.
     Woodbury
1941 James Evert–Robert Smidl
1942 Budge Patty–Robert
     Falkenburg
1943 Robert Falkenburg–James
     Brink
1944 Robert Falkenburg–John
     Shea
1945 Herbert Flam–Hugh
     Stewart
1946 Herbert Flam–Hugh
     Stewart
1947 Herbert Behrens–Richard
     Mouledous
1948 Richard Mouledous–
     Keston Deimling
1949 Gilbert Bogley–Richard
     Squires
1950 Whitney Reed–Norman
     Peterson
1951 Donald Flye–William
     Quillian
1952 Francisco Conteras–Sam
     Giammalva
1953 Jon Douglas–Myron
     Franks
1954 Earl Baumgardner–Gerald
     Moss
1955 Gregory Grant–Juan Jose
1956 Rod Laver–James Shaffer
1957 Robert Delgado–Allen Fox
1958 Butch Buchholz, Jr.–
     Charles McKinley
1959 Charles McKinley–Marty
     Riessen
1960 William Lenoir–Frank
     Froehling, III
1961 Charles Pasarell–Clark
     Graebner

1962 Jackie Cooper–Martin Schad
1963 Jack Jackson–John Pickens
1964 Dean Penero–Jeff Brown
1965 Marcelo Lara–Jasjit Singh
1966 Albert Carrero–Stanley Pasarell
1967 Zan Guerry–Tony Oritz
1968 Robert McKinley–F. D. Robbins
1969 Dick Stockton–Erik van Dillen
1970 Brian Gottfried–Sandy Mayer, Jr.
1971 Jim Delaney–Chip Fisher
1972 Stephen Mott–Brian Teacher
1973 Billy Martin–Trey Waltke
1974 Francisco Gonzalez–Rocky Maguire
1975 Tony Giammalva–Bill Scanlon
1976 Larry Gottfried–John McEnroe
1977 Robert Van't Hof–Van Winitsky
1978 Scott Bondurant–Blaine Willenborg
1979 Mike DePalmer–Rodney Harmon
1980 Scott Davis–Ben Testerman
1981 Bill Baxter–John Ross
1982 Rick Leach–Tim Pawsat
1983 Ken Diller–Brad Pearce
1984 Luke Jensen–Patrick McEnroe

BOYS' 16 SINGLES

1962 Cliff Richey
1963 Bill Harris
1964 Alberto Carrero
1965 Zan Guerry
1966 Erik van Dillen
1967 Dick Stockton
1968 Jimmy Connors
1969 James Hagey
1970 Fred DeJesus
1971 Billy Martin
1972 Bill Maze
1973 Ben McKown
1974 Walter Redondo
1975 Larry Gottfried
1976 Tim Wilkison
1977 Ramesh Krishnan
1978 Ben Testerman
1979 Matt Anger
1980 Jimmy Brown
1981 Brad Ackerman
1982 Aaron Krickstein
1983 Ricky Brown
1984 Chris Garner

BOYS' 16 DOUBLES

1962 James Hobson–Steven Tidball
1963 Roy Barth–Bob Lutz
1964 William Davidson–James Rombeau
1965 Mike Estep–George Taylor
1966 Dick Stockton–Erik van Dillen
1967 Mike Machette–Dick Stockton
1968 James Hagey–Robert Kriess
1969 Jim Delaney–Chip Fisher
1970 Fred DeJesus–John Whitlinger
1971 Billy Martin–Trey Waltke
1972 Bruce Manson–Perry Wright

1973 Jeff Robbins–Van
  Winitsky
1974 Jeff Robbins–Van
  Winitsky
1975 Larry Gottfried–John
  McEnroe
1976 Murray Robinson–Tim
  Wilkison
1977 Sean Brawley–David
  Siegler
1978 Scott Davis–Ben
  Testerman
1979 Sam Giammalva–Bill
  Quigley
1980 Rick Leach–Tim Pawsat
1981 Brad Ackerman–Rick
  Leach
1982 Ken Diller–Brad Pearce
1983 Joe Blake–Dan Nahirny
1984 Mike Briggs–T. J.
  Middleton

BOYS' 14 SINGLES

1962 Alberto Carrero
1963 Zan Guerry
1964 Mac Claflin
1965 Dick Stockton
1966 Randall Thomas
1967 Bob Kreiss
1968 Fred DeJesus
1969 Billy Martin
1970 Billy Martin
1971 Ben McKown
1972 Juan Farrow
1973 Larry Gottfried
1974 Blaine Willenborg
1975 Peter Herrmann
1976 Ben Testerman
1977 Jimmy Arias
1978 Tim Pawsat
1979 Matthew Frooman
1980 Aaron Krickstein

1981 Jeff Hersh
1982 John Boytim
1983 Greg Levine
1984 F. Montana

BOYS' 14 DOUBLES

1962 Zan Guerry–Richard
  Howell
1963 Zan Guerry–George Taylor
1964 Dick Stockton–George
  Taylor
1965 Dick Stockton–Erik van
  Dillen
1966 Jimmy Connors–Brian
  Gottfried
1967 Fred DeJesus–Jake Warde
1968 Fred DeJesus–Jake Warde
1969 Mark Joffey–Chris Sylvan
1970 Earl Hassler–Gene Mayer
1971 Gary Taxman–Perry
  Wright
1972 Walter Redondo–Donald
  Paulsen
1973 Van Winitsky–John
  McEnroe
1974 Bobby Berger–Blaine
  Willenborg
1975 George Tanase–Tom
  Warneke
1976 Ben Testerman–Scott
  Davis
1977 Chris Huff–Bruce Herzog
1978 Pat Harrison–Tim Siegel
1979 Brad Ackerman–Jimmy
  Brown
1980 Tom Bender–John Schmitt
1981 Jeff Hersh–Jim Kass
1982 John Boytim–Mike Briggs
1983 David Kanstaroom–C.
  Sappington
1984 Martin Blackman–David
  Kass

BOYS' 12 SINGLES

1962 Dick Stockton
1963 Dick Stockton
1964 Brian Gottfried
1965 Jake Warde
1966 Jake Warde
1967 Gene Mayer
1968 Gene Mayer
1969 Ben McKown
1970 Juan Farrow
1971 Teddy Staren
1972 Blaine Willenborg
1973 Peter Herrmann
1974 Ben Testerman
1975 Chris Huff
1976 Jimmy Arias
1977 Rick Leach
1978 Richey Reneberg
1979 Neville Williams
1980 Al Parker
1981 Al Parker
1982 Ty Tucker
1983 J. Palmer
1984 Michael Chang

BOYS' 12 DOUBLES

1962 Rick Devereux–Dick
     Stockton
1963 Brian Gottfried–Dick
     Stockton
1964 Brian Gottfried–Jimmy
     Connors

1965 James Hagey–Paul
     Lockwood
1966 Fred DeJesus–Jake Warde
1967 David Bohrnstedt–Dave
     Sherbeck
1968 Billy Martin–Gene Mayer
1969 Pem Guerry–Howard
     Schoenfield
1970 Juan Farrow–Chip Hooper
1971 Dave Pelisek–Teddy
     Staren
1972 Bobby Berger–Blaine
     Willenborg
1973 Paul Crozier–Boyd Bryan
1974 John Davis–Howard Sands
1975 Greg Holmes–Dick Pardoe
1976 Jimmy Arias–Bobby
     Banck
1977 Jimmy Brown–Richey
     Reneberg
1978 Robby Weiss–Aaron
     Krickstein
1979 Robby Weiss–Aaron
     Krickstein
1980 John Boytim–Steve Enochs
1981 Al Parker–Chris Garner
1982 Francisco Montana–Ty
     Tucker
1983 Andrew Joe–William
     Quest
1984 Scott Davidoff–Matt
     Turner

Subject Index

Author Index

About the Author

ANGELA LUMPKIN, Professor and Director of the Physical Activities Program, University of North Carolina, is the author of *Women's Tennis: A Historical Documentary of the Players and Their Games, History and Principles of Physical Education, Physical Education: A Contemporary Introduction*, co-author of *Racquetball Everyone*, and co-editor of *Sport and American Education*. She has contributed articles to the *Journal of Popular Culture, Journal of Physical Education and Recreation*, and *Quest*.

www.ingramcontent.com/pod-product-compliance
Lightning Source LLC
Chambersburg PA
CBHW020353100426
42812CB00001B/40